Basic
FINANCIAL
MANAGEMENT

THIRD EDITION

Willie Conradie
Welma Fourie
René Pellissier

juta

Basic Financial Management

First published 2011
Second edition 2017
Third edition 2022

Juta and Company (Pty) Ltd
First floor, Sunclare building, 21 Dreyer street, Claremont 7708
PO Box 14373, Lansdowne 7779, Cape Town, South Africa
www.juta.co.za

© 2022 Juta and Company (Pty) Ltd

978 1 48513 164 9 (Print)
978 1 48513 195 3 (WebPDF)

Production specialist: Seshni Kazadi
Editor: Helen Hacksley
Proofreader: Lilané Putter Joubert
Cover designer: Genevieve Simpson
Typesetter: Elinye Ithuba

Typeset in Minion Pro Regular 11 on 14pt

Contents

Preface

Clearly, the South African economy requires businesses to be successful. With that comes jobs and opportunities. Business is becoming increasingly complex. Huge changes brought about by the Fourth Industrial Revolution and the global health pandemic either threaten the existence of business or provide new and different opportunities.

Despite the best ideas, the environment is changing so much that success is not guaranteed. Given the evolution of technology, information has grown in its abundance and value. From a business perspective, most of the information resides in the financial resources of an organisation. It is therefore very important for any entrepreneur or business person to ensure that they have the necessary tools to engage with the organisation's data and information set and, specifically, the organisation's financial information.

In light of this, any business is fundamentally a financial system working on the financial data and information of the business. That means that the business ideas, branding, products and services have to be translated into financial systems that summarise the ability of the business to earn an income, stay afloat and have a reliable, accessible cash flow. The manager must be able to keep track of all income, expenses, assets the business owns and the cash flow. Poor fiscal management and inadequate accounting practices produce weak or incorrect information, preventing management from making well-informed decisions or adapting adequately to changes in the environment.

Basic Financial Management was written to answer the question: What does ANY manager or entrepreneur need to know to guarantee sound financial management?

This updated third edition includes:

- basic financial management and data analytical principles and skills – discussed in an understandable and logical way so that you can easily apply them to your specific profession
- guidelines for managing the finances of any enterprise or institution, including governmental institutions and NPOs/NGOs
- guidelines on the sensemaking process of data to information and what that entails
- relevant examples and exercises, which will give you the confidence to apply the principles and practices in real-life situations.

Enjoy reading and studying this book, but above all, apply these principles in your profession and experience the success of sound financial management. Our very best wishes accompany you on this exciting journey.

About the Authors

Prof Willie Conradie is a retired professor in entrepreneurship, leadership and innovation at the Department of Business Management, University of Johannesburg, and is currently a successful entrepreneur. His involvement with establishing and assisting small business development throughout South Africa and Namibia started in 1970 and still continues. He holds the degrees BA, MBA (University of Pretoria) and DBA (North-West University).

Ms Welma Fourie (CA) SA has been a senior lecturer in Accounting and Financial Management at Stellenbosch University, KwaZulu-Natal University and Technikon SA. She has also gained extensive corporate experience since 2008 as a financial manager and currently is a director of her own accounting and taxation services practice, Balance ur Act (Pty) Ltd.

Prof René Pellissier is a professor of Research and Innovation at UNISA, a visiting professor at the Mechanical and Industrial Engineering, University of Massachusetts; an extraordinary professor at the University of the Western Cape; professor emeritus at the University of South Africa; and faculty associate at The Albert Luthuli Centre for Responsible Leadership, University of Pretoria.

1

An introduction to financial management for any entrepreneur or manager in any position

WILLIE CONRADIE

Learning outcomes

After reading this chapter, you should be able to:

- explain what financial management is
- explain why financial management is important to any manager in any position
- explain how financial management relates to the other functional activities in any enterprise
- explain how financial management is also applicable in the micro environment (eg your own life, your family life) and also applicable in the macro environment (eg managing a local government, a provincial government, and/or a national government)
- explain and define financial management as a concept and as an organisational function
- explain how the generic functions of management are applied in financial management
- explain how financial management is an integrated and crucial discipline in any organisation
- explain the most important concepts used in financial management (eg different forms of assets and liabilities, fixed and variable capital needed, return on investment (ROI) and return on equity (ROE))
- give everyday examples (preferably from your own experience) for each of the above-mentioned aspects of financial management.

1.1 Introduction

The aim of this chapter is to introduce you to the exciting and important world of finance, and specifically (but not exclusively) business finance. Through an explanation of the concepts and elements of basic financial management, you will develop a thorough knowledge and understanding of business finance. (If any of these concepts are unfamiliar to you, don't worry – you will soon find out and will soon understand what they all mean.) By working through the chapters in this book, you will acquire the expertise to be able to apply these concepts to the overall management of an existing enterprise or organisation, or even the launch of a new branch or a totally new venture or project.

Let us start by getting to grips with the basics.

1.1.1   What is financial management?

Financial management refers to the process of attracting and using money efficiently. It involves thinking about money and planning how legally to attract and use it to make a profit or reach certain goals. We use the term 'to finance' when we mean 'to obtain money in order to make/utilise money' – for example for a new business venture or project.

The word 'finances' refers to money, or to various resources that can be converted into money, such as assets, stocks, investments, capital, savings, funds, and so on. In South Africa we commonly measure the money value of things in South African rand (as Britain uses the pound, Europe the euro and the USA their US dollar). Nowadays there are also all kinds of 'crypto' money, eg Bitcoin, but we will not discuss it any further, as it is (not yet) a form of everyday financial management.

Financial management basically refers to the way in which a company manages its money effectively to accomplish its objectives, one of which is to avoid going bankrupt or out of business. **A sound financial strategy enables a company to raise capital, allocate funds, make a profit, grow their business, pay dividends to shareholders, and so on.** Every organisation should have a financial strategy – not only for long-term budgeting but also to help them allocate short-term resources, such as current liabilities.

1.1.2   Why is financial management important?

Managers, in business and in government, face financial decisions every day, and each one of them affects the success of the business/organisation.

The following questions are often asked by managers:
- What is a fair selling price to ask or buying price to pay for a product or service, or for a company or other initiative?
- How many monthly sales or how much gross income must we make to keep the business viable?
- How do we know if the business/organisation will realise a gain/surplus or show a loss/deficit?
- Will the forecasted profit be enough? What criteria should we apply to answer this question?
- Is it safer and more profitable to use only our own capital, or is it better to borrow additional capital?

- If we use borrowed capital as well as our own, what should the balance be between these two sources?
- If we experience a sharp increase in demand for services, goods and stock during a peak season, should these be financed with long-term or short-term funds?
- Should we sell products and services for cash only or should we consider extending credit facilities to clients?
- What are the advantages and disadvantages of selling on credit?
- How can we be sure that the products and/or services we offer (the stock/inventory we buy to resell) will be required, bought and paid for by customers?
- How important is cash flow management?
- How important is effective administration for my business/organisation to achieve its objectives?

These are only some examples of the many questions an enterprising manager or business entrepreneur should ask on a regular basis. The success of any business enterprise and/or organisation depends on being able to answer such questions timeously.

NB! No one can be a successful business entrepreneur or a successful manager without a thorough understanding of financial management.

Enterprising managers or business entrepreneurs do not need to be chartered accountants or specialists in the world of money markets. However, each and every business entrepreneur/manager must have a good understanding of the core concepts of financial management. This area is simply too important to ignore!

EXERCISE 1.1

a) Anna Molele is an excellent, skilled creative manager with more than 10 years of experience at various advertising agencies. She is good at understanding customer needs and creating advertising concepts and designs. Now she is starting her own advertising agency. Just last night while preparing her business plan, she said to her husband: 'All my plans are in place. I am going to invest as much time and money as possible in being creative, recruiting the right staff and marketing my business. At the same time, I will spend as little time and effort as possible on record-keeping, financial budgets and the like. I hate figures and paperwork, and will leave that to a bookkeeper, whose only task will be to satisfy my banker and the Receiver of Revenue once a year.'

b) Jimmy Khoza wishes to become a successful small business consultant and says: 'I have realised that the only two things that true entrepreneurs wish for is to do as little administration possible and to pay as little tax as possible.'

Write down at least five 'common sense' arguments to support and/or oppose Anna's and Jimmy's views of administration and paperwork.

1.2   The financial function in any enterprise/organisation

For any enterprise to become and remain profitable, successful and sustainable, certain functions and activities need to be identified and managed. Typical examples are marketing, human resources, production, security and safety, and the financial management function.

QUESTION

The financial function is just as important as any other, and each of these other business functions has financial implications for the enterprise. Is this statement true or false?

ANSWER

Yes. The financial function is just as important as any other, and each of these other functions has financial implications for the enterprise.

EXAMPLES

A number of functions need to be managed well in any organisation:

- Human resources management ensures that the enterprise has sufficient capable people who are working productively. Unproductive employees have a detrimental effect on the financial performance of the enterprise.
- Marketing management ensures that there are enough clients supporting the enterprise. A lack of effective and appropriate marketing activities will lead to a lack of income.
- Production management (also called operations management) ensures that the enterprise delivers or produces high-quality products and/or services. Accruing or purchasing services and products for resale that are not in demand in the marketplace leads to high storage and other costs, with no acceptable rewards for the initiative

1.3   Responsibilities of financial managers

Financial managers must make sure that a business/organisation has access to appropriate and needed financial resources and that it makes optimal use of these to ensure the best financial results over both the short and the long term. Basically, financial managers ensure that the enterprise obtains and makes the best use of its financial resources.

1.3.1   Examples of financial management

The following are some examples of a financial manager's duties:

- Arranging with the owners/shareholders and/or the treasury department (within the organisation) and/or a bank manager (when the enterprise is an own business) to obtain enough of the required funds at the best terms possible (ie acquiring the needed financial resources) well before the time
- Ensuring that all financial transactions are recorded accurately and systematically (ie keeping track of all financial resources, inflow and outflow)
- Ensuring that payments and cash received from sales are safeguarded and banked as quickly and as efficiently possible (ie protecting financial resources).

1.3.2   Comparison with other business functions

Although all activities in an enterprise or business have a financial implication, we cannot say that financial management is responsible for all of them or that it must have the final say over each and every other business activity. To understand this principle, let us look at an example.

Emily Ngobeni is the brand manager of a well-known financial institution. She is considering placing an advertisement in a national Sunday newspaper in order to establish a better image of and a higher demand for the brand she is responsible for. She must decide which aspects of this project are mainly financial management issues and which are marketing management issues.

QUESTIONS

1. The availability of applicable funds, the method of paying for the advertisement, the timing of the payment and the possibility of negotiating for a discount are all aspects that mainly and in essence relate to which function of the business – marketing or financial?
2. The wording of the advertisement, appropriate illustrations, colour, placement (page allocation) and size of the advertisement relate to which function – marketing or financial?

ANSWERS

1. All are mainly financial management aspects.
2. These are mainly marketing aspects.

NB! In many smaller enterprises, one person (the owner/manager) handles all the managerial and business functions. This means that there is less of a need to distinguish which issues are financial, marketing or other functional management issues (such as those of production or human resources). In larger organisations, different managers are responsible for different functions, so it is important to make clear distinctions.

1.3.3 The definition of financial management

Financial management involves the responsibility of timeously acquiring needed financial resources under the best conditions possible, and ensuring optimal use of these resources over the short and long term.

1.4   The managerial functions of financial management

The generic functions of management are planning, organising, activating and controlling, but how do we apply them to financial management?

1.4.1   Financial planning

Financial budgets are the most visible and most common outcomes of the financial planning function, but there are also the monetary results of a number of other planning activities in the business/organisation, for example sales forecasts, future production plans, etc. The importance of all planning can be summed up in the following saying: 'If you fail to plan, you plan to fail!'

Financial planning is, however, not only concerned with financial budgets, but typically includes planning, developing and finalising an appropriate administration, bookkeeping or accounting system and deciding on effective pricing, credit policies and practices, and other financial procedures and processes. This process is continuous, and certainly not a once-off (or annual) activity. Ideally, the annual financial and all other budgets should be 'rolling' budgets. If another month is added to the end of the annual budget period as soon as the first month has passed, the enterprise will always have a detailed financial plan for any of the following 12 months.

1.4.2   Financial organising

Another part of financial management is the responsibility to arrange and organise needed financial activities, equipment and people in the most effective way to carry out the financial function. This includes the delegation of financial responsibility to other people: for example who will be authorised to sign requisitions/cheques/payments to suppliers? Who will be responsible for keeping track of all the direct expenses and costs relating to a customer's specific assignment? Who will be in charge of drawing up and discussing marketing cost quotations with a potential customer? The financial organising function and process is also continuous and not just a once-off activity.

1.4.3   Financial activating

Financial activating refers to a financial manager's responsibility to lead and motivate the people in a unit or enterprise (to achieve financial objectives) and to ensure effective communication (regarding any impact on finances).

EXAMPLES

Some examples are the following:

- Ensuring that employees doing financial work (eg bookkeeping, debt collection, banking, budgeting) are motivated to carry out their tasks as diligently as possible
- Working together with other functional managers (eg marketing, human resources, security, production) to prepare all details of the next annual financial budgeting project in good time
- Forecasting the expected need for and application of financial resources for the next 12 months.

NB! Financial management cannot and should not be isolated from these other operational functions; all should work together to ensure the best results for the organisation.

1.4.4 Financial controlling

It is a common mistake for managers and entrepreneurs to focus only on the controlling aspects of the financial management function. They may believe that financial management is only about 'checking' or 'auditing' financial entries, records, bookkeeping and financial transactions. These are all part of the financial management function, but there is more. You cannot control something that has not been properly planned, organised and activated, because any control activity must have a set standard against which an outcome can be measured and judged to be in order or not.

The better you plan, organise and activate, the better you will be able to control the activities of your department or enterprise.

NB! There are four elements in any controlling function (whether financial or marketing, etc):

1. Determining performance criteria (planning what should be done, and what is expected and desired to happen). Drawing up financial forecasts and budgets is a typical example.
2. Measuring the actual performance (the actual results as they happen). Setting up an effective administrative and bookkeeping system to measure spending on any project, with regular reporting outputs, is a typical example.

3. Comparing the expected outcomes with the actual performances to indicate positive and negative variances; this indicates acceptable and unacceptable deviations from the pre-established financial budgets and other performance criteria.

4. Taking corrective action where necessary, for example retraining staff or revising an existing quotation or payment procedure.

1.4.5 Some financial activities in any enterprise

By now, you should have an idea of why financial management is so important in any enterprise or business, how it is defined and its relationships with other functions in any enterprise or organisation.

There are many financial activities in any organisation. The following are some examples:

EXAMPLES

- Collecting external information on financial matters: for example changes in interest rates; the exchange value of the rand; the availability of loan capital; trends in debt collection; the profitability of similar businesses in the same industry.
- Preparing financial budgets: for example working together with the marketing function to forecast expected income and sales volumes in the forthcoming year; working out a cash flow budget.
- Recording all financial transactions: for example making sure that every expense in the business is recorded and allocated to the correct project or cost centre.
- Analysing financial performance: for example continuously and timeously assessing whether actual income, expenses and cash flows are on course according to the agreed annual business plan and budgets. It is of the utmost importance to also timeously identify and report irregular and illegal corruption within the business/organisation.
- Financial reporting: supplying the other functionaries of the enterprise with needed financial information (eg indicating whether direct labour, other developmental costs and equipment expenses per project are still within each agreed financial budget or not).
- Safeguarding cash resources: for example ensuring that cash received from cash sales and debtors' payments is recorded accurately, safeguarded and banked as soon as possible.
- Formulating credit policy: for example investigating the advantages and disadvantages of selling to clients and customers on credit; ensuring that only creditworthy clients are allowed to use your services.

- Debt collection: for example ensuring that debtors honour their commitments regularly and on time.
- Salary administration: for example ensuring that all employees' services rendered are correctly recorded and that they receive their correct remuneration exactly on time.
- Negotiating with suppliers of capital: for example negotiating with treasury or banks or other financial institutions on the availability of needed bridging capital (say, an overdraft facility) at the best conditions possible.

The above are only some examples; a number of other activities could be added.

1.5   Important concepts in financial management

This section briefly explains the meaning of a number of financial management concepts. Most of these will reappear in later chapters where they are more fully explained and illustrated. The following concepts will be covered:

- assets
  - fixed assets
  - current assets
  - other assets
- capital
  - own capital (equity)
  - outside or borrowed capital (long-, medium- and short-term)
  - permanent and variable capital
  - current capital
  - working capital
  - financial structure
- profitability
- liquidity
- solvency.

1.5.1 Assets

The overall objective of a private business is to maximise the rate of return on investment to the owner(s) over the long term, taking into consideration the interests of all relevant stakeholders. To achieve this, the business needs assets, which vary greatly in nature. For example, a manufacturing enterprise will need manufacturing equipment, a transport enterprise will need vehicles, and a retailer will need shop premises, while a services enterprise will need appropriate offices and equipment for its staff to render the applicable services.

In all cases, the assets of an enterprise can be divided into two major categories: fixed and current assets.

Fixed assets are those assets owned and required by the enterprise for a period of longer than 12 months. (Assets that do not belong to the business, such as items that are leased or rented, are still assets needed and used, but are not part of fixed assets for the purposes of the business's balance sheet.) Typical fixed assets are:

- land and buildings
- equipment and machinery
- vehicles
- furniture.

Current/liquid assets are assets owned by the enterprise that will be used for manufacturing, sales or cash within a period of 12 months. Typical current assets are:

- raw materials needed for production/manufacturing
- stock (inventory) – either work in progress or finished goods/services
- outstanding debtors (people who owe the business money)
- cash (on hand or in the bank).

There is a third category: other assets. These are assets not directly involved in the normal operational activities of the business, for example shares in another business or investments (such as a 12-month fixed deposit) deposited at a financial institution.

1.5.2 Capital

In all cases, the assets required by any organisation or business have to be financed, supplied and paid for. For this, the business requires capital. We can identify a number of sources – for example manufacturers, wholesalers or banks – that act as the suppliers of the necessary capital or assets to the business. Capital supplied is also sometimes called liabilities to the enterprise (the capital supplier needs to be repaid at one time or another).

The major types of capital are the following:

- **Owners' capital (equity)**: This is the capital supplied by the owners/shareholders of the business in the form of an initial start-up or later-on investment (generally assets or cash) or as accumulative retained net profits, or both. In the case of a close corporation (CC), this type of capital is called members' interest. In the case of a private or public company, it is also called shareholders' funds.

- **Outside (borrowed, loan, foreign) capital:** This represents all the capital supplied (in the form of assets or cash) or made available to the enterprise by sources other than the owners/shareholders. When such capital is supplied for a period longer than 12 months, it is called medium- (up to five or seven years) or long-term capital (seven years and longer). Short-term outside capital is repayable within 12 months.

- **Trade credit:** This is a form of borrowed short-term capital (when buying stock/ raw materials on credit from suppliers). The same applies to a bank overdraft, while a 20-year mortgage loan (for example to help finance a factory building) is regarded as a long-term loan.

- **Permanent and variable capital:** Permanent capital is the value of assets/ funds/money that is required by an enterprise at all times (say over a year). Variable capital refers to the additional assets/money (over and above the amount of permanent capital needed) that the enterprise needs from time to time – for example during seasonal peaks such as Easter and Christmas.

EXAMPLE

Mavis Tshabalala manages the emergency care unit of a private hospital. A minimum stock level/materials of R600 000 is needed all year round in the unit, but three times a year (during the April, June/July and December/January holidays) she has to increase her stock levels to R1 000 000 to cater for the increase in trauma cases. In her case, the R600 000 needed to finance the minimum stock level all through the year will be regarded as permanent capital, while the additional R400 000 required only for the three peak periods can be regarded as variable capital.

DEFINITIONS

Current (liquid, operational) liabilities/capital: This is capital utilised on a short-term basis (less than a 12-month period) and should normally only be used to finance part of the current assets of the enterprise. Examples are trade credit, bank overdrafts, short-term loans and wages, or tax payments in arrears.

Working capital: This usually refers to the current assets, while net working capital refers to current assets less current liabilities.

1.5.3   Some other concepts

The following sections discuss some other concepts in financial management.

Financial structure

The concept of financial structure relates to the composition of the business's assets in relation to its sources of capital. It also shows the relationships between owners' capital and long- and short-term outside capital, and how these capital resources were utilised together to finance fixed and current assets. An example would be that the equity part of a business makes up 60% of all capital (the remaining 40% will be capital supplied by outsiders, ie non-owners).

Profitability

Many people will say: 'Profitability is what business is all about.' In a sense this is correct. Profitability is one of the most widely used measures available to determine the degree of success or failure of private business operations.

The owners of any business enterprise always expect to earn a satisfactory profit on their investments of money, time, etc. This is called return on investment, or ROI, and is expressed as a percentage. Profitability is one of the most frequently used and best measures available to determine the ultimate degree of success or failure of private business operations, and is therefore one of the most fundamental and important concepts in business.

There are measures of profitability (more than 20 variations). (These and other financial ratios are more fully explained in Chapter 3.)

Return on total investment (ROI): This indicates the rate of return on all capital utilised in the business – that is, the profitability of the business as a whole. A high ROI is proof of management's ability to make good use of all capital and assets. A low (or no) return on investment indicates management's inability to add value to the enterprise.

Return on equity (ROE): This indicates the rate of return on own capital (equity). The owners/shareholders of a business are often more interested in this measure than in ROI. Fundamentally, the owners are in business to maximise the return on their own investment over the long term. This ratio can thus be regarded as the bottom line for the executive manager/CEO.

It is important to point out that the two kinds of profitability mentioned should not be confused. They are very different but related concepts.

ROI concerns the effectiveness of and return on all the capital utilised in the business (including interest earned on outside capital), while ROE concerns only the return on own capital, after the interest on outside capital has been paid to the investors/lenders.

Interest paid on outside capital can be regarded as an operational cost and is tax deductible. ROI measures the utilisation of all capital (total investment) and therefore the cost of outside capital (ie the interest paid) should be excluded from calculating its effectiveness.

ROE refers only to the return/effectiveness of own capital; therefore it is calculated after interest is paid for using outside capital.

EXAMPLE

Jabulani Moloketi has a small business called Moloketi's Marketing Services, which provides a variety of marketing services to clients. At the end of the financial year, his business's financial statements in summary show the following:

Net profit before interest:	R 100 000
Interest paid:	R 30 000
Net profit after interest:	R 70 000
Total capital employed:	R 400 000
Owner's equity:	R 200 000

In Moloketi's business, the two kinds of profitability will be determined as follows:

$$\text{Return on total investment (ROI)} = \frac{\text{Net profit before interest paid} \times 100}{\text{Total capital employed}}$$

$$= \frac{\text{R}100\,000 \times 100}{\text{R}400\,000}$$

$$= 25\%$$

This means that Moloketi has utilised all the capital (or assets, as the value of both are the same) available to his business in such a way as to show 25c net profit for each R1 of total capital (or total assets) employed.

$$\text{Return on equity (ROE)} = \frac{\text{Net profit after interest paid} \times 100}{\text{Owner's equity}}$$

$$= \frac{\text{R}70\,000 \times 100}{\text{R}200\,000}$$

$$= 35\%$$

This means that Moloketi was able to use own capital to earn 35c net profit for each R1.00 of own capital employed.

Liquidity

The liquidity of a business is not directly related to its profitability. Many profitable enterprises go bankrupt because of insurmountable liquidity problems. Liquidity refers to the ability of the enterprise to pay any of its short-term financial commitments continuously and on time. A business has a liquidity crisis if it is unable to pay its creditors when payment is due because of a lack of cash (liquid) resources. The same applies to other liabilities and obligations, such as taxes, rent, wages and salaries, and municipal rates.

Solvency

Solvency is the degree to which the total assets of the business cover its total liabilities. If an enterprise's total commitments or liabilities are larger than the total value of its assets, it is considered to be insolvent. The reliability of the value of the assets in a business is therefore critical in any calculation of solvency.

1.6   Summary

In this chapter, the definition and concepts of financial management were introduced. The chapter explained how financial management fits in with the other functions of any business, organisation or institution, and some major financial concepts (such as assets, capital, profitability and liquidity) were introduced as an important background to the other parts of this book.

NB! A very popular and easy-to-understand video, explaining financial issues in a small enterprise, is 'The Balance Sheet Barrier' and also 'Working Capital' by the internationally known actor John Cleese, but be warned: it is not all-encompassing financial management, sometimes using outdated terms and formulas and relates to UK practices. See inter alia *The balance sheet barrier* (https://www.youtube.com/watch?v=XHx7JeVmW20). There are also quite a number of excellent videos on financial management, eg see *Finance: What Managers Need to Know* (https://www.youtube.com/watch?v=aJsmJsd6Glw).

Another highly recommended video, more in the broader sense of entre-preneurial behaviour (and therefore on money matters) is *The Untold Truth About Money: How to Build Wealth From Nothing* (https://www.youtube.com/watch?v=6mRbDEtDoyA).

NB! Please take note that in each chapter, the self-evaluation questions are for guidance purposes. They can be put in a very simple way (requiring just one straight answer) or in a more complex way (requiring, say, two, three or four sub-elements, giving one or more everyday examples). Marks are allocated accordingly.

Each question requires you to apply the concepts learned in the text of this chapter, and some questions may have multiple correct answers. You should also be able to give everyday examples (preferably from your own experience) for each of the relevant questions.

SELF-EVALUATION QUESTIONS

1. Explain why financial management is important to any manager in any position.

2. Explain how financial management relates to the other functional activities in any enterprise.

3. Explain and define financial management as a concept and as an organisational function.

4. Explain how the generic functions of management are applied in financial management. With each function, give at least one everyday example.
   a) Financial planning
   b) Financial organisation
   c) Financial activating
   d) Financial control

5. Briefly explain the following financial concepts:
   a) fixed assets
   b) long-term capital
   c) current assets
   d) current liabilities
   e) owners' capital
   f) variable capital
   g) permanent capital
   h) profitability
   i) liquidity
   j) solvency
   k) working capital
   l) financial structure
   m) return on total capital
   n) return on equity (ROE)

6. You can review the various concepts above covered in this chapter by considering the following example of a small business. Think about all the concepts discussed in this chapter and try to identify them in the example. You should also be able to explain what each of the concepts means.

    Ismail Naidoo took over his uncle's cafeteria 12 months ago. He inherited the needed furniture and equipment from his late uncle (total value R800 000), but had no money of his own to refurbish the cafeteria or to buy stock or to pay monthly expenses.

    All the trade suppliers to his new business agreed that he could buy his monthly stock (average R100 000) on a 30-day credit basis, but he had to borrow the R80 000 needed for monthly operational expenses (rent, salaries, electricity, etc). His banker agreed to an overdraft facility of maximum R100 000 at 12% interest pa on outstanding balances/amount actually used to cover this expense.

    He had to borrow R320 000 for refurbishments from family and friends (who agreed that he could repay their loans after 10 years passed, but required him to pay 10% interest per annum on a monthly basis).

    Ismail seems to be satisfied now that the first 12 months have come to an end. The net profit (after paying R32 000 interest to his family and friends and R10 000 interest to his bank) was R200 000, while his initial own total investment was only his inheritance: the furniture and equipment (R800 000). Outside capital at the end of the 12 months was worth R500 000 (bank overdraft R80 000, trade creditors R100 000 and long-term loan R320 000). His own capital has increased to R1 000 000 with the initial R800 000 plus the R200 000 net profit over the past 12 months (after interest paid but before income tax paid)

    a) Name at least four financial functions in this business.

    b) Name the managerial functions in this business.

    c) List the different kinds of assets in this business.

    d) List the different forms of capital in this business.

    e) Explain the financial structure at the start of this business.

    f) Calculate the ROI and ROE for Ismail's business.

    g) Based on your calculations, what conclusions can you draw about the ROI and ROE for Ismail Naidoo's business?

ANSWERS

1. The financial function is just as important as any other function, and the manager of any business enterprise must pay close attention to it (together with the other functions). All business functions are interrelated, and together they enable the enterprise to achieve its mission and goals.

2. The financial management function is distinct from the other managerial and business functions and activities, but should never be seen in isolation from them. Each of these other business functions and activities has financial implications for the enterprise.

3. Financial management is responsible for acquiring the necessary financial resources to ensure the most advantageous financial results for the enterprise over both the short and long term. The term 'financial management' also covers the responsibility for making sure the enterprise makes the best use of its financial resources.

   And/or:

   Financial management may be defined as the responsibility for timeously acquiring the needed financial resources at the best conditions possible and ensuring their best use over the short and long term.

4. a) Financial budgets are the most visible and most common outcomes of the financial planning function.

   b) Arranging and organising needed financial activities, equipment and people in the most effective way to carry out the financial function.

   c) Leading and motivating other people in the unit or enterprise and ensuring effective and efficient communications.

   d) Measuring the actual performance (the actual results as they happen), eg setting up an effective administrative and bookkeeping system to measure spending on any project, with regular reporting outputs.

5. a) Those assets owned and required by the enterprise for a period of longer than 12 months.

   b) Capital that is supplied for a period of seven years and longer.

   c) Assets owned by the enterprise that will be used for manufacturing, sales or cash within a period of 12 months.

   d) Capital utilised and repaid on a short-term basis (less than a 12-month period).

   e) The capital supplied by the owners/shareholders of the business in the form of an initial start-up or later-on investment (assets or cash) or as accumulative retained net profits, or both.

   f) The additional amount of assets/money (over and above the amount of permanent capital needed) that the enterprise needs from time to time – for example during seasonal peaks such as Easter and Christmas.

   g) The amount of assets/funds/money required by an enterprise at all times (say, over a year).

   h) The rate of return for capital invested, for example ROI and ROE (there are more than 20 ways of measuring profitability).

   i) The ability of the enterprise to pay its short-term financial commitments continuously and on time.

   j) The degree to which the total assets of the business cover its total liabilities.

   k) Usually the current assets (net working capital refers to current assets less current liabilities).

l) Composition of the business's assets in relation to its sources of capital, which also shows the relationships between owners' capital and long- and short- term outside capital, and how these capital resources were utilised together to finance fixed and current assets.

m) Also called return on total investment (ROI), which indicates the rate of return on total capital – that is, the profitability of the business as a whole.

n) The rate of return on own capital (equity), or the profitability of own capital (equity).

6. a) Identifying not having enough money; negotiating with trade suppliers to supply credit; negotiating with the bank manager for a bank overdraft facility; negotiating with family and friends for financing the needed refurbishments; determining net profit gained at the end of the year.

b) Planning, organising, activating and controlling regarding each and every operational task.

c) Trading stock; furniture, equipment, cash at end of 12 months.

d) Owner's capital (which he inherited plus net profit, after interests and before income tax paid); short-term capital (bank overdraft and trade creditors); long-term loans (friends and family).

e) At the beginning: R800 000 own capital; R100 000 trade creditors; R80 000 bank overdraft; and long-term loans of R320 000, thus R800 000 own capital and R500 000 outside capital and a ratio of 1.6:1 (for every R1.6 capital initially supplied by the owner, R1 was supplied by outsiders).

f) ROI: Total initial investment was R1 300 000 (800 000 + 320 000 + 80 000 + 100 000) and net profit (before interest is paid) of R242 000 gained on the total investment. Therefore return on the total investment of R1 300 000 = 18.6% ROI (242 000 × 100 ÷ 1 300 000). ROE is net profit (after interest is paid to outside investors) of R200 000 × 100 ÷ 800 000. Therefore the return on own capital of R800 000 = 25% ROE.

g) For every R1 (all monies) invested in this business, a net profit of 18.6 cents was gained. For every R1 invested by the owner, he gained 25 cents.

2 Basic accounting and financial statements

WELMA FOURIE

Learning outcomes

After reading this chapter, you should be able to:

- explain the difference between the terms 'bookkeeping' and 'accounting'
- write up the analysis cash book for an enterprise
- carry out a bank reconciliation of the enterprise's cash book and bank statement
- draw up a balancing trial balance from a given list of balances
- draw up a statement of comprehensive income (income statement) and a statement of financial position (balance sheet) from a trial balance
- explain the meaning of a cash flow statement
- define the function of a petty cash record in the enterprise.

2.1 Introduction

Many businesspeople consider bookkeeping and financial statements to be a waste of time. However, up-to-date financial information is the cornerstone of running a business The entrepreneur or director relies heavily on accounting data in order to make constant business decisions, for example:

- Cash management – is there enough available cash for payroll and suppliers? Do your customers pay you in time?

- Gauge the effects of your operational activities, whether this is your gross profit, net profit percentages or effective control of your stock.

- Report on financial implications and return on investment (ROI).

- Interpret financial statements, such as the assets and liabilities statement of financial position and the statement of comprehensive income, especially if you want to start a business or be a director.

In this chapter, we will provide you with the basic knowledge needed to record (write up) a business's income and expenditure using an acceptable method. Ideally, there would be an accountant to draw up your financial statements and as you expand your business, you would rely on your accountant for more complex accounting functions. There are various accounting software packages available, and in this chapter we focus on explaining the basic concepts that can be applied to any of these packages.

> **NB!** Even if your business has an accountant, it is essential that you understand the difference between bookkeeping and accounting:
>
> - **Bookkeeping** represents the writing up (recording) of financial transactions and the collection of data to create a basic trial balance. From the trial balance an Income Statement and Balance Sheet can be drawn up.
> - **Accounting** is the summarising, reporting, analysis and interpretation of financial statements. You must be able to understand the financial implications (results) of all decisions and policies made by the business.

2.2 The business cycle

A **business transaction** occurs when income is obtained from sales made or services provided. This enables the business to pay the expenses that arose to produce the income – for example wages, water and electricity. The various negotiations and transactions performed by a business can be called a business cycle (see Figure 2.1). How does a business cycle work?

The business cycle starts with cash payments for purchases of materials and paying expenses (eg wages) needed to provide services or sell products. Money is received when sales are made or services are provided. This money is deposited in the bank so that expenses can be paid, and so the cycle starts again.

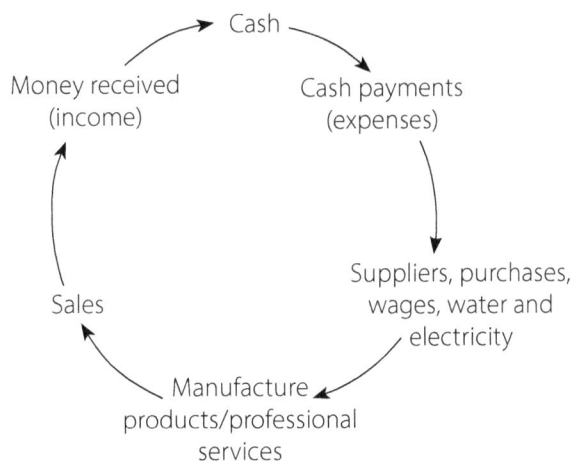

Figure 2.1: A business cycle

Expenses also include the purchase of materials used in providing services, for example wound dressings and baby-care medication used in healthcare.

Transactions are recorded in books to be referred to and processed at the end of each period (usually a month or a year). Figure 2.2 shows this process.

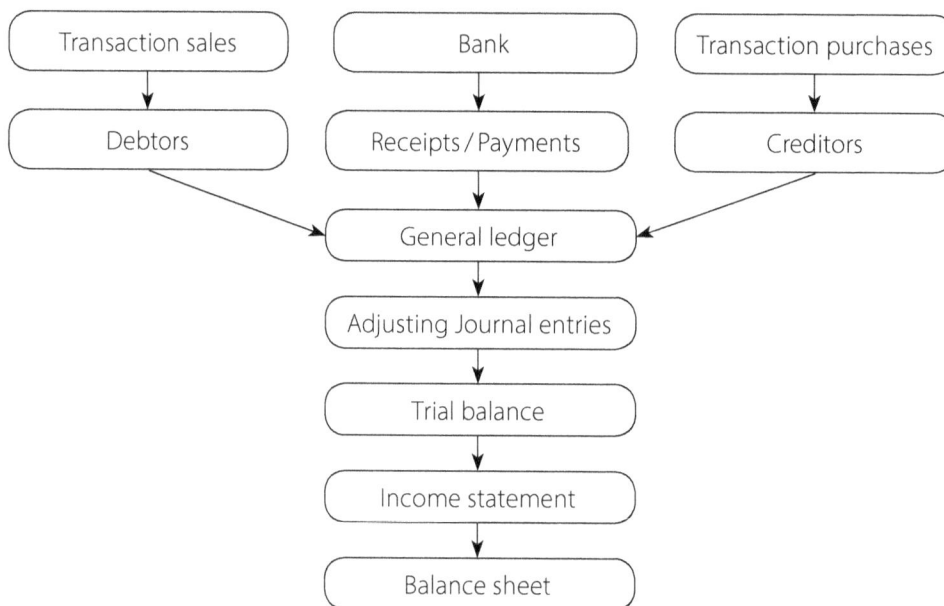

Figure 2.2: The process of recording transactions

2.2.1   The entity concept

For the purposes of accounting, every business is considered to be an entity that is separate from its proprietors (partners/members or shareholders), who we say are not the owners of the business enterprise that is the accounting entity, but merely hold an interest or equity in it. There are two distinct groups of people or institutions that hold an interest or equity:

- **Internal group:** These are the suppliers of capital and funds, which gives them the right to make decisions affecting the entity and its management. This group includes shareholders, members, partners and sole proprietors.
- **External group:** This group mainly furnishes long-term loans and does not usually have any influence on the business activities of the company.

2.2.2   Primary accounting equation

The entity concept is the basis for the primary accounting equation:

Total assets = Equity + Liabilities

> **NB!** The basic principle of accounting is that **for every debit entry there must be a credit entry** of a corresponding (equal) amount. This is the basis of **double-entry accounting – that for every debit entry, which is either an asset or an expense, there must be a corresponding credit transaction**, which will be either a liability, equity or income. The accounting equation must always balance.

EXAMPLE

Contra entries

- Tendayi Advertising and Promotions is a sole proprietorship that was formed by Tendayi Ngubane. The initial capital was a deposit of R100 000 into Quick Save Bank.
- Tendayi bought office furniture for R20 000, which she paid for by EFT/debit card.
- A motor vehicle costing R200 000 was purchased by means of a loan from Entrepreneur Bank.
- To do the accounting, Tendayi bought a computer for R5 000, which she paid for by EFT.

One entry will be the bank transaction, while the contra will be assets, liabilities or bank. The transactions above will be reflected as follows in the balance sheet:

Debit			**Credit**	
1.	Bank (100k – 20k – 5k)	75 000	Capital: Tendayi	100 000
2.	Asset: office furniture	20 000	Loan: Entrepreneur Bank	200 000
3.	Asset: motor vehicle	200 000		
4.	Asset: computer	5 000		
	Total assets	**300 000**	**Total equity and liabilities**	**300 000**

The course of recording a transaction in the enterprise

Depending on the type of transaction and which source documents are produced, the transaction is recorded in the receipts cash book (for sales) or payments cash book (for purchases). If it is not a cash transaction, it is entered in the (general) journal. Then it is posted to the general ledger, from which a trial balance, statement of comprehensive income (income statement) and statement of financial position (balance sheet) are drawn up. You will learn more about all these concepts as you work through this chapter.

DEFINITIONS

A **debtor** is a person who owes you money for goods/services sold to them. A debtor is debited with the amount sold.

A **creditor** is a person to whom you owe money for goods supplied to you. A creditor is credited with your purchases.

The cash book

We will now look at how to record (write up) financial source documents (documents of origin in a transaction). We record cash transactions in one book, namely the **cash book**, which has two sections:

1. **Cash receipts:** All money that is received and banked, such as from cash sales, is recorded here.

   An entry for a sale to a debtor will be as follows:

Day	Details	Sales	Debtors	Sundries	Bank
1	S Small		120		120

   All source documents must be kept as proof of receipts. For example, the **deposit slip** provided by the bank when money is deposited must be kept as proof of the deposit. The deposit slip is also your source document, which you will use to record the details of your deposit in the receipts cash book.

2. **Cash payments:** Cash payments consisting of purchases, electronic funds transfers (EFTs), debit card transactions, debit orders and bank charges payments are recorded here. (The recording of physical cash payments using banknotes is discussed under petty cash.)

   An entry for a cash payment will be as follows:

Cheque	Details	Wages	Purchases	Transport	Bank
0203	Big Five Traders			2 100	2 100

Cheque payments and physical cheques are no longer accepted by banks from 2021.

The EFT method of doing payments on online banking platforms is the most secure and quickest way to transact. To maintain control in a bigger organisation, two people release the payment from the online banking platform. To make sure you record all your transactions, you can either print the **transaction list** from the internet banking or number each one manually. Make sure that all transactions that have gone through on your bank statement are entered into the payments register. Banks also offer the option to extract bank statements as an excel or csf file for easy recording.

2.3 Analysis cash book

2.3.1 How to use the analysis cash book

An analysis cash book is a cash book with various columns to record the cash payments made or income received – for example sales, purchases and salaries. If a payment does not occur regularly, it is entered in the Sundries column. A description of the payment should be provided in the Details column.

EXAMPLE

Entries in a cash book

Entertainment:	R	1 200
Petrol:	R	600
Design and layout computer software:	R	5 000
Goods from ABC warehouse:	R	10 000

Day	Description	Purchases	Entertainment	Transport	Sundries	Details	Amount
1	Cash		1 200				1 200
9	ABC Service Station			600			600
21	Computer Connect (Pty) Ltd				5 000	Computer software	5 000
25	ABC Warehouse	10 000					10 000

In this case, the computer software purchase is a once-off transaction and does not occur regularly, so it is entered in the Sundries column and not the Purchases column. Only goods that you buy to resell should appear in the Purchases column.

NB! All **receipts**, as indicated on the deposit slips from the bank, are entered in the **receipts cash book**.

- **Payments**, money that flows out of the bank, are recorded in the **payments cash book**.
- Only goods that are bought to **resell** should appear in the **purchases** column.

QUESTION

1. Where would you look for information to see whether a debtor has paid you?
   You are not sure if you paid the telephone account for the month. Where do you find the proof?

ANSWER

1. In the receipts cash book or the deposit book/slips or bank statement (direct deposit).
   On the bank statement (EFT) or the payments cash book.

2.3.2   Value-added tax (VAT)

A **value-added tax** (**VAT**) is a type of consumption tax that is placed on a product whenever value is added at a stage of production and at final sale. Currently in South Africa VAT is charged at 15% of the value of goods and services. It is an indirect tax, meaning that it is recovered from wholesalers, retailers and other service providers in the chain of transactions. However, end consumers also pay 15% VAT on most items.

Registering a business for VAT

Entrepreneurs need to consider whether it is viable to register for VAT if they have a very low turnover. All enterprises with a turnover of a certain amount a year must register for VAT. It is mandatory to register for VAT if the entity turnover/sales are in excess of R1 million in any consecutive twelve-month period. A person may also choose to register voluntarily if the taxable supplies made, in the past period of 12 months, exceeded R50 000. (Refer to the SARS website for more guidance about when and whether to register for VAT.)

NB!   VAT is calculated as follows:

$$\frac{\text{Sales}}{100 + 15} \times 15 = \text{Amount of VAT included in your price}$$

EXAMPLES

Calculating VAT

1. Calculate the VAT included in sales of R16 100.

    $$\frac{R16\ 100}{115} \times 15 = R2\ 100$$

2. Calculate the VAT on a cost price of R14 000 and add it to find your selling price.

    Calculate VAT: R14 000 × 15% = R2 100 (rounded off)

    Add VAT to cost price: R14 000 + R2 100 = R16 100

EXERCISE 2.1

1. Calculate 15% VAT on the following cost prices to determine your selling price:

    a) R1 300   b) R2 800   c) R860   d) R10 700

2. Calculate the VAT that has been included in the following sales:

    a) R1 840   b) R575   c) R 14 490   d) R920

EXAMPLE

Entries of deposits and payments in separate cash books

Jane runs an event-planning and PR company called Jane's Events. She has no debtors (people who owe her money) and no creditors (people she owes money to). She pays for everything with cash. The enterprise's cash/cheque transactions for the month of August 2023 are indicated below. Jane is registered for VAT at 15%. At the beginning of the month, Jane showed a positive (favourable) cash book balance of R3 000.

Draw up the transactions given below in order of date in the analysis cash book of Jane's Events in these two sections:

- sales and receipts cash book (deposits)
- purchases and payments cash book (EFTs).

Date	Transactions
1	Jane buys candles for R1 610 from the wholesaler Candles Galore (Pty) Ltd with (EFT 1/7).
	She deposits cash for services to the value of R2 668.
2	She does an (EFT 2/7) for water and electricity for R713. She makes a deposit for cash sales to the value of R2 047.

Date	Transactions
3	She pays the telephone account of R207 for July (EFT 3/7). She pays Ding-Dong Dairy R255 (EFT 4/7); milk is zero-rated for VAT.
4	She banks R1 160 for sales, including R125 for the sale of an unused chair in the office (no VAT was claimed on this chair).
5	She pays R245 to Mr Cotton for flowers for an event (EFT 5/7). The supplier is not registered for VAT.
6	Wages for the week total R2 000 transferred electronically (EFT 6/7).
7	She deposits cash of R1 334 for services. Included in the sales of day 2 were goods to the value of R253 that a client returned and insisted on having an EFT refund for the amount (EFT 7/7). Purchases from the wholesaler total R1 886 (EFT 8/7). She buys a new printer for the company for R2 093 (EFT 9/7) from Magic Q, and sells her old printer to a friend, Riedwaan, for R529 (this is VATable).

Extract from August 2023 Sales and receipts cash book for Jane's Events

Day	Details	Folio	Sales	Sundries	Sundries details	VAT	Amount banked
1	Balance			3 000	Balance		3 000
1	Cash		2 320			348	2 668
2	Cash		1 780			267	2 047
4	Cash		900	125	Furniture sold	135	1 160
6	Cash		1 160			174	1 334
7	Riedwaan			460	Printer sold	69	529
			6 160	**3 585**		**993**	**10 738**

Extract from August 2023 Purchases and payments cash book for Jane's Events

Day	Details	Cheque	Purchases	Water & electricity	Telephone	Wages	Sundries	Details	VAT	Amount paid
1	Wholesale	EFT 1/7	1 400						210	1 610
2	Municipality	EFT 2/7		620					93	713
3	Postmaster	EFT 3/7			180				27	207
4	Ding-Dong	EFT 4/7	255						–	255
5	Mr Cotton	EFT 5/7	245						–	245
6	Wages	EFT 6/7				2000			–	2 000
7	Goods returned	EFT 7/7					220	Sales	33	253
	Wholesale	EFT 8/7	1 640						246	1 886
	Magic Q	EFT 9/7					1 820	Printer	273	2 093
			3 540	620	180	2 000	2 040		882	9 262

The various totals of the cash book are usually posted to a **general ledger,** which contains details of events in all accounts. For each transaction, there must be a debit and a credit entry. The receipts cash book is a debit entry and the payments cash book is a credit entry. If we post it to the general ledger, the receipts cash book entry will be credited to the general ledger accounts, and the payments cash book entry will be debited to the general ledger.

EXAMPLE

Entries in the general ledger

Show the following general ledger accounts for Jane's Events. (Use the information in Jane's Events' cash book entries from August 2023.)

- sales/services
- computer equipment
- VAT
- bank account

Debit				Credit			
Day				**SERVICES**			
7	Goods returned	cb 1	220	30	Cash	cb 1	6 160
	Balance	b/f	5 940				
			6 160				6 160
					Balance	b/d	5 940
COMPUTER EQUIPMENT							
7	Magic Q	cb 1	1 820	7	Riedwaan	cb 1	460
VAT							
30	Payments	cb 1	882	30	Receipts	cb 1	993
BANK							
30	Receipts		10 730	30	Payments	cb 1	9 262

This chapter covers basic accounting, so we will not discuss the general ledger accounts in detail, but will take the totals directly to the trial balance. To ensure that your cash book has been entered correctly, a bank reconciliation (comparison) must be done.

EXERCISE 2.2

Match the terms in column A to the definitions in column B.

A		B	
1.	Bookkeeping	a)	Takes place when the enterprise does business
2.	Transaction	b)	Summary, report and interpretation of financial statements
3.	Deposit slip	c)	Course of business in an enterprise
4.	Source document	d)	Value-added tax
5.	VAT	e)	Is filled in when money is banked
6.	Accounting	f)	Entering and collecting financial data
7.	Business cycle	g)	Source or origin of a transaction

2.4   Bank reconciliation

A bank reconciliation is a comparison of the business's bank statements with the receipts and payments cash book to ensure that the cash book balance will have a correct final balance. This can also be called cash book reconciliation.

> **NB!** Principles of the bank reconciliation:
> 1. The final balance of the cash book (usually at the end of a month) is the basic point of departure in reconciling the balances in the cash book and the bank statement.
> 2. The overall principle is that any entry that appears on the bank statement but is not entered in the same way in the cash book should be corrected in the bank reconciliation and must be accounted for.
>
> Any bank statement item that causes an additional expenditure to the business must be deducted from the final balance of the cash book. Similarly, any bank statement item that gives additional income to the business must be added to the final cash book balance. (The opposite must be done if the cash book balance indicates an overdrawn account.)

2.4.1   How to do a bank reconciliation

The following steps are taken in a bank reconciliation:

Step 1

Check the bank statement. Compare each EFT paid from your bank account against the entries in your cash book.

The amount on the bank statement is usually taken as the correct amount. If it agrees with the amount entered in the cash book, it can be marked as reconciled. If the amount was incorrectly entered (eg an EFT for R1 122 to Mr Confuse is reflected correctly on the bank statement, but was recorded in the cash book as R2 211), then debit (decrease) the payment amount with the difference in the cash book (by R1 122 – R2 211 = R 1 089) to correct the entry.

Step 2

Compare each deposit received with the deposits shown on the bank statement and mark them (with a tick) if the amounts are correct.

Step 3

When the preceding steps have been completed, the payments in the cash book that are not yet reflected on the bank statement (ie not marked off) can be recorded separately as outstanding payments. Deposits shown in the cash book that are not shown on the bank statement (that have not reached your bank account) are recorded as outstanding deposits.

Step 4

All other costs and sundry items on the bank statement that have not yet been ticked – for example service fee costs (bank charges) and other debits – must be recorded in the cash book, and the cash book balance must be adjusted. Once all the above information has been collected, you can calculate the bank reconciliation. In the following example, we will calculate the bank reconciliation for Jane's Events.

EXAMPLE

Show the bank reconciliation for Jane's Events using the July 2023 bank statement.

Extract from bank statement:

KING BANK	20 July 2023	King Bank
Bank statement	No. 12	PO Box 10
		Johannesburg

Month	Day	Details	Ref	Amount		Cumulative total
7	1	Balance		3 000	1	3 000
7	1	Deposit		2 668	2	5 668
7	3	Payment	EFT	(1 610)	3	4 058
7	3	Deposit		2 047	4	6 105
7	4	Deposit		1 160	5	7 265
7	4	EFT – Municipality	EFT	(713)	6	6 552
7	5	EFT – Postmaster	EFT2	(207)	7	6 345
7	5	Interest received		15	8	6 360
7	5	EFT Ding Dong	EFT	(255)	9	6 105
7	5	Bank charges		(72)	10	6 033
7	6	B Sithole	EFT	(2 000)	11	4 033
7	6	Goods returned		(253)	12	3 780

➡

Bank reconciliation statement for Jane's Events as at 30 July 2023

	Balance as calculated in the cash book: at the beginning of the month	3 000	(1)
Plus:	Total of the receipts cash book (10 738 – 3 000)	7 738	
	Interest received	15	(7)
Less:	Total of the payments cash book as adjusted for bank charges, etc.	(9 262)	
	Bank charges	(72)	(9)
	Cash book balance at the end of the month	**1 419**	
Less:	Outstanding deposits	(529)	(a)
	Deposit	(1 334)	(b)
Plus:	Outstanding payments:	4 224	
EFT 5/7	(c)	245	
EFT 8/7	(d)	1 886	
EFT 9/7	(e)	2 093	
	Reconciled bank balance per cash book	**3 780**	

The balance per bank statement (the last figure on the bank statement) and the calculated balance per cash book, written here as 'Reconciled bank balance per cash book', must be the same. In the example you can see they are both R3 780. If they are not equal (ie they do not balance), repeat the process, making sure that the amounts are correct and that items that really are outstanding are shown as such.

EXERCISE 2.3

Mr Dube of ABC Construction CC has started doing his bank reconciliation. The following information has already been collected by Mr Dube:

1. Extract from the receipts and payments cash book of ABC Construction CC:

Cash book for the month ending 31 October

Balance	b/d	5 310	Total payments	3 309
Total receipts		4 641		
		9 951		9 951

2. Deposit of R957 entered in the cash book on 31 October appears on the bank statement as being on 1 November.

3. On the bank statement, an amount of R1 554 was deposited directly into the bank account by a client.

4. List of outstanding debit orders not yet captured in the cash book:

    No. 0389 R 279
         0341 R 387
         0395 R 489
         _____
         R1 155

    (Outstanding debit orders appear on the bank statement but not in the cash book.)

5. EFT payment 0271 was entered in the cash book as R100, but the EFT done shows R127. Mr Dube must adjust the cash book accordingly.

6. On receiving the bank statement, Mr Dube noticed that one of his clients' deposits did not reflect on the bank statement after a proof of payment was received for R720.

7. The bank statement shows a positive balance of R7 578 on 31 October.

8. Bank charges are R69.

    Do the bank reconciliation for Mr Dube using the following format:

	Balance as calculated in the cash book:	_____
Plus:	Total of the receipts cash book	_____
Less:	Total of the payments cash book as adjusted for bank	_____
	Bank charges	_____
	Cash book balance at the end of the month	_____
Less:		_____
Plus:		_____
	Balance per bank statement	_____

2.5   Trial balance

A trial balance reflects the balances of every kind of income, expenditure, asset and liability. If you are certain that the cash book balance is correct, record the amounts in a **trial balance**.

> **NB!** A trial balance is a test to ensure that a **debit** and a **credit** entry were made for each transaction. If this is the case, then the trial balance will balance.

2.5.1   Adjustments trial balance

An adjustments trial balance gives us the opportunity to make adjustments where necessary.

The following kinds of adjustments can be made to a trial balance.

Depreciation on assets

Depreciation is a method we use to decrease the value of an asset over its useful life. Can you think of some reasons for doing this?

We make a depreciation entry as an expense in the income statement, thereby reducing the asset's value as reflected in the balance sheet (the statement of our financial position). The bookkeeper or accountant or shareholder decides what kind of depreciation methods they will apply. The two most common methods are as follows:

- The straight-line method reduces the total remaining by the same amount each month or year during the asset's useful life. The calculation is: (Purchase price – Predicted salvage value, if any) ÷ (Useful lifetime of asset in months or years) = Depreciation amount.

- The reducing balance method reduces the book value (ie the remaining outstanding value) of the asset by a set percentage each month or year. Therefore, a higher amount is deducted earlier in the asset's lifetime, which is logical if the asset's functionality or value decreases over time, eg with computers. The calculation is: (Purchase price – All previous depreciation) = Book value. Book value × Set percentage = Depreciation amount.

EXAMPLE

Jake has a motor vehicle with a cost price of R200 000. Calculate the depreciation by means of the following:

1. The straight-line method over five years with zero salvage value: Annually: R200 000 ÷ 5 = R40 000 a year.

2. The reducing balance method (at 20% a year):
   R200 000 × 20% = R40 000 for the first year; R200 000 – R40 000 = R160 000
   R160 000 × 20% = R32 000 for the second year.

Writing off bad debtors

EXAMPLE

Mr Big Talk's estate has been declared insolvent and he owes you R300. Write the amount off as unrecoverable debt. Make the following journal entry:

	dr	cr
Unrecoverable debt	300	
Debtor: Big Talk		300

Provision for compulsory expenditures that have not yet been paid

It is a good idea to account for fixed expenses that still need to be paid, such as rent and electricity. Each item of expenditure must be debited (increased) by its cost and the total must be credited to the respective parties to whom it is owing and shown as a **running liability** (also called a creditor). This shows that it is an obligation that is still to be paid.

The following expenditures are applicable for the month of August and are owing:

	dr	cr
Water and electricity	600	
Telephone	250	
Rent	1 000	
Expenditures payable		1 850

After we have made all the adjustments to the trial balance, we call the result an **adjustments trial balance**.

EXAMPLE

Adjustments trial balance

Let us look at the example of Jane's Events again and do a trial balance for the month of **December** with several corrections as follows:

- The depreciation on computer software amounts to R219.
- The cost price of the printer that was sold was R250. Calculate the profit on this transaction.
- After a complaint from a customer, a sales credit note was issued for R300 and the money will be refunded to the client, Mrs Complaint.
- Expenses in arrears amount to the following:

	dr	cr
Water and electricity	600	
Telephone	250	
Rent paid	1 000	
Expenses payable		1 850

- The opening bank balance is represented by R3 000 capital.

	Totals		Adjustments trial balance		Final	
ACCOUNT	dr	cr	dr	cr	dr	cr
Capital		3 000				3 000
Computer equipment	1 820			250	1 570	
Accumulated depreciation				219		219
Cash book balance	4 066		250		4 316	
Amounts payable*				2 150		2 150
Sales		7 650	300			7 350
Profit from sale of assets		580				580
VAT control	30				30	
Purchases	2 545				2 545	
Water and electricity	619		600		1 219	
Telephone	150		250		400	
Depreciation			219		219	
Rent paid			1 000		1 000	
Wages	2 000				2 000	
	11 230	**11 230**	**2 619**	**2 619**	**13 299**	**13 299**

* (1 850 + 300)

EXERCISE 2.4

You are given the following trial balance for Krazy Girls Advertising for the month of **December:**

ACCOUNT	dr	cr
Share capital		50 000
Services rendered		250 000
Operating expenses for services rendered	165 000	
Rent	10 000	
Wages	25 000	
Advertisements	2 000	
Electricity	5 000	
Telephone	1 000	
Inventory	9 000	
Furniture (book value)	35 000	
Motor vehicles (book value)	10 000	
Creditors		15 000
Debtors	27 000	
Bank	26 000	
	315 000	**315 000**

You are required to record the following adjustments and then to draw up the adjustments trial balance. The adjustments are as follows.

a) The outstanding telephone account amounts to R85.

b) Additional purchases for operating expenses to the value of R3 050 were paid for on the last day of the year (31 December).

c) Purchases to the value of R50, included in the purchases under (b), were returned as defective.

d) Mr Tick Bird's invoice for R1 500 for accounting services must still be paid.

e) Depreciation must be calculated at 15% per annum (per year) on the book value using the reducing balance method.

2.6 Statement of comprehensive income (also known as the income statement)

If we have a trial balance that balances, we can proceed to draw up a **statement of comprehensive income**, also known as an **income statement**. This is a record of all the income and expenditure of the business in the year or period under review.

Only income and expense items appear on the income statement. These items are involved in the operating of the business, for example the sale of goods and the payment of salaries. The benefit derived from these items, such as the purchase of stationery, is short term. Sometimes an item may have a component in the statement of comprehensive income (eg stationery used during the year), and the remainder or unused portion (longer term) will be reflected as inventory in the statement of financial position, as it contributes to the assets of the enterprise.

Note that receipts and payments for the purchase and sale of **capital items** (eg equipment) are not regarded as operating expenditure, but are shown on the statement of financial position (balance sheet). However, the **profit or loss** from the sale of these assets *is* shown on the statement of comprehensive income (income statement).

The statement of comprehensive income is drawn up according to a fixed format, which helps us to calculate ratios such as the gross profit margin later on. The following is a brief summary of the format of a statement of comprehensive income.

EXAMPLE

Statement of comprehensive income for Jane's Events for the period is as follows:

Services (7 650 – 300)			7 350
Less: Cost of sales			(2 545)
Purchases of utilities		2 545	
Plus:	Opening inventory	–	
	Other direct costs	–	
		2545	
Less:	Closing inventory	(–)	
Gross Profit			**4 805**
Plus:	Other income		580
Less:	Operating expenses		4 838
(All expenditure incurred in the running of the business)			
Water and electricity		1 219	
Telephone		400	
Depreciation		219	
Rent paid		1 000	
Wages		2 000	
Net Profit			**547**

2.7 Statement of financial position (balance sheet)

A statement of financial position shows all the items that contribute to the economic benefit of the business, such as assets, loans and cash. It is also known as the **balance sheet**. Items in the statement of financial position have a **balance** that is carried forward from year to year, in contrast to the items in the income statement, which are closed off against the profit and loss account each year.

Like the income statement, the statement of financial position also follows a fixed format. The first section covers the assets of the business. We can see where capital was applied, whether it comprised non-current assets (fixed assets), new assets purchased by the business, current assets such as debtors or inventory, or cash in the bank.

DEFINITION

Current assets and **current liabilities** are those items that can be converted to cash in a short period (less than one year).

The second section of the statement deals with capital, equity and loans as well as debts of a short-term nature (current liabilities) for financing expansion or other activities. This section tells us how much capital we have and where we obtained it from – for example retained profits, capital deposits, loans or creditors.

NB! The two sections of the balance sheet must balance (ie the total amounts of each section must be **equal**). Again, this reflects one of the fundamental principles of double-entry accounting:

Assets = Equity + Liabilities

EXAMPLE

The statement of financial position (balance sheet) for Jane's Events will be as follows:

Statement of financial position as at 28 February 2023

	2023
	R
Non-current assets (1 570 – 219)	1 351
Current assets	4 346
Inventory	–
Debtors	–
SARS (VAT)	30
Bank balance	4 316
Total assets	**5 697**
Capital	3 000
Retained earnings	547
Current liabilities	2 150
Creditors	–
Arrear expenses	2 150
Bank overdraft	–
Equity and liabilities	**5 697**

EXERCISE 2.5

Indicate whether the following accounts must appear in the statement of comprehensive income (income statement) or in the statement of financial position (balance sheet):

1	Purchases	8	Loan from Z Bank
2	Bank balance	9	Depreciation (annual)
3	Debtors	10	Refreshments
4	Wages	11	Equipment
5	SARS	12	Accumulated depreciation
6	Rent paid	13	Owner's withdrawals
7	Interest received	14	Prepaid expenses

EXAMPLE

Trial balance

The following trial balance was obtained from Bezy Consultants CC.

TRIAL BALANCE	2022 dr	2022 cr
Arrears expenses		3 240
Bank charges	5 114	
Bank balance (overdrawn)		18 315
Electricity	7 575	
Debtors	47 868	
Deposits	1 000	
Repairs	10 261	
Rent paid	46 459	
Cost of sales	536 164	
Commission paid	9 638	
Creditors		72 798
Members' contributions		100
Distributable reserves		205 745
Long-term loan		90 000
Wages and salaries	311 985	
Accountant's fees	1 500	
Interest paid	9 993	
Interest received		17
Accumulated loss the previous year	141 677	
Security	2 448	
Cleaning costs	2 912	
Stationery	330	
Data lines management costs	2 231	
Telephone	5 005	
Inventory	85 000	
Fixed assets – cost price – depreciation	165 094	
Sales		1 124 305
Transport and deliveries	20 596	
Insurance	13 246	
Depreciation	88 424	
	1 514 520	**1 514 520**

EXERCISE 2.6

Draw up the statement of comprehensive income (income statement) and statement of financial position (balance sheet) and fill in the missing amounts (indicated by question marks) in the two tables below. (Comparative amounts from the previous year are not required but are given as an illustration.)

Bezy Consultants CC

Statement of comprehensive income for the year ending 28 February 2022

	2022	2021
	R	R
Income		
Sales	?	782 755
Less: Cost of sales	(536 164)	(424 877)
Gross income	?	357 878
Interest received	17	71
Less: Expenditure	537 717	372 084
Bank charges	5 114	3 937
Electricity	7 575	5 090
Repairs	?	4 356
Rent paid	46 459	41 941
Commission paid	?	12 000
Wages and salaries	311 985	170 337
Accountant's fees	1 500	1 800
Interest paid	?	11 407
Security	2 448	699
Cleaning costs	2 912	738
Stationery	?	524
Data lines management costs	2 231	1 250
Telephone	5 005	2 308
Transport and deliveries	?	12 562
Insurance	13 246	12 930
Depreciation	?	90 205
Net Profit/Loss for the year	**50 441**	**(14 135)**

Bezy Consultants CC

Statement of financial position as at 28 February 2022

	2022	2021
Non-current assets	?	253 518
Current assets	?	130 903
Inventory	85 000	70 000
Debtors	47 868	10 800
Deposits	?	1 000
Bank balance	?	49 103
Total assets	**298 962**	**384 421**
Members' contributions	100	100
Accumulated loss	?	(141 677)
Distributable reserves	?	285 146
Members' shares	14 609	143 569
Non-current loan	?	146 000
Current liabilities	94 353	94 852
Creditors	?	91 612
Arrear expenses	3 240	3 240
Bank overdraft	?	–
Equity and liabilities	**?**	**384 421**

2.7.1 Statement of changes in equity

The statement of changes in equity shows any movement in the equity that belongs to the owners/shareholders of a business.

Bezy Consultants CC

Statement of changes in equity

	Share capital	Share premium	Distributable reserves	Accumulated profits	Total
Balance at 1 March 2020	100	0	285 146	(127 542)	157 704
Net profit/(loss) for the year				(14 135)	(14 135)
Balance at 28 February 2021	100	0	285 146	(141 677)	143 569
Net profit/(loss) for the year				50 441	50 441
Balance at 28 February 2022	100	0	285 146	(91 236)	194 010

2.8   Cash flow statement

A cash flow statement provides information on the flow of funds (cash), namely the inflows and outflows of cash. Non-cash items such as depreciation, profit and loss on disposal of assets, and bad debts are not taken into consideration, so the figures need to be adjusted for these.

The net result of a cash flow statement is the net flow of cash for the year. This must be added to the year's opening bank balance (cash in the bank) to produce the closing bank balance for that year.

A cash flow statement consists of three major sections, which show how cash has been produced and used over a particular period of time.

The three sections are:
1. operating activities, including:
   - income from investments
   - the non-cash component of operating activities, eg depreciation
   - working capital movements
2. investment activities
3. financing activities.

The cash flow statement enables the users of the financial statements to get an impression and make a better judgement about the cash performance of the company. Cash flow statements help interested parties to:

- form an opinion of the risk of the business by paying special attention to its ability to:
  - pay interest and dividends
  - settle (pay off) capital debts on borrowed money
  - access sources of capital, such as banks, to finance the activities of the business
- make projections about the amount of cash that will probably be available in the future to finance expansion
- determine which sources of cash were used for financing operating and investment activities
- evaluate the ability of the enterprise to generate cash from its operating activities to plough back into the business.

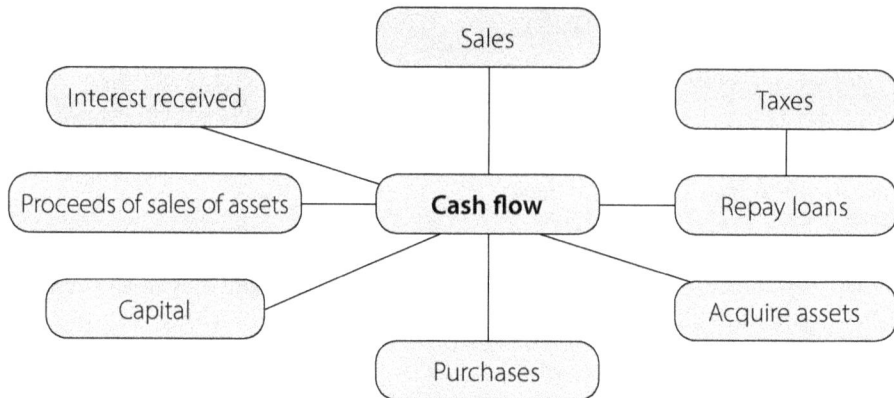

Figure 2.3: Flow of funds

The following is an example of a cash flow statement. You must be able to understand it, but do not need to be able to draw one up.

Bezy Consultants CC

Cash flow statement for the year ending 28 February 2022

	2022
	R
Cash effect of operating activities	**67 983**
Cash receipts from customers (10 800 + 1 124 305 − 47 868)*	1 087 237
Cash payments to suppliers and employees (balancing)	(1 009 261)
Cash generated from operations (Note 1)	77 976
Interest paid	(9 993)
Tax paid	0
Cash effect of investing activities	0
Purchase of fixed assets	
Proceeds from the sale of vehicle	0
Cash effect of financing activities	**(135 401)**
Decrease in long-term loan	(25 401)
Decrease in loan from member	(110 000)
Net cash flow for the year	(67 418)
Opening bank balance	49 103
Closing bank balance	**(18 315)**

* Cash received from customers is calculated by adding the previous year's debtors to this year's sales and subtracting any outstanding debtors at the end of the year. That figure will represent monies received from customers.

Note 1

Reconciliation of net profit before tax to cash generated by operations:	
Net profit before tax	50 441
Adjust for non-cash and separately disclosable items:	
Add: Interest expense	9 993
Depreciation	88 424
	148 858
Adjust for changes in working capital:	
(Increase)/reduction in inventory	(15 000)
(Increase)/reduction in debtors	(37 068)
(Increase)/reduction in creditors	(18 814)
Cash produced by operating activities	77 976

2.9   Petty cash

Every business requires petty cash to cover those expenses that cannot be paid by EFT or debit card – for example postage and parking. Businesses generally keep a small amount of cash on hand to meet such needs, preferably in a small lockable metal box known as the petty cash box. It is important that proof of payment (such as a receipt/invoice) is placed in the petty cash box each time a cash payment is made. To record the petty cash transactions, you follow the same procedure as for an analysis cash book. The only difference is that you must reconcile the payments to obtain a refund that will return your petty cash to the agreed-upon level. For example, if this amount is R500 and you pay out R388 from petty cash, you must reconcile and confirm that you are left with R112 in cash (R500 – R388) in order to be reimbursed for the amount paid out.

2.10   Summary

In this chapter, you learned how a business transaction proceeds and how it affects your financial records. The cash book consists of two sections, namely the cash receipts and sales, and the cash payments and purchases. In the receipts cash book, we enter deposits, whereas in the payments cash book we enter EFTs and other direct bank payments. To check that you have worked correctly, you must be able to do a bank reconciliation. This allows you to summarise all the balances of your accounts in a trial balance; if this balances, it will show that you have worked correctly. From the trial balance, you can determine whether all your figures are accurate and whether you need to provide for payments that fall within the period but have not yet been paid. Then you can draw up the statement of comprehensive income and statement of financial position for the business. Your accounting process has then reached its end.

SELF-EVALUATION QUESTIONS

1. Define the terms 'bookkeeping' and 'accounting' so that the differences between them are clear.

2. You received a quotation for business cards of R1 250 excluding VAT. What amount do you need to pay the supplier and what amount will reflect on the income statement?

3. What are the two sections of the cash book, and what is entered in each section?

4. What is achieved in a bank reconciliation?

5. What does 'an income and expenditure item' mean to you?

6. What important feature do the items that are recorded in the statement of financial position (balance sheet) all possess?

7. Name the three sections of a cash flow statement.

8. Name any three conclusions you can reach from the cash flow statement.

9. Banner Advertising CC drew up the following trial balance for the year ending 31 December 2023.

ACCOUNT	dr	cr
Sales		379 511.38
Materials	200 994.53	
Labour	59 623.86	
Motor vehicle costs	22 782.13	
Telephone	2 729.38	
Travelling expenses	25 060.60	
Bank charges	1 667.24	
Refreshments	159.00	
Water and electricity	6 411.60	
Subscriptions	3 871.48	
Repairs and maintenance	165.00	
Interest received		18.62
Insurance	4 816.28	
Accounting officer	950.00	
Depreciation	5 378.91	
Rent paid	3 000.00	
Salary to member	37 659.23	
Membership fees	359.10	
Entertainment costs	3 660.00	

ACCOUNT	dr	cr
Member's contribution		100.00
Loan from member		54 654.23
Accumulated profits		2 154.48
Assets	82 521.38	
Accumulated depreciation		48 461.94
Bank	8 574.57	
Petty cash	50.00	
Debtors	14 700.00	
Creditors		650.00
SARS	416.36	
Total	**485 550.65**	**485 550.65**

You have been given the following adjustments to enter:

- A further payment of R5 000 must be made to the member.
- Sales of R50 000 to a debtor still need to be recorded on the last day of the month.
- You have just learned that one of your debtors, Mr Little, has been declared insolvent. His debtors account shows a balance of R1 500.
- The following accounts are applicable to the present period: telephone R550; rent paid R450.
- Your tax for the current year has been correctly calculated and amounts to R1 350.

You are required to do the following:

a) Enter the adjustments.

b) Draw up a statement of comprehensive income (income statement) for Banner Advertising for the year ending 31 December 2023.

c) Draw up a statement of financial position (balance sheet) for Banner Advertising for the year ending 31 December 2023.

10. a) An office printer is advertised at R11 500 (including VAT) but is sold at a discount of 15% if paid for in cash. How much will you pay for the printer in cash (cash book entry)? What amount will reflect as the cost of the printer in the asset account?

b) You telephonically enquire about the cost of blinds for the office, and receive a quote of R18 421.05. However, once an email arrives with the official quote, it is R21 000. Explain the difference.

c) You want to determine the selling price of your product: direct cost is R26 000 (incl VAT) and indirect costs are R8 600 (incl VAT). If you order in bulk, you can save 10% on direct costs. Your mark-up is 30% on cost price.

11. Mr Dube of ABC Construction CC has started doing the bank reconciliation for the month of November 2023. The following information has already been collected by him:

a) Extract from the receipts and payments cash book of ABC Construction CC:

Cash book for the month ending 30 November 2023

01 Nov	Balance	65 340	30 Nov	Payments	210 000
30 Nov	Receipts	186 400	30 Nov	Balance	41 740
		251 740			251 740

b) List of outstanding payments in the cash book:

Debit order for insurance	R 6 000
Debit order for December rent	R35 000
Debit order to SARS for VAT	R22 500

c) An EFT payment made on 23 November was entered in the cash book as R11 560, but the bank statement shows it as R11 650. Mr Dube must adjust the cash book accordingly.

d) On the bank statement, Mr Dube notices a foreign transaction for software subscription to the value of R4 000.

e) A deposit of R15 000 entered in the cash book on 30 November reflects on the bank statement only on 1 December.

f) The bank statement shows an amount of R43 000 that was directly deposited into the bank account by a client.

g) The bank statement shows a positive balance of R1 300 on 30 November 2023.

h) Bank charges reflecting on the bank statement are R850.

Required

Do the bank reconciliation for ABC Construction CC for the month of November 2023.

12. The following are extracts from the financial records of Americon Ltd.

Bank reconciliation on 31 May 2022

Balance per bank statement				**15 550**
Less: Outstanding payments	No.	0231	156	
		0259	210	
		0278	468	(834)
				14 716
Plus: Outstanding deposit				3 000
Balance per bank general ledger account				**17 716**

Crab Central Bank: Bank statement of Americon Ltd for June 2022

		dr	cr	Balance
30-May	Balance			15 550
01-Jun	Deposit		3 000	18 550
03-Jun	Payment 0259	210		18 340
	Payment 0231	174		18 166
05-Jun	Deposit		1 730	19 896
	Payment 0301	500		19 396
06-Jun	Correction of error	1 730		17 666
	Deposit	2 468		15 198
12-Jun	Payment 0304	160		15 038
	Payment 0302	836		14 202
14-Jun	Deposit		2 772	16 974
	Payment 0303	692		16 282
	Debit order	200		16 082
18-Jun	Deposit		2 550	18 632
	Payment 0305	2 960		15 672
	Bank costs	10		15 662
24-Jun	Deposit		9 900	25 562
	Payment 0306	1 0 000		15 562
27-Jun	Payment 0307	5 120		10 442
30-Jun	Payment 0309	2 550		7 892

Excerpts from cash receipts and cash payments journals for June 2022

Date	Deposited	Date	Payment no.	Paid
June 6	2 468	June 3	0301	500
14	3 276	10	0302	836
18	2 550		0303	692
30	1 170		0304	1 160
	9 464	15	0305	2 960
		20	0306	10 000
		27	0307	5 120
		30	0308	1 020
			0309	550
				22 838

Additional information

1. The totals of the cash receipt and the cash payment journals have already been recorded in the bank account in the general ledger and the balance of this account is currently R4 342 (debit).
2. The debit order on 14 June on the bank statement was for short-term insurance taken out by Americon Ltd.
3. The deposit on 24 June was a direct deposit made by a debtor, J Smith.
4. According to the duplicate deposit slip, R2 772 was deposited on 14 June.
5. Payment no. 0231 for R156 was for stationery.
6. Payment no. 0309 for R550 was for casual salaries.
7. Payment no. 0304 for R1 160 was cash withdrawal in favour of a creditor, Textiles Pty Ltd.

Required

a) Prepare a supplementary bank account in the general ledger for June 2022 including the correction of all mistakes.
b) Prepare the bank reconciliation statement on 30 June 2022.

13. Trial balance and income statement: You have been supplied with the following trial balance of Dennel (Pty) Ltd and two adjusting entries.

	dr	cr
Property	100 000	
Motor vehicles (book value)	31 000	
Investment	22 500	–
Bank account	52 680	
Debtors control	12 200	
Share capital		10 000
Retained income		60 500
Long-term loan		78 500
Creditors control		24 390
Receiver of revenue		1 810
Sales		63 600
Rent received		25 400
Accounting fees		
Bank charges	430	
Finance cost	5 700	
Depreciation: motor vehicles		
Water and electricity	5 300	
Salaries	34 390	
	264 200	**264 200**

Additional information

1. Depreciation on assets is calculated at 10% using the reducing balance method.
2. An accounting fee of R750 needs to be provided for.

Required

Compile the statement of comprehensive income (income statement) for Dennel (Pty) Ltd for the year ended September 2023.

⟶

ANSWERS

1. Bookkeeping: the writing up (recording) of financial transactions and the collection of data to create basic financial statements.

   Accounting: the summarising, reporting, analysis and interpretation of financial statements. You must be able to understand the financial implications (results) of all decisions or policies made by the business.

2. Amount due to be paid to the supplier: R1 425
   On the income statement: R1 250

3. The receipts cash book is for debit entries and the payments cash book is for credit entries.

4. A bank reconciliation is a comparison of the business's receipts and payments cash book with the bank statements, to ensure that the cash books will have a correct final balance.

5. An income and expenditure item is used in the course of the trading and function of the business, for example the sale of goods and the payment of salaries.

6. The items recorded in the statement of financial position (balance sheet) all have a balance that is carried forward from year to year, in contrast to the items in the income statement, which are closed off against the profit and loss account each year.

7. The three main sections of a cash flow statement are:
   - operating activities, including:
     - income from investments
     - the non-cash component of operating activities, eg depreciation
     - working capital movements
   - investment activities
   - financing activities.

8. Some conclusions you can reach from the cash flow statement:
   - Form an opinion of the risk of the business.
   - Make projections about the amount of cash that will probably be available in the future to finance expansion.
   - Determine which sources of cash were used for financing operating and investment activities.
   - Evaluate the ability of the enterprise to generate cash from its operating activities to plough back into the business.

9. a) **Banner Advertising CC: Adjusted Trial Balance for the year ending 31 December 2023**

ACCOUNT	dr	cr	Adjusting journals	Final trial balance
Sales		379 511.38	−50 000.00	−429 511.38
Materials	200 994.53			200 994.53
Labour	59 623.86			59 623.86
Motor vehicle costs	22 782.13			22 782.13
Telephone (2 729.38 + 550)	2 729.38		550.00	3 279.38
Travelling expenses	25 060.60			25 060.60
Bad debt			1 500.00	1 500.00
Bank charges	1 667.24			1 667.24
Refreshments	159.00			159.00
Water and electricity	6 411.60			6 411.60
Subscriptions	3 871.48			3 871.48
Repairs and maintenance	165.00			165.00
Interest received		18.62		−18.62
Insurance	4 816.28			4 816.28
Accounting officer	950.00			950.00
Depreciation	5 378.91			5 378.91
Rent paid (3 000 + 450)	3 000.00		450.00	3 450.00
Salary to member (37 659.23 + 5 000)	37 659.23		5 000.00	42 659.23
Membership fees	359.10			359.10
Entertainment costs	3 660.00			3 660.00
Income tax			1 350.00	1 350.00
Member's contribution		100.00		−100.00
Loan from member		54 654.23		−54 654.23
Accumulated profits		2 154.48		−2 154.48
Assets	82 521.38			82 521.38
Accumulated depreciation		48 461.94		−48 461.94
Bank (8 574.57 − 5 000)	8 574.57		−5 000.00	3 574.57
Petty cash	50			50.00
Debtors (14 700 − 1 500 + 50 000)	14 700.00		48 500.00	63 200.00
Creditors (650 + 550 + 450)		650	−1 000.00	−1 650.00
SARS (416.36 − 1 350)	416.36		−1 350.00	−933.64
Total	**485 550.65**	**485 550.65**	**0**	**0**

b) **Statement of comprehensive income for Banner Advertising for the year ending 31 December 2023**

INCOME		
Sales	200 994.50	429 511.38
Less: Cost of sales	59 623.86	260 618.39
Materials Labour		
GROSS PROFIT		**168 892.99**
EXPENSES		**126 151.33**
Accounting officer	950.00	
Bad debt	1 500.00	
Bank charges	1 667.24	
Depreciation	5 378.91	
Entertainment costs	3 660.00	
Insurance	4 816.28	
Interest received	−18.62	
Membership fees	359.10	
Motor vehicle costs	22 782.13	
Refreshments	159.00	
Rent paid (3 000 + 4 500)	3 450.00	
Repairs and maintenance	165.00	
Salary to member (37 659.23 + 5 000)	42 659.23	
Subscriptions	3 871.48	
Telephone (2 729.38 + 550)	3 279.38	
Travelling expenses	25 060.60	
Water and electricity	6 411.60	
Net income before taxation		**42 741.66**
Income tax	**1 350.00**	
NET INCOME AFTER TAXATION		**41 391.66**

c) **Balance sheet of Banner Advertising on 31 December 2023**

Equity and reserves		**98 300.37**
Own capital	43 646.14	
Member's contribution	100.00	
Accumulated profits (2 154.48 + 41 391.66)	43 546.14	
Loans	54 654.23	
Loan from member	54 654.23	
Current liabilities		**2 583.64**
Creditors (650 + 550 + 450)	1 650.00	
SARS (416.36 – 1 350)	933.64	
Total equity and liabilities		**100 884.01**
Assets		
Non-current assets		**34 059.44**
Fixed assets	82 521.38	
Accumulated depreciation	–48 461.94	
Current assets		**66 824.57**
Bank (8 574.57 – 5 000)	3 574.57	
Petty cash	50.00	
Debtors (14 700 – 1 500 + 50 000)	63 200.00	
Total assets		**100 884.01**

10. a) Calculate the discount amount:

11 500 × 15%	=	1 725
Cash price: 11 500 – 1 725	=	9 775
Calculate the VAT included: 9 775 × 15 ÷ 115	=	1 275
Cost of printer: 9 775 – 1 200	=	8 500

b) Explain the difference:

Suppliers sometimes give quotes excluding VAT:

VAT on the blinds: 18 421.05 × 15%	=	2 736.15
Total costs = 18 241.05 + 2 736.15	=	21 184.20

c) You want to determine the selling price of your product. Calculate the cost of direct costs after discount:

Saving 26 000 × 10% (incl VAT)	=	2 600
Cost of direct costs 26 000 – 2 600	=	23 400
Indirect costs (incl VAT)	=	8 600
Total costs (incl VAT)	=	32 000
Total costs (excl VAT @ 15%)	=	27 826
Add: Mark-up of 30%	=	8 347.80
Total selling price (rounded)	=	36 174

11. **Bank reconciliation of ABC Construction CC on 30 November 2023**

30 November	Cash book closing balance		41 740
Plus:	Outstanding deposits:		43 000
Less:			–68 440
	Debit order not processed	–6 000	
	Debit order not processed	–35 000	
	Debit order not processed	–22 500	
	Correction of payment 23 Nov	–90	
	Bank charges	–850	
	Foreign software	–4 000	
30 November	**Reconciled cash book balance**		**16 300**
Less:	Outstanding deposit		–15 000
30 November	**Balance per bank statement**		**1 300**

12. a)

Supplementary bank account for Americon June 2022					
	Balance	4 342	Payment	Short-term insurance	200
24 June	J Smith	9 900	0231	Stationery correction	18
14 June	Correction of deposit	–504	0304	Textiles (–1 160 + 160)	–1 000
			0309	Salaries (2 550 – 550)	2 000
				Bank charges	10
		13 738			1 228
				Balance	**12 510**

b) **Bank reconciliation of Americon on 30 June 2022**

Balance per bank statement		7 892
Less: Outstanding payments		−1 488
	−468	
0308	−1 020	
Plus: Outstanding deposits		3 638
06-Jun	2 468	
30-Jun	1 170	
Bank correction: reverse entry of deposit reflected as payment 06 June		2 468
Balance per bank general ledger account		**12 510**

13.

Dennel (Pty) Ltd	
Statement of comprehensive income for the year ended 2023	
Income	
Sales	63 600
Rent received	25 400
	89 000
Expenses	
Accounting fees	750
Bank charges	430
Depreciation: motor vehicles	3 100
Water and electricity	5 300
Salaries	34 390
	43 970
Operating profit	45 030
Finance cost	5 700
Total comprehensive profit for the year	**39 330**

3

Analysing the annual financial statements

WELMA FOURIE

Learning outcomes

After reading this chapter, you should be able to:

- explain briefly the purpose of analysing the financial statements
- define a financial ratio
- calculate and interpret the liquidity ratios
- calculate and interpret the most important activity ratios
- calculate and interpret the basic solvency ratios
- calculate and interpret the profitability ratios.

3.1   Introduction

In Chapter 2 you learned about compiling financial statements. An analysis of financial statements assists the user in determining whether the business is profitable, its current cash position and return for owners, whether its financial position is sound and whether it is achieving its goals (eg a 20% return on capital). Analysis is also useful to determine which product lines are profitable and where marketing can be employed more successfully. Financial institutions will also apply ratios to determine whether they want to extend loans to a company. A financial analysis gives a very clear picture of what has occurred over a particular period of time, and indicates the present financial position of the business.

> **NB!**
> 1. **Set targets** with the help of the budget, for example: 'We aim to achieve 15% growth on overall sales based on the R10 million being spent on marketing.'
> 2. **Measure the actual results** that were achieved (using record-keeping and administration).
> 3. **Compare the actual results with earlier plans or forecasts** and establish whether any deviations have occurred (eg if the actual results are much lower than those forecast).
> 4. **Take corrective steps if necessary** (eg determine how the activities of the business should be adjusted to eliminate the major deviations) from your targets.

The information from the financial analysis can therefore also be used to plan for the future. Knowledge of the present position of the business is the starting point in determining what can be achieved. You can see therefore how financial statements are also vital for financial planning. Financial planning based on what has happened in the past creates the opportunity to reduce or even avoid mistakes in the future. An analysis of the financial statements allows you to compare the financial performance of one year with that of a previous one, and to make comparisons with other businesses in the same industry. There are several ways to analyse financial statements. In this chapter, we will discuss the analysis of financial statements using financial ratios.

3.2   Financial ratios

A financial ratio is a comparison that indicates the relation between two sets of values (items) from the financial statements, such as the statement of comprehensive income (income statement) and statement of financial position (balance sheet). Do you still remember the significance of these statements? If you need to, refer to Chapter 2.

> **NB!**
> The **statement of comprehensive income** (income statement) gives a summary of the income and expenditure of the business during a specific period.
>
> The **statement of financial position** (balance sheet) gives an indication of the financial position of the business at a point in time.

For example, the current ratio shows the relation between the current assets and current liabilities:

$$\text{Current ratio} \quad = \quad \frac{\text{Current assets}}{\text{Current liabilities}}$$

Financial ratios can help us to manage and operate a business enterprise successfully. It is very important not to look at a financial ratio in isolation, as a ratio on its own is not an indication of the success or failure of the business. It must be compared with a norm and assessed together with other ratios. Only then does it provide the starting point for an investigation into the financial performance of the business.

In this chapter, we will look at the following four groups of ratios:

- liquidity ratios
- activity ratios
- solvency ratios
- profitability ratios.

These financial ratios are shown in Figure 3.1.

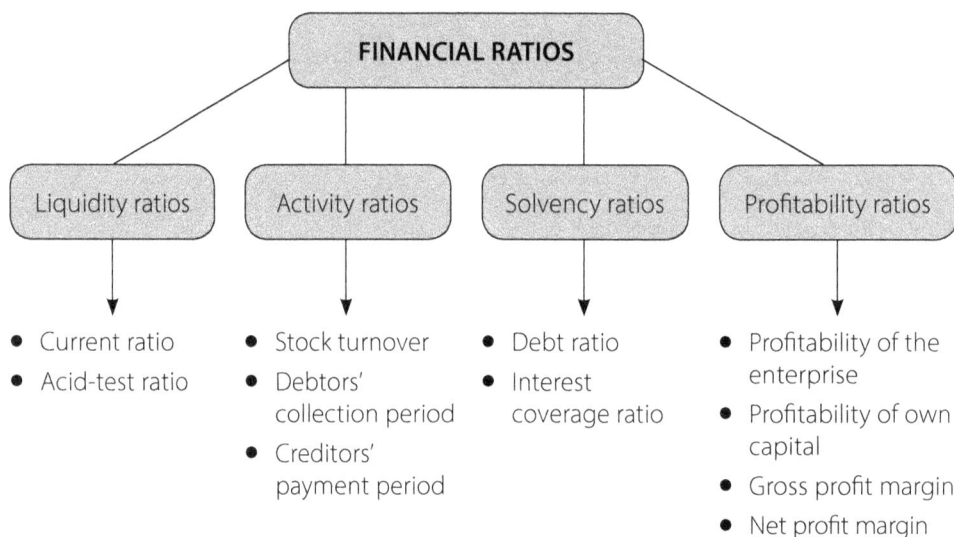

Figure 3.1: Financial ratios

To help in our discussion of financial ratios, we will use the example of Jane's Events CC.

In Chapter 2 you were asked to look at the statement of comprehensive income (income statement) and statement of financial position (balance sheet) of Jane's Events CC. Review what you learned in that section with the aid of the complete statements shown on the following pages.

EXAMPLE

Jane's Events CC

Statement of comprehensive income (income statement) for the year ended 29 February 2023

	2023	2022
	R	R
INCOME		
Sales	1 124 305	782 755
Less: cost of sales	536 164	424 877
Gross income	588 141	357 878
Interest received	17	71
EXPENDITURE	**527 724**	**360 677**
Bank charges	5 114	3 937
Electricity	7 575	5 090
Repairs	10 261	4 356
Rent paid	46 459	41 941
Commission paid	9 638	12 000
Wages and salaries	311 985	170 337
Accountant's remuneration	1 500	1 800
Security	2 448	699
Cleaning costs	2 912	738
Stationery	330	524
Information technology (IT) costs	2 231	1 250
Telephone	5 005	2 308
Transport and deliveries	20 596	12 562
Insurance	13 246	12 930
Depreciation	88 424	90 205
NET PROFIT/(LOSS) BEFORE INTEREST	**60 434**	**(2 728)**
Less: interest paid	9 993	11 407
NET PROFIT/(LOSS) AFTER INTEREST	**50 441**	**(14 135)**

- Credit sales equal 20% of Jane's Events CC total sales.
- 50% of Jane's Events CC purchases were on credit.

Jane's Events CC

Statement of financial position (balance sheet) as at 29 February 2023

	2023	2022
	R	R
ASSETS		
Non-current assets	165 094	253 518
Current assets	133 868	130 903
Inventory	85 000	70 000
Debtors	47 868	10 800
Deposits (investment)	1 000	1 000
Bank balance	–	49 103
TOTAL ASSETS	**298 962**	**384 421**
Members' contributions	100	100
Accumulated loss	(91 236)	(141 677)
Distributable reserves	205 745	285 146
Members' interest	114 609	143 569
Non-current loan debt	90 000	146 000
Current liabilities	94 353	94 852
Creditors	72 798	91 612
Arrear expenses	3 240	3 240
Bank overdraft	18 315	–
TOTAL EQUITY AND LIABILITIES	**298 962**	**384 421**

Jane's Events CC
Statement of changes in equity

	Share capital	Share premium	Distributable reserves	Accumulated profits	Total
Balance – 1 March 2018	100	0	285 146	(127 542)	157 704
Net profit/(loss) for the year				(14 135)	(14 135)
Balance – 28 February 2022	100	0	285 146	(141 677)	143 569
Net profit/(loss) for the year				50 441	50 441
Balance – 29 February 2023	100	0	285 146	(91 236)	194 010

3.3 Liquidity ratios

Liquidity ratios are used as an aid to assess the liquidity position of the enterprise.

EXERCISE 3.1

Do you still remember what liquidity is?

Liquidity refers to the enterprise's … to make all payments on a …

The two ratios that are most commonly used to assess the liquidity of an enterprise are:
- the current ratio
- the acid-test ratio.

3.3.1 Current ratio

The formula for current ratio is as follows:

$$\text{Current ratio} = \frac{\text{Current assets}}{\text{Current liabilities}}$$

If we take the figures from the statement of financial position (balance sheet) of Jane's Events CC, the current ratio for 2023 will be as follows:

$$\frac{133\,868}{94\,353} = 1.42{:}1$$

EXERCISE 3.2

From the statement of financial position:

	2023	2022
Current assets	**133 868**	**130 903**
Inventory	85 000	70 000
Debtors	47 868	10 800
Deposits (investment)	1 000	1 000
Bank balance	–	49 103
Current liabilities	**94 353**	**94 852**
Creditors	72 798	91 612
Arrear expenses	3 240	3 240
Bank overdraft	18 315	–

Calculate the current ratio of Jane's Events CC for 2022.

The current ratio indicates to what extent the current liabilities (short-term debt) of the business are covered by the current assets. In other words, the current ratio tells us whether the business has the means (liquidity) to meet its obligations in the short term (eg the payment of interest, rent, water and electricity). The suppliers of credit are especially interested in the current ratio as they want to know whether the business will be able to pay what it owes them.

The general norm for the current ratio is 2:1. This means that the business must possess R2 in the form of current assets for every R1 that it owes in the short term. A low current ratio can mean that an enterprise will have trouble meeting its short-term obligations (eg the payment of its creditors).

In 2023, for every R1 that Jane's Events CC owed as current liabilities, the business had current assets worth R1.42. At the end of the previous year the current ratio was 1.38:1. This means that the current ratio of the business has improved slightly over the past year. If similar businesses have a current ratio of 2:1, this means that Jane's Events CC is not performing as well as they are. The current ratio will have to improve during the next year.

A weak current ratio can be the result of many factors, among which are the following:

- too many creditors
- inventory cost is too high
- a large bank overdraft.

QUESTION

Can you suggest any ways that an enterprise can improve a weak current ratio?

ANSWER

How do your ideas compare with the following suggestion?
- Pay creditors more quickly.
- Plough sufficient profits back into the enterprise.

3.3.2 Acid-test ratio

When we calculated the current ratio, we assumed that all current assets could be turned into cash equally quickly. However, this is not necessarily the case in reality. For example, it sometimes takes longer to turn inventory into cash than it does to liquidate debtors or an investment in the bank. This is because inventory is sold on credit, which leads to the creation of debtors. For this reason we use another ratio, which excludes inventory, to assess the ability of the business to meet its short-term obligations regularly and on time. This ratio is called the acid-test ratio.

The formula for the acid-test ratio is as follows:

$$\text{Acid-test ratio} = \frac{\text{Current assets} - \text{Inventory}}{\text{Current liabilities}}$$

Again, if we use the figures from the Jane's Events CC statement of financial position (balance sheet) for 2023, the acid-test ratio will be:

$$\frac{133\ 868 - 85\ 000}{94\ 353} = 0.52{:}1$$

EXERCISE 3.3

	2023	2022
Current assets	133 868	130 903
Inventory	85 000	70 000
Debtors	47 868	10 800
Deposits (investment)	1 000	1 000
Bank balance	–	49 103
Current liabilities	94 353	94 852
Creditors	72 798	91 612
Arrear expenses	3 240	3 240
Bank overdraft	18 315	–

Calculate the acid-test ratio of Jane's Events CC for 2022.

The general norm for the acid-test ratio is 1:1. This means that for each R1 of short-term debt, the business must have R1 of liquid assets that can be converted to cash quickly. In the case of Jane's Events CC, in 2023 the business has only R0.52 of current assets for every R1 it owes as current liabilities. A year ago, the ratio was 0:64, so we can see that it weakened during the year.

A low acid-test ratio indicates that the business has possible cash flow problems. By this we mean that it is not able to pay its current liabilities, such as creditors. This makes suppliers of credit – for example banks – hesitant about granting additional credit/financial aid. These suppliers cannot be certain that settlement (interest payments, for instance) will be made regularly.

> **NB!** A low acid-test ratio can be the result of:
> - **too much inventory** – before this can be known, however, the business must assess inventory turnover
> - **a lack of sufficient cash resources**
> - **many debtors** who have already settled their accounts.

If we look at the example of Jane's Events CC, we can see that both the current and the acid-test ratios are below the general norm. This means that the business will have trouble paying short-term debts on time and regularly, and will somehow have to make provision for these payments. (If you look at the statements of the business, you can see that the bank balance has moved from positive to overdrawn over the course of the year.) If the current and acid-test ratios do not improve, the business is likely to develop serious liquidity problems. Persistent cash flow problems can lead to the failure of the business.

3.4 Activity ratios

The activity ratios give an indication of how effectively the assets of the business are being used to realise sales. After all, the goal of acquiring assets is to sell products/services (and thereby obtain income). There are several activity ratios. The ones that you will find most useful are:

- inventory turnover rate (inventory turnaround speed)
- debtors' collection period
- creditors' payment period.

3.4.1 Inventory turnover rate

This is the number of times that the average inventory, which is [(Opening inventory + Closing inventory) ÷ 2], is turned into sales during the year. An ice cream company will experience a much higher inventory turnover in the summer months than in winter.

$$\text{Inventory turnover rate} = \frac{\text{Cost of sales}}{\text{Average inventory}}$$

The calculation for Jane's Events CC for 2023 is as follows:

$$\frac{536\ 164}{(85\ 000 + 70\ 000) \div 2} = 6.92$$

EXERCISE 3.4

From the statement of comprehensive income:

	2023	2022
Sales	1 124 305	782 755
Less: cost of sales	536 164	424 877
Current assets	133 868	130 903
Inventory	85 000	70 000
Debtors	47 868	10 800
Deposits (investments)	1 000	1 000
Bank balance	–	49 103

1. Calculate the inventory turnover rate for Jane's Events CC for 2022 (inventory for 2018 = R6 500).
2. How does this figure compare with the figure for 2023?

The inventory turnover rate gives an indication of how fast its products are moving, relative to the company's cash flow, and measures the company's efficiency in managing the inventory. The challenge for the entity is to find the balance between having the right amount of inventory on hand to minimise the holding costs while not missing sales due to no inventory. The higher the ratio, the more inventory are sold. As a result it is more likely that the company's cash flow is good. Moving inventory means that the money is changing hands and that no excess cash is tied up in slow-moving products.

In order to realise its projected sales for the year, the business's inventory has to 'turn over' a certain number of times. In the example of Jane's Events CC, the firm's inventory had to turn over 6.92 times to realise the sales for the year.

There is no single norm for the inventory turnover rate of a business, because this rate differs from industry to industry.

EXAMPLE

According to the USA Census Bureau, inventory turnover ratios are as follows for these diverse types of businesses:

Manufacturing sector: all goods	1.2 to 1.39
Manufacturing sector: durable goods	1.4 to 1.82
Manufacturing sector: non-durable goods	0.91 to 1.14

If a company based in a coastal area is selling T-shirts and shorts, they must ensure that their stock turnover rate is neither too low nor too high.

If the rate is low, it can mean that:

- inventory is being carried that is not really in demand, eg winter season stock of long-sleeved T-shirts (wrong type of inventory)
- the inventory is obsolete (out of date) or damaged
- the business is carrying too much inventory
- the price of the individual items might be too high for the demographic of the area.

A higher inventory turnover rate means that the business will need less capital to carry inventory, and that capital can be used more frequently during a specific period to finance new inventory. However, there are also dangers in a high inventory turnover rate, which could be the result of carrying too little inventory in comparison with the volume of sales of the business. This could lead to a risk of inventory shortages when sales surge, which would create additional costs for the business (see Chapter 9).

3.4.2 Debtors' collection period

$$\text{Debtors' collection period} \quad = \quad \frac{\text{Average debtors} \times 360}{\text{Credit sales}}$$

EXAMPLE

From the statement of comprehensive income (income statement):

	2023	2022
Sales	1 124 305	782 755
From the statement of financial position (balance sheet):		
Current assets	**133 868**	**130 903**
Inventory	85 000	70 000
Debtors	47 868	10 800
Deposits	1 000	1 000
Bank balance	–	49 103

20% of the sales of Jane's Events CC were on credit for 2023, ie R224 861.

$$\text{Average debtors} \quad = \quad \frac{(47\,868 + 10\,800)}{2} \quad = \quad 29\,334$$

$$\text{Debtors' collection period for 2023} \quad = \quad \frac{29\,334 \times 360}{224\,861} \quad = \quad 47 \text{ days}$$

The debtors' collection period is an indication of the number of days it takes, on average, for the business to collect from its debtors. It enables the business to compare the genuine collection period with the theoretical one. If there are big differences, the business ought to review its credit policy and collection practice.

A long debtors' collection period is an indication of slow and overdue payments by debtors. This has a direct influence on the cash flow of the enterprise and can, in a short space of time, give rise to liquidity problems. (The debtors' turnover rate – a variation on the debtors' collection period – gives an indication of the number of times a year that debts are converted to cash. However, it is much easier to use the debtors' collection period as an aid.)

> **NB!** The credit period that the business grants with credit sales can be used as a guideline in the assessment of the debtors' collection period.

In the case of Jane's Events CC, the debtors' collection period of 47 days for 2023 means that the enterprise had to wait an average of 47 days before its debtors paid their accounts. If the enterprise grants a credit period of 30 days, this means that its debtors are paying their accounts reasonably regularly and on time. (A theoretical credit period of 30 days usually has a collection period of 45 days.)

EXERCISE 3.5

1. Calculate the debtors' collection period for 2022. The average amount owing by debtors for 2022 is R24 868.
2. How does the debtors' collection period for Jane's Events CC for 2022 compare with that of 2023?
3. Can you see that Jane succeeded in shortening the debtors' collection period during 2023?

3.4.3 Creditors' payment period

$$\text{Creditors' payment period} = \frac{\text{Average creditors} \times 360}{\text{Credit purchases}}$$

EXAMPLE

From the statement of comprehensive income (income statement):

	2023	2022
Sales	1 124 305	782 755
Less: cost of sales	536 164	424 877
From the statement of financial position (balance sheet):		
Current liabilities	94 353	94 852
Creditors	72 798	91 612
Arrear expenses	3 240	3 240
Bank overdraft	18 315	–

50% of the purchases of the enterprise are on credit = R268 082 for 2023.

$$\text{Average creditors} = \frac{(72\,748 + 91\,612)}{2} = 82\,205$$

$$\text{Creditors' collection period for 2023} = \frac{82\,205 \times 360}{268\,082} = 110.39\,\text{days}$$

The creditors' payment period gives us an indication of the number of days that elapse before the business pays its creditors. In the case of Jane's Events CC, the creditors wait an average of 110.39 days before they are paid.

EXERCISE 3.6

Calculate the ratio (ie the creditors' payment period) for 2022 with average creditors of R85 204.

As a guideline or norm for assessing this ratio, the business can use the average credit period that is granted to it by creditors.

The real creditors' payment period should correspond with the credit period that was granted.

Large deviations from the granted credit period can be an indication of possible cash flow problems – in other words, the business does not have the cash to pay its creditors.

External credit suppliers, especially in the short term, are very interested in this ratio (together with the current ratio) because it gives an indication of how long the business takes to pay its creditors (whether it has the ability to pay). If the business takes too long to pay its creditors, it may be considered a weak payer. A favourable creditors' payment period also has a positive influence on the current ratio of the enterprise.

If a creditors' payment period is much shorter than the credit period granted, this is not necessarily a good sign. Sometimes creditors put pressure on the business to pay as soon as possible (perhaps as a result of slow/late payments in the past). A very favourable creditors' payment period must be considered together with, among other things, the cash flow of the business and the debtors' collection period. (If the enterprise pays sooner than the credit period granted, it should be possible to negotiate a cash discount from the creditor.)

Jane's Events CC has a very long creditors' payment period compared with the credit period of 45 days that is granted. The business waits a very long time before paying its creditors. The reason for this could be a lack of sufficient cash resources – we saw that this was a problem for the company when we calculated the current and acid-test ratios.

3.5 Solvency ratios

The ability of the business to pay all its debts at any time – even if its activities come to a stop – is known as the solvency of the enterprise. The total liabilities (money that the business owes to its creditors and capital suppliers) must be covered by the total assets. The business must always be able to repay all its debts. If the business cannot give this assurance to the suppliers of borrowed capital (in both the short and the long term), it will be difficult, if not impossible, to attract any initial and/or additional capital from an external source. A lack of capital can threaten the continuity and survival of the business. For solvency ratio we are going to look at debt ratio as well as interest coverage ratio.

EXERCISE 3.7

Why do you think it is essential for a company to have a favourable solvency ratio?

3.5.1   Debt ratio

The solvency ratio that you will find most useful is the debt ratio.

$$\text{Debt ratio} \quad = \quad \frac{\text{Total assets}}{\text{Total liabilities}}$$

EXAMPLE

From the statement of financial position (balance sheet):

	2023	2022
Non-current assets	165 094	253 518
Current assets	**133 868**	**130 903**
Inventory	85 000	70 000
Debtors	47 868	10 800
Deposits	1 000	1 000
Bank balance	–	49 103
TOTAL ASSETS	**298 962**	**384 421**
Non-current liabilities (loan debt)	90 000	146 000
Current liabilities	**94 353**	**94 852**
Creditors	72 798	91 612
Arrear expenses	3 240	3 240
Bank overdraft	18 315	–
TOTAL LIABILITIES	**184 353**	**240 852**

$$\text{Debt ratio for 2020} \quad = \quad \frac{289\,962}{184\,353} \quad = 1.62{:}1$$

The debt ratio reflects the extent to which the total liabilities (long-term liabilities plus current liabilities) of the business are covered by its total assets. For example, a debt ratio of 2:1 means that the business has R2 in assets for each R1 of debt (in both the short and the long term). Jane's Events CC has a debt ratio of 1.62:1, meaning that the business has R1.62 in assets for each R1 of debt. The lower the debt ratio of a business, the greater the financial risk. A debt ratio of 1:1 means that the business is technically insolvent, and if the owner does not take drastic action, it could fail. A debt ratio of 1:1 and lower means that the enterprise is totally owned by external capital suppliers, who can decide to liquidate the business at any time. Prospective capital suppliers are very interested in the debt ratio of a business, precisely because they want to know how safe it is for them to invest in it.

The solvency of the enterprise must be maintained in the long term. The supplier of a loan with a repayment period of 20 years wants to be sure that the business will continue to pay its interest commitments as well as the capital over the term of the loan. In addition to the requirement that total assets must be greater than total liabilities, the business must also have the income potential to meet its commitments in the long term. (This ratio can also be calculated in the liquidity ratio as it reflects the enterprise's ability to make payments.)

3.5.2 Interest coverage ratio

$$\text{Interest coverage ratio} = \frac{\text{Income before interest and tax}}{\text{Interest commitments for the year}}$$

$$\text{Interest coverage ratio for 2023} = \frac{60\ 434}{9\ 993} = 6.05 \text{ times}$$

EXAMPLE

From the statement of comprehensive income:

	2023	2022
EXPENDITURE	**527 724**	**360 677**
Bank charges	5 114	3 937
Electricity	7 575	5 090
Repairs	10 261	4 356
Rent paid	46 459	41 941
Commission paid	9 638	12 000
Wages and salaries	311 958	170 337
Accountant's fees	1 500	1 800
Security	2 448	699
Cleaning costs	2 912	738
Stationery	330	524
Information technology (IT) costs	2 231	1 250
Telephone	5 005	2 308
Transport and deliveries	20 596	12 562
Insurance	13 246	12 930
Depreciation	88 424	90 205
NET PROFIT/(LOSS) BEFORE INTEREST	**60 434**	**(2 728)**
Less: interest paid	9 993	11 407

The interest coverage ratio indicates the number of times the enterprise can pay its interest commitments for the year from its income before interest and tax. Jane's

Events CC's interest coverage ratio for 2023 is favourable, which means that the enterprise can cover its interest commitments six times out of net income before interest and tax. (Note that this does not tell us whether the business has the cash to make the payments.)

3.6   Profitability ratios

In Chapter 1 we explained the concept of profitability and saw that, as well as the profitability of the business, we can also calculate the profitability of own capital. The profitability ratios of the business reflect how profitably the available capital has been employed – has the business obtained a satisfactory return on the available capital? Businesses try to increase the profitability of available capital as much as possible. In this section, we will look at four profitability ratios:

- profitability of the enterprise (return on total assets)
- profitability of own capital
- gross profit margin
- net income margin.

3.6.1   Profitability of the enterprise (return on total assets)

$$\text{Profitability of the enterprise} = \frac{\text{Net income before interest and tax} \times 100}{\text{Total assets}}$$

$$\text{For 2023} = \frac{60\,434 \times 100}{298\,962} = 20.2\%$$

EXAMPLE

From the statement of comprehensive income (income statement):

	2023	2022
NET PROFIT/(LOSS) BEFORE INTEREST	60 434	(2 728)
Less: interest paid	9 993	11 407
From the statement of financial position (balance sheet):		
Non-current assets	165 094	253 518
Current assets	133 868	130 903
Inventory	85 000	70 000
Debtors	47 868	10 800
Deposits	1 000	1 000
Bank balance	–	49 103
TOTAL ASSETS	298 962	384 421

The return that the business earns on the capital invested (both own and borrowed capital) must meet the goals of the business. The profitability of the business must:

- at least exceed the inflation rate
- be higher than alternative investments (eg fixed deposits or unit trusts)
- be considerably higher than interest rates (costs of borrowed capital).

In other words, it must be worthwhile for the owner(s) of the business to invest their capital.

In the case of Jane's Events CC, the profitability of the enterprise for 2023 equals 20.2%. In the previous year, the return on total assets was negative. We can therefore see that the profitability of the business has increased. The owner of Jane's Events CC must look at the inflation rate, the rate of return on alternative investments and the interest rates on borrowed capital as guidelines to determine whether she is satisfied with the return on her investment in the business.

3.6.2 Profitability of own capital

$$\text{Profitability of own capital} = \frac{\text{Net income after interest and before tax} \times 100}{\text{Own capital (owner's interest or members' interest)}}$$

$$\text{For 2023} = \frac{(60434 - 9\,993) = 50\,441 \times 100}{114\,609} = 44\%$$

The profitability of own capital is an indication of the return that the owner(s) of the business have earned on their capital annually. The profitability of own capital is influenced by many things, but particularly the extent to which the business makes use of borrowed capital. The owner(s) strives to raise this ratio as high as possible so that it will be worthwhile to continue with the enterprise. This ratio is also know as return on equity.

EXERCISE 3.8

Jane realised a return of 44% on own capital. How does this compare, in your opinion, with the general guideline (of earning interest on a fixed deposit)?

During the analysis of the financial statements, the profitability of the business can also be expressed in terms of the sales of the enterprise. This brings us to the last two profitability ratios: the gross profit margin (or gross income percentage) and net income margin (or net income percentage).

3.6.3 Gross profit or gross income margin

$$\text{Gross profit margin} \quad = \quad \frac{\text{Gross profit} \times 100}{\text{sales}}$$

$$\text{For 2023} \quad = \quad \frac{588\ 141 \times 100}{1\ 124\ 305} \quad = \quad 52.31\%$$

> **NB!** Gross profit = Sales for the year – Cost of sales

The gross profit margin of the business is calculated by expressing the gross profit as a percentage of the total sales for the year. This number should agree with the mark-up policy of the business. If the gross profit margin is too high compared with market trends, there is a danger that the business's prices are too high. This will eventually lead to a decline in sales (in favour of competitors with lower prices). (A higher gross profit margin can also be the result of better purchasing prices – the business negotiates better prices than the competitors – in which case it is to the advantage of the business.)

EXAMPLE

The cost price of a product is R10. The business marks the product up by 25% – that is, R2.50. The selling price of the product is R12.50. The gross profit percentage on the product is:

$$\frac{2.50 \times 100}{12.50} \quad = 20\%$$

The gross profit margin of Jane's Events CC is 52.31% in 2023. If the general norm for similar enterprises is 34%, Jane's Events CC's gross profit margin is much higher. As we have already said, this can cause problems: Jane's Events CC's product prices may be too high, which can cause a drop in sales. However, a high gross margin could also be the result of better purchasing.

EXERCISE 3.9

- Calculate the gross profit margin of Jane's Events CC for 2022.
- How does it compare with 2023?

3.6.4 Net income margin

$$\text{Net income margin} \quad = \quad \frac{\text{Net income after interest and before tax (NPBT)} \times 100}{\text{Sales}}$$

$$\text{For 2023} \quad = \quad \frac{50\,441 \times 100}{1\,124\,305} \quad = \quad 4.49\%$$

NB! Net income = Gross profit – Operating expenses

In this ratio, the net income before tax is expressed as a percentage of sales. The net income margin is directly influenced by the gross profit margin as well as the operating expenses of the enterprise – including interest payable. In the case of Jane's Events CC, the net income margin is very low. High operating expenses and low sales could be among the reasons for this.

The net income margin of the business can be favourably influenced by:

- lower operating costs
- higher sales
- higher selling prices
- more favourable purchase prices (lower costs of sales).

3.7 Financial leverage

It is important to realise that the use of borrowed capital can have both favourable and unfavourable effects on the profitability of own capital. This is caused by the financial leverage effect. The financial leverage effect has a positive influence on the profitability of own capital if the enterprise profitability is greater than the commitment to the suppliers of borrowed capital (interest on borrowed capital).

To explain the positive effect of the financial lever, let us consider the following three ways in which a business can finance assets:

EXAMPLE

	1	2	3
Own capital	50 000	25 000	5 000
Borrowed capital	–	25 000	45 000
Total capital	50 000	50 000	50 000
Net income before interest and tax	10 000	10 000	10 000
Interest paid @ 18% per annum	–	4 500	8 100
Profitability of the business (= row 4 ÷ row 1)	20%	20%	20%
Profitability of own capital	20%	22%	38%

The profitability of the business for all three examples is 20%, but you can see that the return on the owner's capital becomes considerably higher as more borrowed capital is used. The basic reason for this is that the cost of the borrowed capital is lower than the return that is realised from its investment in the business. Although it is beneficial to make use of borrowed capital, the business cannot use it to an unlimited extent. The business still needs to repay the capital. If the enterprise cannot do this, the owner loses control of the business and it will fail. The excessive use of borrowed capital leads to problems: as the amount of borrowed capital grows, external suppliers of capital become unwilling to carry the increasing levels of risk. Eventually the business will not be able to borrow any more money.

As soon as the fixed interest commitments become greater than (exceed) the return on the investment in the business (enterprise profitability), the profitability of own capital will decline due to the use of too much borrowed capital.

We can explain the negative effect of the financial lever by considering the following three possible ways in which an enterprise can finance assets:

EXAMPLE

	1	2	3
Own capital	50 000	25 000	5 000
Borrowed capital	–	25 000	45 000
Total capital	50 000	50 000	50 000
Net income before interest and tax	10 000	10 000	10 000
Interest paid @ 21% per annum	–	5 250	9 450
Profitability of the business	20%	20%	20%
Profitability of own capital	20%	19%	11%

If the costs involved in the borrowed capital exceed the return on the investment in the enterprise, the profitability of own capital declines.

3.8   Performance ratio

Although industry ratios provide useful benchmarks, it is sometimes difficult to find suitable comparisons. Many businesses will need to redefine their own ratios and key performance indicators (KPIs). Using these monitors can assist in measuring the performance of a company that mainly deals with stock.

For a manufacturing company, the most important ratios will be the following:

- average days to sell (how long it takes to buy or create goods and turn them into sales)
- inventory write-offs (goods that no longer have any value)
- average inventory (a measure of how fast inventory is selling and the average cost of inventory on hand from the beginning of the financial period to the end)
- inventory turnover (number of times the entire inventory is sold in a period)
- holding cost of goods (cost incurred for storage and maintenance of goods).

For a car rental company, the utilisation of the fleet is used as a measure of performance:

$$\text{Utilisation of the fleet} = \frac{\text{Actual car rental days}}{\text{Available car rental days}}$$

EXAMPLE

John has a rental fleet of three cars. For a normal month, his available car rental sales days will be $3 \times 30 = 90$ days.

John added the number of days that the cars were actually rented out, which totalled 62 days.

Therefore, the utilisation % will be:

$$\frac{\text{Car rental days actual}}{\text{Available car rental days}} = \frac{62 \text{ days}}{90 \text{ days}} = 69\%$$

This can now be used to make a month-on-month as well as a year-on-year comparison.

3.9 Summary

In this chapter, we saw that we can use financial ratios to analyse the financial condition of the business. This is done by calculating and analysing various financial ratios using figures from the statement of financial position (balance sheet). The ratios alone do not tell the owner(s) anything – they must be compared with specific goals, trends and guidelines/norms in order to draw conclusions.

The financial statements should be analysed with the aid of the following financial ratios:

- Liquidity ratios, which reveal the ability of the enterprise to meet its commitments regularly and on time
- Activity ratios, which investigate the degree of effectiveness to which the assets are employed to realise sales
- Solvency ratios, which determine the ability of the enterprise to pay all its debts at any given time
- Profitability ratios, which assess the profitability of the enterprise and calculate return on the available capital.

1. Do you agree with the following statements?
   a) An analysis of the financial statements of the business is an important aid to planning. (YES/NO)
   b) By analysing financial statements, you can determine how the business has performed over the previous five years. (YES/NO)
   c) The liquidity ratios of the business are one of the groups of ratios that must be calculated. (YES/NO)
   d) The business can adjust its policy on the management of current assets based on an analysis of the financial statements. (YES/NO)
   e) Suppliers of borrowed capital are interested in the activity ratios and the solvency ratios. (YES/NO)

2. Give reasons for your answers to the statements in question 1.

3. The financial statements of Mama Bake (Pty) Ltd appear below:
   - 50% of the business's sales are on credit.
   - The credit period that the business grants is 30 days.
   - The value of inventory at the beginning of 2023 was R75 000.
   - The enterprise buys 75% of its purchases on credit.
   - The mark-up percentage of the business is 30%.

Mama Bake (Pty) Ltd

Income statement for the year ended 31 December 2023

INCOME	R'000	R'000
Sales	4 125	
Less: cost of sales	−3 000	
Gross profit		1 125
Less: current costs	−750	
Net income before tax and interest		375
Less: interest	−54	
Net income before tax		321
Less: tax	−90	
Net income after tax		231

Mama Bake (Pty) Ltd Statement of financial position (balance sheet) as at 31 December 2023

	R'000	R'000
ASSETS		
Fixed assets		375
Current assets		250
Cash	50	
Debtors	113	
Inventory	87	
TOTAL ASSETS		**625**
Own capital		200
Reserves		175
Total own capital		375
Borrowed capital		
Non-current loan		125
Current liabilities		125
Creditors	125	
EQUITY AND LIABILITIES		**625**

Required

a) Calculate the liquidity ratios.

b) Calculate the activity ratios.

c) Why are suppliers of credit interested in the liquidity position of the enterprise? Give reasons for your answer.

d) Calculate and analyse the solvency ratios of Mama Bake (Pty) Ltd.

e) Assess the profitability of Mama Bake (Pty) Ltd making use of the profitability ratio.

4. Why is it beneficial for a business also to make use of borrowed capital to finance the capital requirements of the business?

5. You are presented with the financials of White Rose Trading (Pty) Ltd for the years ending 31 December 2022 and 31 December 2023. Before you seek advice from your investment adviser, you as an investor would like to analyse the financials objectively.

Statement of financial position (balance sheet) of White Rose Trading (Pty) Ltd at 31 December 2022 and 31 December 2023

	2022	2023
Non-current assets	85 000	58 010
Current assets	95 000	95 000
Stock	72 500	40 000
Debtors	22 500	35 000
Bank	–	20 000
TOTAL ASSETS	180 000	153 010
Members' interest	70 000	55 000
Distributable reserves	40 000	15 010
Total members' interest	110 000	70 010
Long-term liabilities	30 000	25 000
Current liabilities		
Creditors	40 000	58 000
EQUITIES AND LIABILITIES	180 000	153 010

Statement of comprehensive income (income statement) of White Rose Trading (Pty) Ltd for 2022 and 2023

	2022	2023
Gross revenue (all sales were on credit)	248 400	200 000
Cost of sales	(123 480)	(85 000)
Gross profit	124 920	115 000
Operating expenses	(70 320)	(45 000)
Net profit before tax	54 600	70 000
Tax	(19 110)	(24 500)
Net profit after tax	35 490	45 500
Ordinary dividends	(10 500)	(12 500)
Net profit for the year	24 990	33 000

Balances at 31 December 2018

Inventory   R35 000
Debtors   R30 000

Required

Based on the financial statements of White Rose Trading (Pty) Ltd for the years ended 31 December 2022 and 2023, calculate the following ratios (and compare them with the industry norms):

		Industry norm
a)	Current ratio	2:1
b)	Stock turnover ratio	2.5 times
c)	Number of days in stock (assume a 360-day year)	75 days
d)	Number of days in debtors (assume a 360-day year)	45 days
e)	Gross profit	50%
f)	Net profit ratio	25%
g)	Return on equity (profitability of own capital)	40%

6. Analyse profitability: You need to assist in a decision regarding whether a big deal is profitable enough to proceed. The company has a chance to sell goods with a selling price of R1 000 000 on condition that a discount of 25% is granted. This would result in savings on advertising costs of R50 000. The company has the following yearly information:

Sales	3 000 000
Gross profit %	40%

Operating expenses	750 000
Net profit %	15%

Required

Calculate whether the required 25% discount should be granted to obtain the same return on net profit.

7. Analyse liquidity: The marketing manager is proposing a big Christmas campaign and this will require that inventory be increased by R3 500 000, which will need to be paid immediately.

The current applicable figures are as follows:

Inventory	3 000 000
Debtors	10 400 000
Bank	2 000 000
Creditors	8 000 000
Provisions	3 000 000

Required

a) Calculate the current ratio before and after the additional inventory has been bought.

b) If the shareholders require a ratio of 1.4:1, what can you do to conform to this ratio?

8. Utilisation ratio: A young entrepreneur started a car rental company. He has a total of five vehicles, which he rents out per day. He realises that the efficient utilisation of his fleet is a key performance measure for his business and gathers the following information for the month of June:

Vehicle number	Rental period in days
1	10
2	21
3	30
4	17
5	19

Required

Calculate his utilisation based on the information supplied for the month of June.

ANSWERS

1. a) YES
   b) YES
   c) YES
   d) YES
   e) YES

2. a) The analysis of financial statements is a useful aid in determining profitability for different product lines and to show where marketing can be successfully employed.

   b) If you have the information for the last five years, an analysis of financial statements assists the user in determining whether the business is profitable, the cash position and the return for owners, and whether the financial position of the business is sound and whether it is achieving its goals (eg a 20% return on capital).

   c) The ratio groups are the following: liquidity ratios, activity ratios, solvency ratios, profitability ratios.

   d) Use the activity and liquidity ratios to assess the usage of current assets.

   e) These ratios will enable the funders to determine the ability of the entity to repay their capital.

3. a) **Liquidity ratios:**

$$
\begin{array}{ccc}
\text{Current assets} & : & \text{Current liabilities} \\
250\,000 & : & 125\,000 \\
2 & : & 1
\end{array}
$$

Acid test ratio:

$$
\begin{array}{ccc}
(\text{Current assets} - \text{Current inventory}) & : & \text{Current liabilities} \\
(250\,000 - 75\,000) & : & 125\,000 \\
175\,000 & : & 125\,000 \\
1.4 & : & 1
\end{array}
$$

b) **Activity ratios:**

$$\text{Inventory turnover rate} = \frac{\text{Cost of sales (cost price of sales)}}{\text{Average inventory}}$$

$$= \frac{1\,000\,000}{(87\,500 + 75\,000)/2}$$

$$= \frac{1\,000\,000}{81\,250}$$

$$= 12.3 \text{ times}$$

$$\text{Debtors' collection period} = \frac{\text{Average debtors} \times 360}{\text{Credit sales}}$$

$$= \frac{112\,500 \times 360}{1\,375\,000 \times 50\%}$$

$$= \frac{40\,500\,000}{687\,500}$$

$$= 58.9 \text{ days}$$

$$\text{Creditors' payment period} = \frac{\text{Average creditors} \times 360}{\text{Credit purchases}}$$

$$= \frac{125\,000 \times 360}{(1\,000\,000 \times 75\%)}$$

$$= \frac{45\,000\,000}{750\,000}$$

$$= 60 \text{ days}$$

c) The suppliers of credit are interested in the liquidity position because this is a good indication as to whether they will be able to repay the interest and capital when it is due.

d) **Solvency ratios:**

$$\text{Debt ratio} = \frac{\text{Total assets}}{\text{Total liabilities}}$$

$$= \frac{625\,000}{125\,000 + 125\,000}$$

$$= 2.5$$

The assets cover the liabilities 2.5 times.

$$\text{Interest coverage ratio} = \frac{\text{Income before interest and tax}}{\text{Interest commitments for the year}}$$

$$= \frac{106\,250 + 18\,750}{18\,750}$$

$$= 6.67 \text{ times}$$

As per the solvency ratio, the entity's assets are well covered by its liabilities, and the profit will cover the interest payment 6.67 times.

e) **Profitability ratios:**

$$\text{Profitability of the enterprise} = \frac{\text{Net income before interest and tax} \times 100}{\text{Total assets}}$$

$$= \frac{(106\,250 + 18\,750) \times 100}{625\,000}$$

$$= \frac{12\,500\,000}{625\,000}$$

$$= 20\%$$

$$\text{Profitability of own capital} = \frac{\text{Net income after interest and before tax} \times 100}{\text{Own capital (owners' interest/members' interest)}}$$

$$= \frac{(55\,250 + 18\,750) \times 100}{200\,000}$$

$$= \frac{74\,000 \times 100}{200\,000}$$

$$= 37\%$$

Gross income percentage, also known as gross profit margin:

$$\text{Gross profit margin} = \frac{375\,000 \times 100}{1\,375\,000} = 27\%$$

Net income percentage, also known as net profit margin:

$$\text{Net profit margin} = \frac{\text{Net income after interest and before tax} \times 100}{\text{Sales}}$$

$$= \frac{106\,250 \times 100}{1\,375\,000}$$

$$= 7.7\%$$

Conclusion:

The profitability of both the assets as well as capital (equity) is very good in comparison with the return that would be received from putting the money into a savings account.

4. Paying interest has a tax benefit and can be negotiated depending on the credit profile of the company. The cost of interest for the borrowed funds is cheaper than the cost of capital (refer to calculation in 3(e)).

5. a) Current ratio : Current ratio

    Current assets : Current liabilities

        95 000 : 40 000

                   = 2.37:1

This current ratio is better than the industry norm of 2:1.

b) Inventory turnover rate

$$= \frac{\text{Cost of sales (Cost price of sales)}}{\text{Average inventory}}$$

$$= \frac{123\ 480}{(72\ 500 + 40\ 000)/2}$$

$$= \frac{123\ 480}{56\ 250}$$

$$= 2.19 \text{ times}$$

The inventory turnover is not as fast as the industry average of 2.5 times.

c) Calculate the days in inventory by dividing the number of days in the period by the inventory turnover ratio (as calculated above).

Days in inventory

$$= \frac{\text{Number of days in the period}}{\text{Inventory turnover ratio}}$$

$$= \frac{360}{2.19}$$

$$= 164 \text{ days}$$

It takes 164 days to sell all the inventory in comparison with the industry of 75 days.

d) Debtors' collection period

$$= \frac{\text{Average debtors} \times 360}{\text{Credit sales}}$$

$$= \frac{(22\ 500 + 35\ 000) \div 2 \times 360}{248\ 400}$$

$$= 41.6 \text{ days}$$

The debtors' collection period will depend on the credit term granted by the entity but currently it is 3.4 days shorter than the industry, which is very good.

e) Gross income % $= \dfrac{124\,920 \times 100}{248\,400} = 50\%$

The gross profit % is in line with the industry.

f) Net income margin $= \dfrac{\text{Net income after interest and before tax} \times 100}{\text{Sales}}$

$= \dfrac{(35\,900 + 19\,110) \times 100 \ (\text{NPBT})}{248\,400}$

$= 22.1\%$

Net profit percentage is just under the industry norm of 25%.

g) Profitability of own capital $= \dfrac{\text{Net income after interest and before tax} \times 100}{\text{Own capital (owners' interest/members' interest)}}$

$= \dfrac{(35\,490 + 19\,110) \times 100 \ (\text{NPBT})}{110\,000}$

$= \dfrac{54\,600 \times 100}{110\,000}$

$= 49.6\%$

The return on equity is higher than the industry of 40%.

6. First calculate the gross profit, cost of sales and net profit based on ratios given:

		Yearly info
	Sales	3 000 000
Step 2	Cost of sales	−1 800 000
Step 1	Gross profit	1 200 000
Step 3	Operating expenses	750 000
Step 4	**Net profit**	450 000
		15%

Calculate the effect of the transaction on a discounted price:

		Calculation	Discount transaction
Step 1	Sales	1 000 000 × (100% − 25% = 75%)	750 000
Step 2	Cost of sales	1 000 000 × 60%	−600 500
Step 3	Gross profit	GP (1 000 000 × (40% − 25%)	112 500
Step 4	Operating expenses	Saving on expenses	−50 000
Step 5	**Net profit**		200 0000

Add the yearly amounts and discounts transaction together:

	Yearly info	Discount transaction	Yearly info plus discount transaction
Sales	3 000 000	750 000	3 750 000
Cost of sales (3 000 000 – 1 200 000)	–1 800 000	-600 500	–2 400 000
Gross profit 3 000 000 x 40%	1 200 000	150 000	1 350 000
Operating expenses (1 200 000 – 450 000)	750 000	–50 000	700 000
Net profit (R3 000 000 x 15%)	450 000	200 000	650 000
Net profit %	**15%**		**17%**

Conclusion:

It is more profitable to grant the 25% discount on the bulk sales transaction.

7. a) Current ratio before inventory increase:

$$\frac{\text{Current assets}}{\text{Current liabilities}} = \frac{(3\ 000\ 000 + 10\ 400\ 000 + 2\ 000\ 000)}{(8\ 000\ 000 + 3\ 000\ 000)} = 1.4{:}1$$

After inventory increase:

$$\frac{\text{Current assets}}{\text{Current liabilities}} =$$

$$\frac{(6\ 500\ 000 + 10\ 400\ 000 + (2\ 000\ 000 - 3\ 500\ 000))}{(8\ 000\ 000 + 3\ 000\ 000)} = \frac{15\ 400\ 000}{11\ 000\ 000} = 1.4{:}1$$

b) Increase debtors' collection so that the company has sufficient cash to pay for the entire inventory and does not need to obtain an overdraft.

8. Use the following formula:

$$\frac{\text{Car rental days actual}}{\text{Available car rental sales days}} = \frac{97\ \text{days}}{150\ \text{days}} = 64.7\%$$

4

The capital requirements of any enterprise or organisation

WILLIE CONRADIE

Learning outcomes

After reading this chapter, you should be able to:

- identify and illustrate the costs involved in researching and developing a viable initiative or business idea
- distinguish between the initial research and development costs and the capital required to establish a new initiative or enterprise
- understand the various capital needs for fixed assets
- understand the various capital needs for current/liquid assets
- explain the difference between the need for permanent capital and the need for variable capital
- draw a diagram showing the needs for permanent and variable capital in any organisation or business enterprise
- explain the two principles ruling what kind(s) of capital sources should be used to finance either the permanent or the variable need for capital
- identify and explain the impact of the following factors on an enterprise's need for capital:
  - the type of industry
  - the length of its working capital cycle
  - forecasted and future income or sales figures
  - a period of high growth in income or sales
  - an ongoing initiative
  - a new start-up business or project/new department.

4.1   Introduction

All organisations, institutions and businesses need certain things in order to function well – for example human resources, money, machines and materials. As these resources are usually scarce and costly, the manager/business entrepreneur has to be able to acquire and combine them in the most productive ways possible.

When it comes to acquiring and combining scarce resources, we need to be aware of two separate but related concepts.

> **NB!** Firstly, the manager/business entrepreneur has to decide what is needed and required for the enterprise to achieve its goals and objectives. For example, they must decide what machinery and equipment is needed for the new and/or existing initiatives. There are many factors to be investigated and considered, such as models, makes, capacities and capabilities, and expected lifespan. These decisions are called **investment decisions**.
>
> Secondly, the manager or owner needs to make decisions about the best ways to finance the required assets and resources. This is the responsibility of financial management – to acquire the applicable needed capital for a business and to ensure that the best use is made of it (as discussed elsewhere). These decisions are called **financing decisions**.

> **NB!** There are many excellent videos available on determining the needs for capital, from the most basic to the very sophisticated. One is *Calculating Your Business Capital Needs* (https://www.youtube.com/watch?v=8lFfuVCzz0w).

In this chapter, we will look at the qualitative and quantitative nature of financial planning. Management planning is a prerequisite for the success and future wellbeing of any enterprise and its stakeholders. Directly related to management planning is financial planning – translating management's plans into financial terms and plans.

Financial planning aims:

- to determine the variety of needs for assets and therefore the required capital
- to decide on the best way to finance these needs.

In this chapter we will discuss the most important elements of the capital need (the investment decision). Elsewhere we will look more closely at the elements of the financing decision.

4.2   The capital need for evaluating viability

Creating and developing a new business idea and transforming it into a realistic business plan, with its many elements and requirements, is something that demands a huge investment in time and other resources.

> **NB!** There are two kinds of investments involved in this phase:
> 1. the initial research and development costs
> 2. the once-off setup costs.

4.2.1   Initial research and development costs

An idea for any new initiative can come from many sources. For example, you might see an advertisement in a newspaper for a business that is up for sale. Perhaps you saw some innovative products and/or services in another city or country while you were on holiday. Sometimes a client/customer or a supplier will mention something that indicates a need in the market place.

> **NB!** An important thing to remember about research and development costs is that you must be able to afford and absorb these costs without knowing whether the final product or service will be viable. However, such costs are generally of a once-off nature. Once your business is established, you will not need to keep spending as much money on research and development.

Although initial research and development is considered a once-off cost, it is a good idea for a business to engage in ongoing research and development activities. The business environment is constantly changing, and the manager and business entrepreneur must always look for new ways to improve their existing business/organisation and to identify new business opportunities.

4.2.2   Investigating the idea

You need to investigate the idea and to assess it according to all the principles and functions of business management. You may need to visit an existing business that is for sale, and to hold discussions with the seller and their agents, with lawyers, bankers and accountants and perhaps even with business consultants. Sometimes it is necessary to develop a business model, to test-market a product and to undertake costly and extensive market research.

4.2.3   Initial setup costs

Once you have established that your business idea is viable, there are many things to put into place before the business can be regarded as ongoing. All of these things involve costs, and the following are some examples of these.

Agreements (legal costs)

Before a business can be established, there are costs involved in drawing up purchasing contracts and/or rental agreements, and/or finalising partnership agreements.

Rental and other deposits

Apart from the required monthly rental, the owner of the business premises will usually demand a deposit – often equivalent to (but sometimes three times as much as) the monthly rental. A deposit may also be required by the local authority before it will provide water and electricity services.

Adhering to rules and regulations

Depending on the nature of the new enterprise or initiative and its location, there may be costs involved in obtaining the required authorisations. For example, a local authority may stipulate that additional fire extinguishers be purchased, a site may need alterations before it will be approved for a particular use, or health requirements may dictate that the kitchen walls of a hired site must be tiled up to ceiling level. There are also costs involved when you register formally as an employer, as a tax collector (PAYE from employees and VAT) and as a taxpayer, and for satisfying the legal requirements in registering a new company as a (Pty) Ltd.

Acquiring assets

Every enterprise needs assets, and these cost money. Some of them are once-off in nature – for example installing machinery and equipment; fitting shelves and display units; producing signage, billboards and display windows; and designing a website, letterheads and other stationery.

Capital needed to break even

A very important aspect of financial management is the financial break-even point. No generation of net profits is possible until the break-even point (number of units and sales volumes required to cover all costs) is reached and passed. The break-even point is covered in detail in a later chapter.

Usually, new retail businesses and new ventures in the marketing services industry need to trade for several months before they reach and pass the break-even point. In manufacturing, this may take one or more years (eg a well-known steel manufacturer in Mpumalanga took more than 10 years to break even).

Apart from the initial legal costs, deposits and once-off fitting costs, the business manager/entrepreneur must also provide for monthly operational costs during the period before the business reaches the break-even point. During this time, more cash is going out than is coming into the business, and this gap needs to be financed. Especially in a services enterprise, where salaries and wages will be a major cost (up to 80% of operational costs) right from the start, this requirement cannot be ignored. Normally, a new business will also need to finance at least three to nine months of budgeted operational costs during this phase. Once break-even is reached and passed, and cash flow becomes positive, the need for initial establishing capital will fall away.

4.3   The need for fixed and current assets

As we have seen, every organisation needs assets to carry out its operations. Some of these have a relatively long life expectancy, while others are needed to do business within the shorter term.

4.3.1   Fixed assets

> **NB!** Fixed assets are those assets needed in an organisation or business for periods exceeding 12 months. These assets are used by the business to do business and are not sold as part of its product range.

When it is deemed necessary for the business to acquire assets, this creates a fixed capital need, as such assets must be procured and financed. If they are rented or leased, there is a need for operational capital because rent is an operational cost.

Following are some typical examples of fixed assets in a business:

- land and buildings
- machinery and equipment
- furniture and fittings
- vehicles.

4.3.2   Current assets

> **NB!** Current assets include things that are needed to do business, and which will usually be consumed or turned into sales and/or cash within 12 months. Current assets are also called liquid or operational assets.

All these assets need to be acquired and financed. To become operational to do business, an enterprise may need the following current assets:

- **Raw and supplementary materials** include all the raw materials needed in the manufacturing process, for example the chemicals and other ingredients needed by a pharmaceutical company, or the various kinds of metals, wood, glue and nails used by a billboard manufacturer.

- **Stock** (inventory) includes goods that are meant for consumption or resale purposes. In a manufacturing concern, stock refers to both work-in-progress and finished products.

- **Outstanding debtors** shows the total amounts that clients owe the business, and represents past credit purchases (by these clients) of services rendered to those clients that are not yet paid for. Usually the enterprise will expect these amounts to be paid within a month or two.

- **Cash** in the business is the ultimate current asset in a business. It includes short-term investments (eg deposits in a savings or cheque account).

> **NB!** Note that what is considered a fixed asset in one type of industry may be regarded as a current asset in another.

EXERCISE 4.1

Koos van der Merwe's Mobile Delivery Agency specialises in selling advertising space on his trucks to a variety of businesses in Limpopo province. He has 10 huge trucks, with plenty of advertising space, making daily deliveries to a variety of clients all over the province.

Ashraf Cassiem's Commercial Ambulances, on the other hand, specialises in buying and selling second-hand ambulances. At present he has 10 vehicles for sale on his showroom floor.

1. Would the 10 trucks belonging to Koos van der Merwe's Mobile Delivery Agency be classified as fixed or current assets? Why?
2. Would the 10 vehicles belonging to Ashraf Cassiem's Commercial Ambulances be classified as fixed or current assets? Why?

4.4   The need for permanent and variable capital

A business's need for capital can also be split into the need for permanent and variable (short-term) capital.

4.4.1   The permanent (or continuous) capital need

Permanent capital refers to capital that is needed at all times or for a certain fixed period. This is the absolute minimum amount of capital that the business requires to operate continuously and do business.

A business needs permanent (or continuous) capital because it must acquire minimum amounts of both fixed and current assets in order to operate. Usually, the total need for fixed assets is part of the need for permanent capital. The other part of permanent capital is that portion of current assets that is a constant, non-variable part of the required current assets.

We can also express this concept as a formula:

Permanent capital = Capital needed for all fixed assets + Permanent part of the capital needed for all current assets

The following are some examples of current assets for which permanent capital is needed:

Stock

Although the levels of stock in a shop may change between a low level of R800 000 per month and a peak level of R1 500 000 per month, the low level may be regarded as a permanent capital need (as it is the absolute minimum level of stock required for the business to operate continuously at all times).

Outstanding debtors

There are often large variations in the total amount of monies owed to the business by clients and customers. Usually, this total amount will reach its lowest level after the first week of the month (the time when payments are usually made), and is highest near the end of the month. The minimum level of outstanding debtors during the year represents the amount of permanent capital required to finance this minimum level of outstanding debt on a continuous basis.

Cash

A minimum level of cash (on hand or in the bank) is needed at all times in a business. This may be cash floats for project managers or cashiers, or for certain daily expenses (eg staff refreshments). This minimum level represents a permanent need for capital.

4.4.2   The variable (short-term) capital need

Variable capital consists of additional capital required by the business from time to time, over and above the amount of capital required on a permanent basis. During certain periods, the business may find that it needs more than the minimum levels of capital. During these periods, usually referred to as peak periods, additional assets (especially current assets) are required to do well in business.

Typical peak periods are during the winter or summer and the April, June/July and December school holidays, and particularly the Christmas season. At these times, businesses require much more than the minimum level of stock and have much higher operational expenses (such as hiring temporary staff). During April,

June and July, and during October, November and December, retailers may carry two to four times more stock than their minimum stock levels. This is especially true for businesses in and around holiday resorts and other popular holiday areas. This increase in the need for stock – the difference between the minimum level of stock required at all times and the maximum level of required stock during peak periods – represents the short-term need for additional variable capital. In other words, it is capital that is needed for a short period of time only.

In the same way, there are times when a business needs to carry a certain additional level of outstanding debtors (over and above the permanent minimum level) and/or a certain additional level of cash (over and above the permanent minimum level). These additional amounts of current assets represent the variable (short-term) capital need of a business.

The permanent and variable needs for capital can be illustrated on a graph, as shown in Figure 4.1. Note that the arrows in the diagram indicate the relative differences in value between types of assets over time.

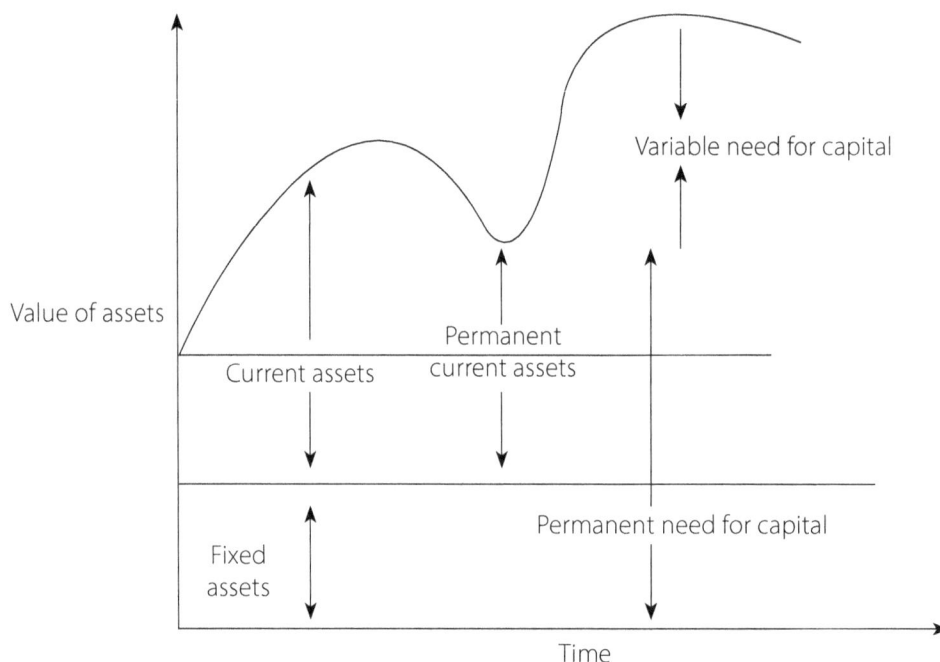

Figure 4.1: Permanent and variable needs for capital

4.4.3 Two important principles

There are two principles we can use to help us understand a business's need for fixed and current assets, and to link this understanding to the nature of the need for permanent capital.

> **NB!** The permanent capital needs of a business should only be financed through long-term capital sources. This means that (a) all the needed fixed assets (land and buildings, machinery and equipment, vehicles and furniture) as well as (b) the permanent part of the needed current assets (the minimum levels of stock, debtors and cash required at all times) must be financed from long-term capital sources. We will look more closely at long-term capital sources elsewhere in this book.

The variable capital needs of a business are the only part of the total capital needs that should be financed from short-term capital sources.

This means that only the seasonal need for additional current assets (over and above the minimum levels required at all times throughout the year) should be financed through short-term capital sources.

> **NB!** Many managers and business entrepreneurs make the mistake of using an overdraft facility or suppliers' credit (both short-term capital sources) to buy fixed assets, or to pay for the permanent part of current assets. This practice can be very costly to the business, and can lead to a serious and sometimes fatal liquidity crisis.

Some owners/managers argue that they are forced to do this because they do not have access to long-term capital. This may be true, but it still does not make the practice a good idea. You must try hard to adhere to the two very important principles given above.

4.5   Other factors influencing the capital need

Thus far, all the factors we have discussed in this chapter have been common and generic to all types of organisations and businesses, in any industry. However, there are a number of additional factors influencing the capital requirement of an enterprise. In this section we look at the following:

- the type of industry
- the length of the working capital cycle
- forecasted sales figures
- external factors
- growth and expansion
- the differences between ongoing and new businesses/projects.

4.5.1   Type of industry

Certain types of industries – for example manufacturing, or producing (especially television) advertising material – may need to invest a substantial portion of their total investment in fixed assets. Such businesses typically require huge investments in equipment, and/or land, and/or machinery, and/or specialised vehicles. Such businesses are commonly known as capital-intensive businesses.

On the other hand, a services business may require the biggest part of its total investment to be allocated to labour requirements (full-time and/or part-time professional staff). We refer to this type of business as being labour intensive. A retailer (buying and selling products) may find that up to 80% of all the capital requirements of the business arise from its need for stock. We can thus see that the type of industry has a direct influence on a business's need for capital.

4.5.2   Length of the working capital cycle

The length of the working capital cycle also plays an important role in the eventual capital requirements of an enterprise. The working capital cycle refers to the average number of days from the date of the initial investment up to the date that full income is received from it.

EXAMPLE

Zara Jacobs owns a manufacturing firm specialising in making sophisticated medical care furniture. If we examine the workflow in her factory, we can observe the following:

- Zara first places an order for the raw and supplementary materials she needs to manufacture the specialised furniture.
- After a few days, she receives the materials ordered.
- She now has to pay for her purchases, say by means of cash on delivery or on a credit basis. For our purposes, we assume that she must pay for the goods within 30 days of delivery.
- The materials now need to be transformed into finished goods. This requires an investment of production labour (wages) and machinery. Production takes 10 days.
- The finished goods are now sold, either for cash or on a credit basis. It takes 10 days to find a willing client to buy the goods. Let us say that the client then takes 100 days to pay.

⏹➡

We can illustrate this process as follows:

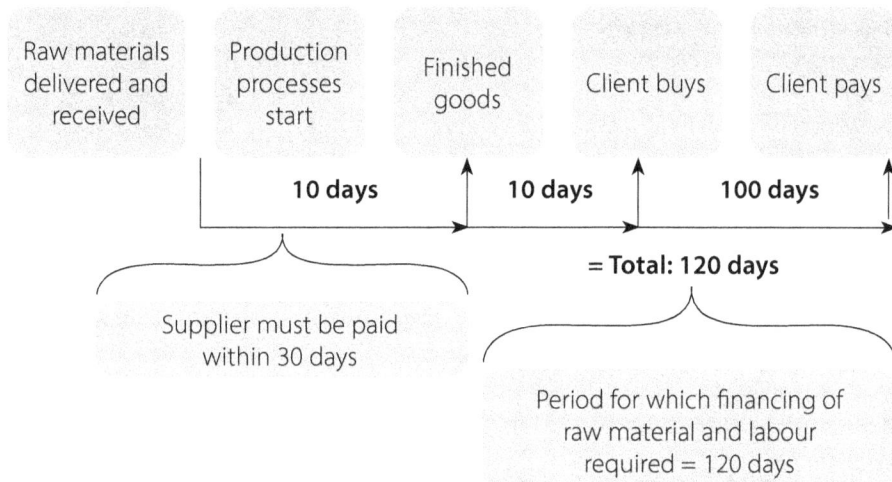

From delivery of the ordered materials to the day payment is received from the client, we can see that the whole cycle takes 120 days. For 30 of these days, the supplier financed the needed raw materials. However, additional short-term capital is required for the remaining 90 days.

NB! The owner/manager should do everything possible to shorten the working capital cycle without causing stock-outs, overstocking or other problems. The shorter the working capital cycle, the sooner profit and a positive cash flow can be realised. The longer the cycle, the more capital is required and the greater the financing costs.

EXERCISE 4.2

List four areas where a working capital cycle could be shortened. Will this indicate any additional risks?

4.5.3 Forecasted sales/income figures

The sales/income forecasted for the new or existing enterprise/organisation forms the basis of most financial plans and budgets because this information will determine the size and nature of all other detailed budgets (eg the sales budget, purchases budget, human resources and production budgets).

DEFINITION

Sales/income forecasting is the process where all relevant external and internal factors are taken into consideration in order to make a calculated prediction of the specific demands/requests for products or services by clients (mostly expressed in monetary terms) for each of the enterprise's services and/or products during a particular future period – usually the following 12 months.

4.5.4   External factors

For both new and ongoing businesses/organisations, there are a number of external factors that play important roles.

The general economic, political, social and technological environment

Will the country/region/town experience economic growth or turmoil in the foreseeable future? Is it politically stable? Are there significant technological changes looming? What about potential social upheavals?

The economic, political, social and technological outlook for my specific industry

How will each of these factors impact my enterprise (and my suppliers and customers) when I am in the manufacturing, retailing or services industry?

The influence of economic, political, social and technological changes on my target market and customers

How will these factors impact on my existing and potential clients and customers?

The competitive environment in my industry

What steps are my existing competitors likely to take next year? And what are the chances of new competition entering my industry?

4.5.5   Growth and expansion

It is not commonly known or understood that high growth and expansion have caused the downfall of many smaller organisations and businesses (as well as some very big ones). Most owners/managers of business enterprises have visions of rapid growth, and expansion is one of their most cherished wishes. So how can high growth possibly result in failure?

The answer lies in whether the growth and expansion is well managed or not: was it foreseen, and were its implications studied and the necessary precautions taken to ensure controlled (rather than uncontrolled) growth resulting in the desired interim and end results? Or was growth unexpected, unforeseen and uncontrolled?

> **NB!** Any growth in business activities has a direct impact on additional capital requirements. The faster the growth, the higher the demands for additional capital (more staff, more space, more storage, better security, etc). An increase in business activities automatically creates a need for extra capital – for fixed and current assets and for higher levels of permanent and variable capital. The right types of capital sources need to be identified and convinced to invest in the business – and at the right time. If this does not happen, the problems created by high growth may prove to be insurmountable and eventually devastating for the business.

EXAMPLES

The following are some typical examples of problems created by high growth:

- An urgent need for additional production capacity (eg more machines and equipment)
- An urgent need for more trained and experienced staff
- An urgent need for more stock (whether raw and supplementary materials or finished goods)
- An urgent need for more facilities (eg storage space, telephones, transport and training)
- More reactive and less proactive management practices (ie solving day-to-day crises instead of directing energy towards planning for growth)
- A surge in customer complaints (as a result of declining quality of rendered services and/or manufactured products, late deliveries, wrong invoicing and accounts, etc).

> **NB!** The recent Covid19 international pandemic is an extreme example and case study of sudden, unforeseen and extreme decline or high growth demands for applicable products and services.

EXERCISE 4.3

Think about each of the above-mentioned problem areas and try to give at least one everyday practical example or illustration from your own experience to illustrate each one.

4.5.6 Capital requirements for ongoing and new enterprises

Determining the capital requirements of an ongoing business is a fairly straightforward matter, and firstly involves collecting the relevant information. Such information includes past and present financial performance (particularly regarding income, expenses and expenditure) and is used to determine present and future trends.

Because this information is readily available in an ongoing business, management only needs to forecast how all these business activities will behave in the future (taking into consideration the impact of external and internal factors and any new plans for the coming period).

Determining the capital requirements of a new unit, enterprise or business is a much more challenging task. There are no past client or customer figures, no past sales and income figures and no figures for direct and indirect operational costs (such as stock levels, production costs, wages and salaries) to use as a basis for forecasting. No past trends can be calculated and used to predict the future. No past and/or present internal sources of information are available.

There are, however, a number of external sources of information available to the management of a new business. Local and national chambers of commerce and industry and some universities or other research institutions can help in supplying specific and localised ratios and trends applicable to a specific industry or business.

EXAMPLE

A marketing entrepreneur is planning to open a ladies' boutique retail business. She may find that for ladies' boutique businesses in upmarket shopping centres in Gauteng the average monthly sales per square meter of rented area is R 50 000. The entrepreneur can thus project her own forecasted/expected monthly sales figures by taking this piece of information and multiplying it by the number of square meters of the premises the business will rent in an upmarket shopping centre.

The same can be done with many other ratios and indicators. Care should be taken, however, when using these external sources of information. Every business is a unique entity with its own strengths and weaknesses, and you should never assume that a new venture will indeed follow the average past performances of other similar businesses in that industry. Search for these external sources of information, study them carefully and then use the information as a base to project your own figures for the future. Remember that you can write anything you wish on paper, but to actually make it work out in the real world of business management is quite a different thing!

> **NB!** It is good practice to create three possible future scenarios and plans for a new enterprise/project: a low/pessimistic road; a high/optimistic road and a middle-of-the road scenario … for the next three years at least!

4.6 Summary

In this chapter, we highlighted the capital requirements for any organisation or enterprise. Capital will always be needed because any enterprise needs all kinds of assets in order to operate, and these have to be supplied and financed by someone. Certain once-off costs have to be incurred when starting an enterprise or a new initiative. These initial costs need to be financed until the business passes its financial break-even point. The business also needs fixed and current assets on an ongoing basis and these require certain capital investments.

Fixed and current assets have different life expectancies and the manager/business entrepreneur therefore has to distinguish between the needs for permanent and variable capital. It is important to keep in mind the principle that permanent capital needs should only be financed from long-term capital sources, while variable capital needs are the only part of the total capital need that should be financed from short-term capital sources.

Other factors that influence the need for capital are the type of industry, the length of the working capital cycle, expected demand for services and/or sales volumes, and the impact of exceptionally high growth (or decline) in business activities.

Finally, it is important to remember that the capital needs of an ongoing enterprise are determined in different ways to those of a new one. In the latter case, the lack of information about past results and performance seriously hampers accurate calculations of the business's future needs for capital.

SELF-EVALUATION QUESTIONS

1. Name and explain at least three types of activities associated with the research for and the development of a new business opportunity that will need to be financed *(see Section 4.2.2)*.

2. Indicate at least three typical costs involved in the initial establishment of a new initiative. Give a practical example in each case *(see Section 4.2.3)*.

3. Explain and illustrate, by means of examples, an enterprise's capital needs for:
   a) fixed assets (three types) *(see Section 4.3.1)*
   b) current assets (three types) *(see Section 4.3.2)*.

4. Explain the difference between an organisation's needs for permanent and variable capital. Give everyday examples of each *(see sections 4.4.1 and 4.4.2)*.

5. Use a graph to explain your answer in question 4 *(see Figure 4.1)*.

6. Explain and illustrate the two important principles when financing the permanent as well as the variable capital needs of an enterprise *(see Section 4.4.3)*.

7. Explain, giving everyday examples, how each of the following factors influences an enterprise's need for capital:
   a) the type of industry *(see Section 4.5.1)*
   b) the length of its working capital cycle *(see Section 4.5.2)*
   c) the forecasted demand for services and expected sales figures *(see Section 4.5.3)*
   d) the occurrence of a phase of rapid growth *(see Section 4.5.5)*.

Financing the capital requirements of an enterprise

WILLIE CONRADIE

Learning outcomes

After reading this chapter, you should be able to:

- define the two primary sources of finances or capital: own capital (share capital, equity, retained earnings) and outside capital (foreign, borrowed, external, loan)
- describe the major characteristics of:
  - ◆ permanent finance/capital and its sources
  - ◆ long-term finance/capital and its sources
  - ◆ medium-term finance/capital and its sources
  - ◆ short-term finance/capital and its sources
- explain which principles are involved in correctly choosing sources of finance/capital
- discuss the typical problems experienced by small enterprises in obtaining finance/capital.

5.1 Introduction

The **investment decision** determines what assets are required to do business successfully. The manager/entrepreneur must decide what fixed assets (land and buildings, machinery and equipment, vehicles and furniture) and what kind of current assets (cash, stock or inventory and size of the debtors' book) are required by the enterprise.

In this chapter we will look at the other side of the finance/capital requirement: **the financing decision**. Once you have decided on all the required fixed and current assets for your enterprise or strategic business unit, you need to ask yourself a number of important questions:

- How will I acquire these assets?
- How will I pay for them?
- If my own/the shareholders' capital is not enough, who would be willing to finance them?

- Is it wise to use only own capital or should I invite and allow other parties to invest?

- What are the important principles involved in ensuring that I make the right financing decisions?

- What are the requirements and motives of those who may be able to assist me?

- Will their contribution be to my advantage or only theirs?

- What are the problems experienced by the average business manager/entrepreneur, and how can I learn from them?

We will now show you how to find the answers to these questions.

5.2   Sources of finance/capital

The two major sources of finance for any enterprise are own capital (internal sources) and outside capital (external sources). Each of these has its own characteristics, advantages, disadvantages and requirements.

> **NB!** It is important to understand that the words 'capital' and 'finance' do not necessarily refer to physical cash or money. Finance may be supplied as cash (in one of a variety of forms), but may also be supplied as an asset. The value of the capital is the monetary value of that asset.

5.2.1   Own capital (equity, share capital, retained earnings)

Own capital (also known as owner's capital, shareholders' funds or owner's interest or equity) is one of the most important sources of finance for any business enterprise. The characteristics of own capital are as follows:

- Often it is the first source of capital available when starting a business.

- It is that part of the total capital that is legally recognised as the total value (at a certain point in time) of contributions made by all legal owners of the business.

- It serves as the basis from which other (mostly outside) capital can be attracted.

- Without own capital invested in the enterprise, it is very unlikely that other potential suppliers of capital will be interested in putting money into the business.

- Own capital is permanent. The investment will last as long as the business itself, provided that the business is not sold or terminated (although exceptions to this rule are possible).

- It is not easy and/or advisable to withdraw a part of own capital, especially if the business is not a sole proprietorship, for example when it is a partnership, close corporation or private company with other shareholders.

- There are a variety of sources of own capital, including owner's savings, pension payouts and existing owned assets put to use in the business. It may even consist of unrelated assets (eg a house or household furniture) that are sold or bonded and changed into cash.

- A person starting an enterprise does not need to depend solely on their own contribution to complete the full picture of own capital. There are two other supplementary sources of own capital:

  ◆ If the founder borrows money from someone else in their personal capacity (and not on behalf of and in the business's name) and invests it in the business, such monies are considered to be own capital.

  ◆ If the founder wishes to bring co-owners (partners, other shareholders) into the business, these co-owners may also provide own capital.

  ◆ Another very important source that adds to the value of own capital is the reinvestment of net profit (after tax) as time goes by. This is sometimes called 'retained earnings'.

EXERCISE 5.1

1. Vusi, the founder of Vusi's Marketing, had no cash to invest in his business when he started it, but he owned appropriate photographic and other graphical and editing equipment to the value of R1 300 000 and a vehicle to the value of R200 000. He was also able to convince his previous employer to sell additional needed equipment to his business. They agreed that his business needed only to repay the total value of R1 600 000 in five years' time. Interest on the outstanding money will be calculated at 10% per annum and payable monthly.

   a) How much capital did Vusi initially invest in his new business? Is this own or outside capital?

   b) How much did Vusi's previous employer invest in the new business? Is this the business's own or outside capital?

2. Talk to the owner of any business enterprise that you know, and ask how the business was started. Ask the owner to indicate to you the different sources of assets/capital that they had available to them at the beginning. Your written answer must include the following:

   a) the name of the business enterprise

   b) the owner's name

   c) the enterprise's initial assets/capital

   d) who supplied/financed these assets.

5.2.2 Outside capital (foreign, borrowed, external, loan)

DEFINITION

As the name suggests, **outside capital** is finance/capital that comes from sources outside the business. A more formal definition is that outside capital is the sum total of all legal claims by other parties (other than the legal owner(s) of a business) who have supplied the business with assets and/or cash and have not yet been repaid in full.

To understand the nature of outside capital, note the following points:

- Outside capital is usually made available to the enterprise on a short-, medium- and/or long-term basis. This is different from own capital, which remains in the business permanently.
- Outside capital therefore has to be repaid at some time in the future. In contrast, it is rare that own capital must be repaid.
- Suppliers of outside capital are paid financing fees (ie interest) as remuneration (reward or payment) for helping to finance the business. The exception is trade creditors (businesses that supply the enterprise with commercial goods and services on a credit basis). In contrast, the suppliers of own capital are usually paid a dividend as remuneration (they also benefit from the growth in the value of their investment).
- If the business is liquidated or sold, the suppliers of outside capital usually have distinct and preferential claims when it comes to being paid. Usually, employees (salaries in arrears) and SARS have first priority. The last parties to be paid (if anything is left) are the suppliers of own capital.

Table 5.1: Own capital vs outside capital

Own capital	Outside capital
Has a permanent nature	May be of a short-, medium- or long-term nature (no permanence)
Is seldom withdrawn	Must be repaid eventually
Suppliers of own capital are remunerated in the form of dividends and growth in value	Suppliers are remunerated in the form of interest paid and/or goods or services sold/supplied to the enterprise
Suppliers of own capital are in full charge of the management of the business	Suppliers have very little or no control at all over the business
Suppliers of own capital are the last claim to be remunerated if the business is liquidated/terminated	Represents a preferential claim on assets (before owner(s)) should the business be liquidated

{Chapter 5: Financing the capital requirements of an enterprise}

5.3   Forms and sources of finance

We explained elsewhere that the capital needs of any enterprise include fixed and current assets. Remember too that any enterprise has both a permanent and a variable need for capital.

We also emphasised how important it is to satisfy the need for permanent capital only from long-term sources of capital. Similarly, the need for variable capital should be satisfied by using short-term sources of capital.

The unit manager/business entrepreneur must make use of the appropriate forms and sources of finance to satisfy these needs and requirements. In this section we will look at four forms and sources of finance that are relevant to the business sector.

5.3.1   Permanent finance and its sources

Normally the only source of permanent finance for a small, start-up business is own capital. The only other source may be the reinvestment of net profit (after tax) in the form of undistributed reserves (also called retained earnings). There is quite a variety of forms of own capital (eg share capital and loan accounts by shareholders).

It is not uncommon to find suppliers of outside capital who are interested in taking up shareholding in a viable small business. The Industrial Development Corporation (IDC) and Business Partners are two such organisations.

5.3.2   Long-term finance and its sources

DEFINITION

Long-term finance consists of those monies or goods made available on credit to the enterprise for a period of five/seven years or longer (normally not more than 20 years).

The major characteristics of long-term finance and its sources are as follows:

- Normally a formal, written, legal document drawn up by an attorney and signed by all parties will spell out the detailed conditions of the agreement between the supplier and receiver of such monies or goods.
- In most cases, interest has to be paid to the supplier. In the past, it was not uncommon to have a fixed interest rate lasting for the full period. Nowadays, the interest rate will most likely be linked, say, to regular changes in the prime banking rate and will be adjusted accordingly as time goes on.

Basic Financial Management

- In most cases, long-term finance will be made available to the enterprise only if it can be directly linked to a long-term fixed asset. Normally, such a fixed asset will be legally registered as collateral for the amount due to the supplier of capital. This form of finance will usually be treated as a long-term loan on an enterprise's balance sheet.

- In some cases, long-term shareholders' loans may also be supplied by the owners of a business, and are not regarded as equity. In most of these cases, no form of collateral will be required.

- In rare cases, outside parties (such as a family member or a friend) may supply a long-term loan without expecting or insisting on adequate collateral.

Table 5.2: Examples of assets and appropriate collateral

Nature of asset	Form of collateral	Contribution
Land	Mortgage bonds (1st, 2nd or 3rd)	Money to buy land from seller
Buildings	Mortgage bonds (1st, 2nd or 3rd)	Money to buy or erect buildings
Equipment with a life expectancy longer than five years	Contract of pledge	Equipment to use or sell, or money to buy equipment

QUESTION

What are the assets most commonly financed with long-term loans? What are the most likely sources of finance for acquiring them?

ANSWER

- Land, which is financed by own capital, banks, other financial institutions and/or the seller of the asset.

- Buildings, which are financed by own capital, banks, other financial institutions, the seller of the asset and/or the building contractor themselves.

- Machinery and equipment (with a five-year-plus life expectancy), which is financed by own capital, banks, other financial institutions and/or the seller of the asset.

> **NB!** Wealthy private individuals (so-called 'business angels') may also be possible sources of long-term finance for a viable business. These are wealthy people who are looking for alternative investment opportunities. They prefer to invest their capital in local businesses (instead of international stock markets and the like) where they can take a personal interest in its progress. If the business grows and becomes more profitable, these investors will expect to be additionally remunerated. They may even wish to become minority co-owners/shareholders of the business.

5.3.3   Medium-term finance and its sources

DEFINITION

Medium-term finance consists of assets and/or monies supplied to the business for periods lasting between one and seven years.

The major characteristics of medium-term finance and its sources are as follows:

- A legally drafted, signed document is usually an integral part of the transaction.
- Normally, interest will have to be paid by a business. In some cases, it will be a fixed interest rate, but in most cases, the interest rate may change according to changes in the official banking rate.
- Repayments of the initial capital (plus interest and other finance charges) are usually made in equal monthly payments for the whole period. Sometimes only interest and finance charges are initially paid monthly, and the capital is repaid only at the end of the period (or every six or twelve months).
- Renting (or leasing) an asset is also a form of financing. There are a variety of renting/leasing options, each with its own characteristics and conditions.
- A hire-purchase agreement is also a common form of medium-term finance.

> **NB!** It is important to know that the conditions applicable to this type of finance are generally negotiated and packaged to suit the requirements and circumstances of individual enterprises. The suppliers of medium-term finance are generally able to offer a wide variety of conditions.

Remember that the manager/business entrepreneur should never blindly accept the initial conditions and demands put forward by the willing supplier of goods or capital. The manager/entrepreneur has to make sure that each and every condition is to the advantage of the enterprise. Before signing anything, the manager/entrepreneur should negotiate and query all conditions of the credit transaction.

QUESTION

What assets are most commonly financed with medium-term finance? What are the most likely sources of medium-term finance for acquiring these assets?

ANSWER

- Machinery and equipment, which is financed by own capital, banks, other financial institutions, the seller of the asset, and/or private individuals.
- Vehicles, which are financed by own capital, banks, other financial institutions, the seller of the asset, and/or private individuals.
- Furniture, which is financed by own capital, banks, other financial institutions, the seller of the asset, and/or private individuals.

EXERCISE 5.2

Visit a branch of one of the well-known banks and ask to speak to a loan officer. Ask this person to explain to you the variety of forms of finance that the bank makes available to business enterprises. List at least five forms and then note the major characteristics of each.

NB! Another form of medium-term finance, offered by most banks and some specialised financing institutions, is **factoring**. Factoring takes place when the business sells (as a once-off transaction or even on a monthly basis) its debtors' book (all or some of its debtors' accounts) to the bank or a specialised financing institution. The latter will pay cash for the debtors' book and will then collect the outstanding monies for their own pockets. Remember that a buyer (known as a **factor**) will not want to run the risk of bad debts, and thus will negotiate to buy the debtors' book at, say, only 60–90% of its invoice value. This form of finance is not readily made available to most start-up businesses.

5.3.4 Short-term finance and its sources

DEFINITION

Short-term finance is made available to the business enterprise for a period of less than 12 months. Normally, the specified period of availability is 30–90 days (in the case of suppliers' credit) or even 24 hours (a bank overdraft facility may be withdrawn within 24 hours, although usually it will be available for much longer).

The major characteristics of short-term finance and its sources are as follows:

- When short-term goods or services, stock and materials are made available on credit to an enterprise, we say that such goods or services are being temporarily financed by the suppliers – the suppliers are then considered to be the suppliers of short-term finance to the business.

- Normally, suppliers or creditors of short-term goods and services (eg raw materials, stock or inventory) will not charge interest on the outstanding balance owed by the business. However, they may charge a high interest rate on accounts in arrears.

- The suppliers of short-term cash loans to the enterprise (banking overdraft facilities or loans forwarded by individuals) will usually charge the business interest.

- Suppliers of short-term goods and services on credit are usually not very strict or disciplined in assessing the creditworthiness of their credit-purchasing customers. This is because they especially wish to encourage sales, among other reasons. However, they may become very strict and unforgiving if and when their trust in a business customer proves to be unjustified.

- Suppliers' short-term credit is not only restricted to those goods the business owner/manager needs for reselling purposes (called stock or inventory). Other goods and services needed to facilitate business activities (eg marketing or bookkeeping or security and/or administration services) may also be paid for on a credit basis.

DEFINITIONS

The term **trade creditors** refers to the credit suppliers of goods and/or services needed for reselling purposes (manufacturing works in exactly the same way). The term **other creditors** refers to the parties to which outstanding monies are owed as the suppliers of goods/services (other than for manufacturing and/or reselling purposes) that are needed for support operations.

In some cases, the short-term capital needs of an enterprise may even be partially financed by one or more customers (such as when a customer places an order with a manufacturer/contractor and pays a deposit at the same time).

> ### EXERCISE 5.3
>
> Visit a manufacturer (or a wholesaler) and ask to speak with the credit control officer/ manager. Ask this person to explain to you the variety of credit forms available to business clients when they need short-term assets/services.
>
> Your written answer must include:
> - the forms of at least two types of credit offered
> - the main characteristics of these forms of credit.

5.4 Choosing sources and forms of finance

Over the long term, the business entrepreneur/manager is responsible for maximising the value added to the business's equity. To do this, they need to make sure that the specific sources and forms of finance used will help to achieve this goal.

This section will look at the critical considerations that must be analysed before each financing decision is made.

5.4.1 Matching life expectancy of assets and credit time available

As mentioned elsewhere, it is extremely important to match the life expectancy of the asset(s) with the length of time for which the source of credit is made available. We saw, previously, that an understanding of a business's needs for fixed and current assets requires an understanding of the needs for permanent and variable capital.

5.4.2 Availability and accessibility issues

In real business situations, it is sometimes not possible for the business entrepreneur/manager to follow prudent financial management principles. Sometimes the appropriate sources and forms of finance are not available. However, you should take care not to be tricked into dubious sources because they seem like the most available form of capital.

5.4.3 Costs associated with a specific source

Often, business entrepreneurs/managers are so relieved to find willing sources of finance that they completely forget to negotiate the best possible conditions and requirements. Always and on a regular basis negotiate with suppliers of credit.

5.4.4 Independence versus dependence and control

One of the strongest motivations for starting one's own business enterprise is the desire to be independent – to initiate your own plans and to do things your own way.

However, the more outside capital you use in the business, the more your independence is threatened. If you do not have enough own capital resources, a needed piece of equipment will only become available if and when you find an outside supplier of finance. The same goes for bringing in extra partners or shareholders. This not only strengthens the own capital base, but also reduces the independence of the business entrepreneur.

5.4.5 Freedom of application of finance

Most of the sources and forms of finance available in the marketplace will only be made available to the business entrepreneur on condition that the money is used for a specific and predetermined purpose (see Table 5.3).

Table 5.3: Forms of finance and their uses

Form of finance	Uses
Mortgage bonds	Can only be used for the acquisition or renovation of land and fixed buildings
Rental/leasing/hire purchase	Can only be used for the acquisition of certain and specified equipment and/or machinery, and/or vehicles, and/or furniture and fittings
Suppliers' credit	Can only be used for the acquisition of specific goods and services bought on credit from a supplier
A bank overdraft	One of the rare cases in which the entrepreneur has almost total freedom of use
Own capital in the form of cash	The owner has total freedom of use

5.4.6 The effects of financial leverage

Financial leverage is related to the cost and use of borrowed capital in the enterprise. If the profitability of the enterprise (ROI) is greater than the interest rate on borrowed capital, the use of borrowed capital results in an increase in the profitability of own capital/equity (ROE). The enterprise therefore uses borrowed capital in the hope that it will cause the profitability of own capital to rise. However, if the interest rate on borrowed capital is greater than the overall profitability of the enterprise, the profitability of own capital is negatively influenced and it drops. It is important to remember certain factors, namely:

- the relationship (ratio) between own and outside capital
- the profitability of the whole enterprise (its return on total investment, or ROI)
- the costs/interest of outside capital compared to the ROI
- the effect that financial leverage will have on the return on equity (ROE). In an attempt to attract own or outside capital, the business entrepreneur/manager must not forget to work out whether the result of the decision will lead to a positive or negative leverage on own capital (ROE).

5.4.7   Considerations of liquidity and profitability

Deciding on the specific form of finance has a direct impact on the business's liquidity and profitability. This is closely related to the considerations in sections 5.4.3 and 5.4.6.

Sometimes over the short term it is wise to forget about profitability issues and to make sure that major liquidity threats do not sink the ship – **there are many examples of highly profitable businesses that have had to close down because of a sudden liquidity crisis.**

5.4.8   Taxation considerations

There are important taxation issues that are relevant to the wellbeing of a private enterprise. For now, remember that almost every decision about required assets, as well as on the sources and forms of finance, has tax implications.

EXAMPLES

Peter Nkosi needs a sophisticated and professionally well-equipped 4×4 vehicle to use in his wildlife adventure tourism business. He has three options:

1. If he pays cash for the vehicle (using own capital), he will not be able to deduct any part of the purchase price from his business's income for income tax purposes (although insurance premiums and maintenance costs may be deductible).
2. If he purchases the vehicle on a hire-purchase basis, he may pay a deposit (not tax deductible) and a monthly instalment (where only the interest and insurance part of the instalment and accrued maintenance costs may be tax deductible, but not the capital down payment part of the instalment).
3. If he rents the vehicle without ever becoming the legal owner, the total cost of renting may be deductible for income tax purposes.

5.4.9 Building long-term relationships

One of the major strengths of small business owners/managers (compared to those of very large businesses) is their dedication and expertise in building and developing strong networks. This is something to remember and to build on.

There are many people involved in a small business: the owner(s), relatives and friends, bankers, lawyers, suppliers, existing and potential customers, employees, local authorities, the local communities and even the staff of SARS.

The more the business entrepreneur/manager succeeds in building and developing sound relationships with the vast range of constituencies, the more they will be able to combine the wisdom and strengths of all these resources. If these networks are neglected, isolation and failure may result.

5.5 Typical problems in obtaining finance

Small businesses have certain advantages when compared to big businesses (eg building strong personal relationships and networks), but the size and influence of a small business can be a disadvantage when it comes to obtaining finance.

This section deals with typical problems experienced by small business entrepreneurs in their quest for the right sources and forms of finance.

5.5.1 When own capital's contribution is too small

To finance all the assets needed in a business, prudent financial management dictates that the contribution of own capital should be at least 50%. In other words, own capital should never be less than half of the business's total capital.

To start a business, an entrepreneur generally uses all available savings and own capital. As the business grows and expands, so does its increased need for assets (and for sources of finance to acquire them). Because the entrepreneur's original savings have been depleted, they depend more and more on outside capital sources.

A related problem is that potential suppliers of outside finance also want to know about the financial structure of the small business. The smaller the relative proportion of own capital to total capital, the less willing these suppliers will be to provide additional funding. If they do so, there will always be an additional cost to the business.

5.5.2 Lack of experience in financial management

Usually the small business entrepreneur will have excellent experience and knowledge in a number of disciplines (eg manufacturing, and/or selling and marketing, and/or supplying unique goods/services to customers), but very few entrepreneurs are also experienced in financial management. This lack of expertise creates many difficulties inter alia when approaching potential suppliers of needed finance, and the entrepreneur may not be able to convince them to help. Such owners/managers should admit this fact and seek assistance in this field.

5.5.3   Lack of financial expertise

A lack of experience in financial management specifically affects the management and running of the business. An entrepreneur who is experienced and knowledgeable about, say, marketing and/or manufacturing will tend to be heavily involved in these activities. An entrepreneur/manager who does not understand financial management will be more inclined to ignore or avoid them. This tendency is very dangerous for any small business/enterprise and its sustainability.

EXERCISE 5.4

Try to relate the three statements under headings 5.5.1–5.5.3 to an everyday small business operation. Do you agree or disagree with the statements above? Give two reasons for each answer.

5.5.4   Too much emphasis on collateral by suppliers of finance

Inexperienced entrepreneurs may only be aware of some of the sources and forms of finance – perhaps only the large national banks and a few other major financial institutions and trade creditors. If they approach only these sources, the results can be disappointing. Generally, the first question asked by these suppliers is: 'How much collateral can you put up to guarantee your debts?' Banks in particular are often accused of using this quick and easy method of credit assessment. This approach is like saying to someone: 'If you don't already have an umbrella, I can't help you get one!'

Although this is a valid criticism of banks, they often have no other choice. If the entrepreneur has not done their 'homework' and chosen the right form of finance, the banker can only accurately assess one of the aspects of their creditworthiness, such as collateral.

5.5.5   Lack of planning

The planning function is an important part of business management. The saying 'If you fail to plan, you plan to fail' contains a great deal of truth. On the other hand, if you prepare an elaborate business plan and then do not implement it, you will have wasted a lot of energy and other resources.

Many business textbooks discuss the steps, contents and issues that should be addressed in the business plan. Many claim that the major purpose of a business plan is to convince potential suppliers of finance to invest in the business or to supply capital. However, the very first use of a business plan is for the entrepreneur to determine the viability of their business ideas, and then to make a success of implementing them.

5.5.6 Creditworthiness

Just as an entrepreneur/manager needs to make a careful analysis to determine the creditworthiness of a client, so the suppliers of finance need to analyse the strengths and weaknesses of an applicant.

The challenge for the business manager/entrepreneur is therefore to be prepared, to have substantiated facts and motivations ready to convince the selected source of finance to provide needed capital, and then to maintain this trust into the future.

5.6   Summary

In this chapter, we discussed the major issues relating to how a business's assets should be financed. We explained the differences between own and outside sources and forms of finance. In direct relation to these issues, we examined the various sources and forms of permanent and variable finance available in the marketplace. These include permanent, long-term, medium-term and short-term finance.

There are a number of critical considerations involved in choosing the best form and source of finance. However, the availability and accessibility of a finance source often forces the entrepreneur/manager to disregard these considerations. The chapter concludes by discussing some typical problems encountered by small business entrepreneurs in their attempts to obtain finance.

SELF-EVALUATION QUESTIONS

1. Name and explain at least four characteristics of 'own capital' in any private business. *(see Section 5.2.1).*

2. Name and illustrate at least five characteristics of 'outside capital' *(see Section 5.2.2).*

3. What are the nature and sources of permanent finance? *(see Section 5.3.1).*

4. Briefly discuss at least five characteristics of long-term finance and their sources *(see Section 5.3.2).*

5. Explain in your own words what 'business angels' are *(see Section 5.3.2 about wealthy individuals).*

6. Briefly discuss at least five characteristics of medium-term finance and its sources *(see Section 5.3.3).*

7. Briefly discuss at least five characteristics of short-term finance and their sources *(see Section 5.3.4).*

8. There are at least nine important considerations in choosing the right sources and forms of finance. Can you think of five of these? Give a short explanation for each of your answers *(see sections 5.4.1–5.4.9).*

9. Small business entrepreneurs face unique problems in obtaining finance. What are five of the problems they face? Give a short explanation for each of your answers *(see sections 5.5.1–5.5.6).*

6

The financial break-even analysis

WILLIE CONRADIE

Learning outcomes

After reading this chapter, you should be able to:

- indicate some of the most important things to consider in starting and managing a new initiative
- explain in simple terms what is meant by the financial break-even principle
- explain in simple terms what is meant by the financial break-even point
- name, explain and illustrate the three pieces of information required to calculate the financial break-even point
- calculate the financial break-event point using three formulas
- explain the break-even concept using a graph
- assess the impact on the break-even point when any one of the three critical elements changes
- explain in simple terms why the financial break-even point is of importance to the ongoing venture
- explain the advantages and disadvantages of the financial break-even analysis.

> **NB!** There are many excellent videos available on the financial break-even point, from the most basic to the very sophisticated. See, for example, *Break-even Point – easily explained!* (https://www.youtube.com/watch?v=ZihWEVWCJYk).

6.1 Introduction

A business entrepreneur/manager must answer many important questions when considering starting a new initiative (be it a totally new venture or a new initiative/department for an existing enterprise). Some of these questions are the following:

- At what cost prices will I be able to acquire the products and services I intend to sell?
- At what selling prices will I be able to convince potential customers to buy from me rather than from my competitors?

- Apart from the actual direct cost price of the products and services, what other costs will I incur in order to acquire and sell these products and services?

- How can I know in advance how many products I need to acquire and sell in order to realise a satisfactory profit (or end-result if the gaining of an acceptable profit is not my objective as will be the case with a governmental or not-for-profit institution)?

- After I have started the enterprise/venture, if there is a change in one or more of my cost prices, how will that influence the quantity of products and services that I need to sell in order to realise the same profit as before? (This question is also relevant whenever a change may occur in the selling prices and/or other costs of business operations.)

In this chapter, we will answer these questions by looking at some realistic everyday examples.

Critical aspects of starting any initiative or business

In this section we will review some of the factors that must be considered before starting a new enterprise or initiative. To do this, let us use the example of an entrepreneur selling fast food.

EXAMPLE

Mary Khoza is a second-year marketing student and needs to improve her financial position. Because she is good at making hamburgers and her friends always ask her to make hamburgers for them, she is considering running a weekend hamburger stall called Super-Duper Burgers at a popular flea market near the campus.

EXERCISE 6.1

What are the most important things to consider when starting such an initiative (or any other kind of venture)? What information does Mary need to establish whether her hamburger stall will be viable? List at least 10 things she will need to investigate.

6.1.1 Common factors to consider

Here are a few (among many) of the factors Mary will have to consider:

Location

Is there an appropriate site available at the chosen flea market? How much will the rent per day be? What about alternative flea markets or another type of location?

Competition

Are there other suppliers of hamburgers at (or near) the flea market? At what price do they sell their hamburgers? How many hamburgers do they sell on average? What can Mary offer her customers that will give her a competitive advantage?

Equipment

What kind of equipment will Mary need at the stall to make and sell her hamburgers? Is this equipment available on a rental basis or will Mary have to buy it?

Raw materials

In Mary's case the raw materials are the ingredients she will use. She needs to make a list of all the ingredients to make her Super-Duper hamburgers (eg meat, spices, rolls and sauces). It is very important that she calculates exactly what it will cost to make a single hamburger.

Salary and wages

A basic principle of business management is that the profit of the business and the salary/remuneration of the owner or manager are two separate things, even if the entrepreneur is also the manager. An entrepreneur who operates and manages their own business should pay themselves a competitive, market-related salary – the same salary one would have to pay someone else to be a manager in the entrepreneur's place. This forms part of the overall expenses of the business. Profit is determined by deducting all applicable business expenses (including the manager's salary) from the related income. Mary should therefore make provision for her own market-related remuneration. If business is good, she may need to employ one or more assistants, and work out how much to pay them.

6.1.2 The marketing factor

It is not enough to have an excellent product or service; you also have to inform and convince the target market about it and make it attractive and easy for customers to buy it. These activities are part of marketing. Mary will need to market her hamburgers in an efficient and effective way, otherwise her business will not succeed.

Mary's investigations, inquiries and negotiations yielded the following results:

- **Site:** Mary finds a well-located site close to where visitors enter the flea market at a daily rate of R1 600 (payable in cash on the previous Monday).

- **Selling price:** There is one competitor in the flea market selling hamburgers at R50 each. Mary reckons that she will do well selling her hamburgers at the same price (so as not to compete on price, but rather compete by differentiating on taste and quality of service). She could not find out how many hamburgers this competitor sells per day, but the landlord reckons that an average of 10 000 people visit the market daily on weekends.

- **Equipment:** After investigating many alternatives, Mary determines that the best option would be to rent a fully equipped trailer, custom-made for a hamburger stall, including gas bottles, utensils, signboards, etc. The daily rent is R400 and is payable one week in advance.

- **Wages:** Mary reckons that a market-related daily wage for herself could be R900 per day (R90 per hour for 10 hours). Her younger sister is willing to assist her for R300 per day (R50 per hour for six hours). Her sister expects to be paid this figure regardless of the number of hamburgers they sell per day.

- **Ingredients**: With the help of a friend who qualified as a chef, Mary laboriously calculates that the total cost price of all the ingredients needed for one Super-Duper hamburger is exactly R20. This includes the bread roll, meat patty, butter, mustard, onions, lettuce, her 'mystery' Super-Duper sauce, salt and pepper, and packaging.

- **Marketing:** Mary's sign-writer neighbour offers to make a striking billboard (3 m × 2 m) for the top of Mary's trailer to advertise her Super-Duper hamburgers. He and Mary work together on the design and wording of the billboard. It will cost Mary a once-off amount of R2 000.

- **Transport and communication:** After considering all the relevant aspects, Mary estimates that her transport and communication costs will be about R80 per day.

6.2   The break-even point per single product unit

This very important question needs to be asked of any existing or new business venture: How many products must be sold over any given period of time to cover all costs and not incur a loss/negative end result? Let us see how to work this out.

Now that Mary has worked out the costs of everything she needs to start and operate her hamburger stall, she needs to calculate how many hamburgers she must sell each day to cover all her costs. This is called the break-even point.

DEFINITION

The **break-even point** of a business (or of any initiative) can be defined as the level of sales (expressed in number of units and/or monetary value) at which neither a profit nor a loss is realised. It is the level of sales where the gross income is equal to the total direct and indirect costs/expenses of the enterprise/initiative. At this point, the business is neither making any profit nor realising any loss – it is breaking even in terms of costs and income.

EXAMPLE

How many units (hamburgers) must be sold by Mary per day to break even? To answer this question, we need three pieces of information:

1. **The selling price of a single product/service:** Mary has decided that she will sell her hamburgers for R50 each.

2. **The direct cost price of a single product/service:** The direct cost price relates to all the costs directly incurred in acquiring/manufacturing a single product. In Mary's case this will be R20, representing the accumulated cost prices of all the ingredients needed to make and sell one hamburger. If a staff member is employed solely to make hamburgers (the production process), such a person's salary should also be regarded as a direct manufacturing cost and must be divided by the number of hamburgers that the staff member will make per day to get to a figure for direct labour costs per unit. For the purpose of this exercise, we will for now ignore this principle of direct labour costs.

3. **The total indirect costs (also called operational or fixed costs or overheads) of the business:** The total indirect costs cover all other costs (other than the direct costs required to acquire/manufacture the product/service) necessary to operate the business. In Mary's case, these costs seem to be the daily rental of a site (R1600), the daily rental of the custom-made trailer (R400), the daily wages to be paid (R900 + R300 = R1200) and the transport and communication costs of R80 per day. Added together, this amounts to R3 280 per day. But what about costs that do not have a straight-forward daily/weekly or monthly cost?

QUESTION

The R2 000 Mary has to pay for the billboard (ie marketing costs) needs some further discussion. This amount is not a daily expense (as is the case with the daily rental of equipment or daily wages or site rental) but it is a once-off expense. How should this kind of cost be included in determining the actual daily cost?

➠

ANSWER

There is a logical answer to this. If one argues that the life expectancy of the billboard can be regarded as, say, 12 months and it will be used over 50 weekends (allowing two weeks of holiday per year for Mary), it will be used for 100 days per year. The daily cost for this billboard will therefore be R2 000 divided by 100, which equals R20 per day. The same principle applies when a business buys machines or equipment or vehicles. The life expectancy (time period of productive usage) and the purchase value of each of these durable assets are used to determine their monthly or annual cost to the enterprise (normally indicated as monthly or annual depreciation costs).

The total and actual indirect costs (or operational or fixed costs or overheads) to Mary's business will thus be R3 300 per day (R1 600 for the rental of the site, R400 for the rental of the custom-made trailer, R1 200 for wages, R20 for the allocated billboard costs, plus R80 budgeted for transport and communication costs).

6.2.1   Using the break-even formula

The following formula can be used to answer the question of how many hamburgers Mary must sell per day in order to break even:

$$\frac{\text{Total overheads}}{\text{Selling price} - \text{Direct cost price per unit}} = \frac{\text{R3 300}}{\text{R50} - \text{R20}} = \begin{array}{l}\text{110 hamburgers must be made}\\\text{and sold per day to break even}\end{array}$$

This shows that Mary needs to sell 110 hamburgers per day in order to break even. If she sells more, she will make a profit. If she sells fewer than 110 units on a specific day, she will make a loss.

6.2.2   Verifying your answer

How can you be sure that you have correctly calculated Mary's break-even point? You can easily verify the answer by answering the following questions.

QUESTIONS

1.   How much will Mary's daily total gross income be if she sells 110 hamburgers per day at R50 each?
2.   How much will her total daily direct costs be when making and selling 110 hamburgers at a direct cost price of R20 per hamburger?
3.   How much are her total daily indirect costs to operate the business?

ANSWERS

1. 110 × R50 = R5 500 total income
2. 110 × R20 = R2 200 total direct costs/manufacturing costs
3.   R   400 for trailer rental
        + R1 600 for site rental
        + R20 for advertising
        + R1 200 for wages
        + R80 for transport and communication
            = R3 300

So: Gross sales per day (110 @ R50 each)   = R5 500

Less: Direct costs (110 @ R20 each)

                                           = R2 200

Gives: Gross profit   = R3 300

Less: Indirect costs (overheads)   = R3 300

        Gives: Net profit (or net loss)   = R0

NB! Remember, you need the following three pieces of information to calculate the break-even point:

1. selling price per unit
2. direct cost price per unit
3. total indirect costs (overheads) of the business initiative as a whole.

6.3   Other financial concepts

Now that you understand what is meant by the break-even point, let us look at some other important concepts in financial management. First we will examine terms we have used already in our calculation of the break-even point, namely indirect costs (or the same in other words: overheads or fixed costs or operational costs) and direct costs. We will then discuss gross profit/marginal income.

6.3.1 Overheads

Overheads (also called indirect costs, operational costs, fixed costs or non-variable costs) are those costs, other than the direct costs (see Section 6.3.2), that are unavoidable in business. If sales are low, the fixed costs will still be incurred. If sales rise, fixed costs will still be the same (up to a certain point, of course).

DEFINITION

Overheads (also known as fixed costs, indirect costs and operational costs) are committed, unavoidable costs that are not directly related to the volume of sales. Normally, overheads consist of the costs of the facilities and resources that enable the business to operate, eg buildings, equipment, vehicles and such facilities needed to operate. They are the expenses incurred in order to do business whether one or 1 000 items are sold.

Typical examples of overheads are:

- rent paid for business premises and equipment
- wages and salaries paid to management and other non-manufacturing employees
- monies paid for marketing campaigns, insurance premiums, fees for municipal services, etc.

Overheads are an essential part of doing business, but are not related directly to the cost price of a product unit. These costs are, however, indirectly related to all products and services offered to the target market.

EXAMPLE

Mary has to pay R2 000 for the advertising billboard. She has to pay this money to the sign-writer whether she sells one hamburger per day or 1 000. The same applies to the R400 rental for the trailer, the R1 600 rental for her site and the R1 200 needed for wages. All these costs are therefore regarded as **indirect costs** (ie overheads).

A useful way of determining whether a cost is direct or indirect is to ask the following question: If I sell no products or services on a single day, will that specific cost/expense be more or less, or will it remain the same? If I sell 1 000 hamburgers (products or services) on a single day, will that cost be more or less, or will it remain the same?

In our example of the hamburger stall, Mary's fixed costs (overheads) are the costs of renting the site and the trailer, and paying for the advertising sign and her sister's wages. Whether she sells one or 1 000 hamburgers per day, she will still have to pay these costs in full.

In business, fixed costs are only fixed for particular periods of time. For example, after a period of 12 months, the rent on the premises may be raised or employees may demand higher salaries. If an increase in sales creates the need for more employees, the fixed cost of wages will increase as well.

6.3.2 Direct costs

Direct costs (also called variable costs, cost of sales or manufacturing costs) are the direct costs incurred to acquire (or manufacture) and sell a single product/service. For a retailer, direct costs usually consist of the amount that the retailer pays to the supplier of the product, usually to a wholesaler. For a manufacturer, direct costs per unit normally consist of the accumulated cost prices of the raw materials (ingredients) and the cost of the labour used in manufacturing the product.

EXAMPLE

Mary with the help of her qualified chef friend calculated the combined cost of all the ingredients needed to make one Super-Duper hamburger at R20 per hamburger. If customers do not order a single hamburger on a specific day, Mary will accrue no direct costs in making the hamburgers. If she sells 200 hamburgers, the variable cost to the business that day will be $200 \times R20 = R4\ 000$. Thus we can see that **direct costs are directly related to the volume of sales**. If sales volume is low, direct costs will be low; if sales volume increases, the direct cost will increase proportionally.

In real life, Mary might consider making hamburgers beforehand, to build up an inventory in advance of the flea market day. This aspect of real-life business operation will change the above equations and is dealt with later in this book.

DEFINITION

Direct costs are those costs incurred and directly related to acquiring and selling a single product/service. The accumulated direct costs of the items that are sold is also called cost of sales or manufacturing costs.

6.3.3 Gross profit (marginal income)

Gross profit (also known as marginal income) represents the positive difference between the selling price per unit and the direct cost price per unit, and is very much a function of the pricing strategies and practices followed by the manager/entrepreneur.

EXAMPLE

In Mary's case, the R50 selling price less the R20 direct cost yields R30 'gross profit' or marginal income per unit. This means that for each hamburger sold at R50, R20 is needed to pay for ingredients (direct costs), while the R30 gross profit/marginal income contributes to the payment of the indirect costs (overheads, fixed or operational costs). Once the total indirect costs have been defrayed (covered) by the marginal income, the business starts to make a profit. If the accumulated gross profit/marginal income is not enough to cover the total overheads, the result will be a net loss.

Whenever the gross profit (marginal income) of a product is expressed as a percentage, it is calculated either as a percentage of the selling price (gross profit percentage) or of the cost price (mark-up percentage) of that product.

Gross profit percentage

$$\text{Gross profit percentage} \quad = \quad \frac{\text{Gross profit} \times 100}{\text{Selling price}}$$

In Mary's case:

$$\text{Gross profit percentage} \quad = \quad \frac{\text{R30} \times 100}{\text{R50}}$$

$$= \quad 60\%$$

This means that for every R1 of sales, a gross profit of 60 cents is realised.

Gross profit percentage is different from the mark-up percentage, which is the percentage a manager/entrepreneur will add to the cost price of a product in order to arrive at that product's selling price. The mark-up percentage is therefore calculated as the gross profit (marginal income) expressed as a percentage of the cost price (and not the selling price) of that product.

Mark-up percentage

$$\text{Mark-up percentage} \quad = \quad \frac{\text{Gross profit} \times 100}{\text{Cost price}}$$

In Mary's case:

$$\text{Mark-up percentage} \quad = \quad \frac{\text{R30} \times 100}{\text{R20}}$$

$$= \quad 150\%$$

This means that for every R1 spent on direct costs (acquiring or manufacturing a product), R1.50 is added to arrive at the selling price.

QUESTION

We can now ask: How many hamburgers must Mary sell if she wishes to make a net profit of, say, R1 500 per flea market day? After all, she is not in business to break even, but to make a profit. Note that her salary of R900 per day is not considered profit, but is a staff expense her business must be able to afford (whether it is to pay Mary or another person for doing the work is irrelevant).

ANSWER

The same three pieces of information are required as for the calculation of the break-even point. We need to know Mary's selling price per unit, her direct cost price per unit and her total indirect costs per day. Now add Mary's required net profit to her indirect costs and then recalculate the total, which includes profit desired.

The formula now is:

$$\text{Break-even point} = \frac{\text{Total indirect costs} + \text{Required net profit}}{\text{Selling price per unit} - \text{Direct cost price per unit}}$$

In Mary's case:

$$\frac{\text{R3 300} + \text{R1 500}}{\text{R50} - \text{R20}} = \frac{\text{R4 800}}{\text{R30}} = 300 \text{ units to be sold per day to achieve R 1 500 net profit}$$

So Mary must sell 160 hamburgers per day in order to make her desired R1 500 daily net profit.

Verifying your answer

Once again it is quite easy (and also a good idea) for you to check whether the answer of 160 hamburgers is correct. All you have to do is answer the following questions.

QUESTIONS

1. How much will Mary's total gross income be per day if she sells 160 hamburgers at R50 each?
2. How much will her total direct costs be per day when making and selling 160 hamburgers at a direct cost price of R20 per hamburger?
3. What are the total indirect costs involved in operating Mary's business?

6.4 The break-even point per multiple products with different pricing structures

Most organisations deal with quite a large number of different products/services, rather than with a single product and/or service as per our example of the Super-Duper Hamburger business. Bigger businesses normally have quite a variety of different products and services. For example, a retail store may have separate men's, women's and children's clothing sections and even a hardware and a garden section/department. Similarly, a hardware retailer may have a tool section, a paint section and a lumber section, because each section/department has a different nature and serves customers with different needs. Enterprises are divided into departments for more effective management and also to facilitate direct, easy access for customers to the products/services they require.

How then must the entrepreneur/manager also determine and manage break-even, not only of a specific product unit, but of a specific section/department and of the business/project/enterprise as a whole?

Two points are important here:

1. First, it remains very important even for a well-established business continuously to monitor its direct costs, indirect costs and required overall break-even volumes. The reason for this is quite obvious because acquiring and selling prices are seldom stagnant;

2. Second, the contribution of each product/service (or at least each of the subdepartments with the same kind of products, costs, pricing practices and income structures) to the overall break-even point and profitability must be known in order to make sure only the most profitable and greatest contributors to the success of the business/enterprise are maintained and expanded.

> **NB!** The 80/20 Pareto principle must always be borne in mind as it is applicable to every business or organisation: 20% of products/services/team members will always contribute 80% to the outcomes. The opposite is also true: 80% of products/services/team members will always contribute to only 20% of the outcomes.

The gross profit percentage planned/achieved by the business is more than a handy tool to answer this question. It may even apply to a range of products/services that have similar gross profit percentages. For example, a retailer may have a grocery department, a hardware department and a fresh produce department, in which different pricing policies (mark-ups and gross profit percentages) are required and implemented.

When we know the marginal income percentage (gross profit percentage) of any business, we can use the following formula to indicate its break-even point in terms of monetary sales volume:

$$\text{Break-even point} = \frac{\text{Total indirect costs} \times 100}{\text{Gross profit percentage}}$$

$$= \text{Sales in monetary value needed to break even}$$

EXAMPLE

Lerato's Store is selling a wide variety of goods. Her pricing policy is to implement a 200% profit margin to whatever she pays her suppliers for any product bought. Her average gross profit margin will therefore be 66.67% (eg a cost price of R100, plus a 200% mark-up of R200, adds up to a selling price of R300; the R200 gross profit gives a gross profit percentage of 66.67%, worked out as follows: R200 x 100 ÷ R300). Her total overheads (fixed or indirect costs) per month are at present R900 000.

Calculating the break-even point for Lerato's Store in monetary terms:

$$\text{Break-even point} = \frac{(\text{Total indirect costs OR Overheads})}{\text{Gross profit percentage}}$$

$$= \frac{\text{R900 000}}{66.67\%}$$

$$= \frac{\text{R900 000} \times 100}{66.67}$$

$$= \text{R1 349 932.50 Sales per month required to break even}$$

Therefore monthly sales of R1 349 932.50 are required to break even.

Test: Sales   =   R 1 349 932.50

Less: Gross profit   = $\underline{\text{R 449 932.50}}$ (66.67% of R 1 349 932.50, in other words: 66.67 × 1 349 932.50 ÷ 100)

                 =   R 899 999.99

                 =   R 900 000 (rounded up)

Balance to pay overheads: R900 000

Result: No net profit or net loss

In Mary's case:

$$\frac{\text{R3 300} \times 100}{60} = \text{R5 500 (the same as calculated in 6.2)}$$

So, Mary needs R5 500 monetary sales per day to break even (110 hamburgers at a selling price of R50 each).

You can also use this formula to calculate the needed monetary volume of sales in order to realise a given net profit. In this case, you must first add the required profit to the total indirect costs.

In Mary's case, if she wants a profit of R1 500, this will be:

$$\frac{(\text{Total indirect costs} + \text{Required profit}) \times 100}{\text{Gross profit percentage}} = \frac{(\text{R3 300} + \text{R1 500}) \times 100}{60} = \frac{\text{R8 000}}{}$$

So, Mary needs total sales of R8 000 per day to realise a R1 500 net profit (160 hamburgers at R50 each).

6.5 Using a graph to explain the break-even point

6.5.1 Indirect (fixed, operational) costs

As mentioned before, the total indirect (fixed, operational) costs of a business remain the same regardless of the sales volume of the enterprise. They do not change whether one or 1 000 items are sold during a period. This is illustrated in Figure 6.1, which shows that the indirect costs (R3 300 per day) for Mary's hamburger stall stay the same regardless of how many hamburgers she sells per day.

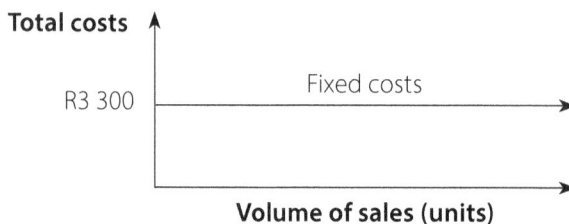

Total costs

R3 300   Fixed costs

Volume of sales (units)

Figure 6.1: Indirect/fixed costs

6.5.2 Direct (variable) costs

The accumulated direct costs needed to purchase (or manufacture) a single product vary according to the volume of sales. If Mary makes and sells only one hamburger, her direct costs will be only R20; if she makes and sells 1 000 hamburgers, her direct costs will increase in direct relation to the increase in sales volume, thus 1 000 × R20 = R20 000.

Figure 6.2 shows the direct costs for Mary's hamburger stall.

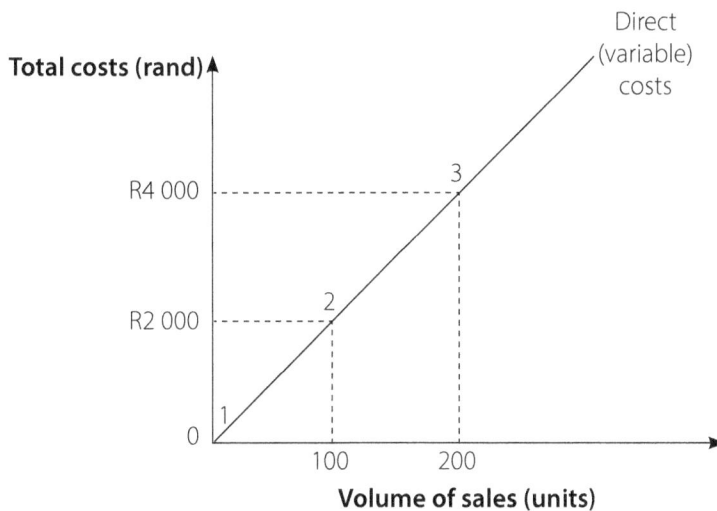

Figure 6.2: Direct costs

At point 1 on the graph, no hamburgers are made and sold and therefore the direct costs are zero. At point 2, 100 hamburgers are made and sold and therefore the total direct costs are 100 × R20 = R2 000. At point 3, 200 hamburgers are made and sold, and thus the total direct costs are 200 × R20 = R4 000.

6.5.3 The complete graphical break-even point

You know by now that three critical cost figures are needed to calculate the break-even point, namely the total indirect costs of the business, the direct cost price per unit and the selling price of a product/service. We can now illustrate the break-even point by means of a graph (see Figure 6.3) that combines the information presented in figures 6.1 and 6.2.

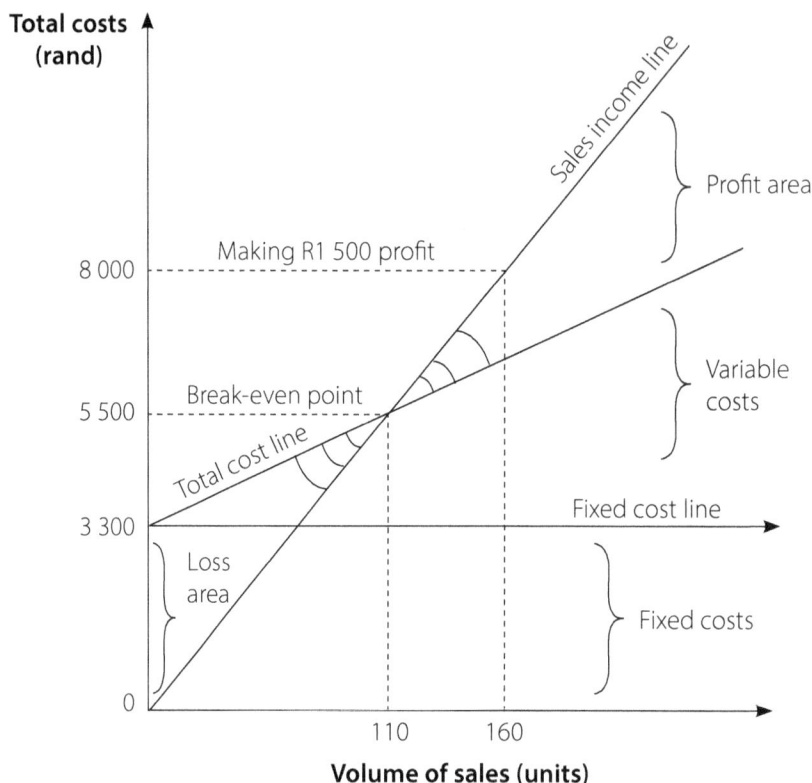

Figure 6.3: The break-even point

Once a business enterprise or any organisation has reached its break-even point, it is in an excellent position (but only then) to start making a net profit.

In Mary's case, each additional hamburger she sells (after 110) will mean a net profit to her of R30. Before break-even, this R30 gross profit was needed to contribute to covering her indirect costs (overheads). After reaching break-even, a product's gross profit will become net profit because all indirect costs are already paid.

6.6   Advantages and disadvantages of the break-even analysis

The break-even analysis is an extremely useful tool for the business manager/entre-preneur. There are no real disadvantages to it, although it can be misunderstood, for example:

- Sometimes it is not easy to distinguish between direct and indirect costs. For example, if you make a phone call to order a product, should you regard this cost (*if* you know and have recorded the exact cost) as a direct cost in acquiring the product?

- The costs involved in calculating and recording expenses should be less than the advantages gained from it. And *always* remember: if you cannot measure something, you cannot manage it. And the better you measure something, the better you can manage it.
- Having a pricing strategy without measuring its effects is no good.
- The elements affecting the direct cost price per unit, as well as those making up the total indirect costs of a business, are not constant, but change continually.

In spite of these potential pitfalls, doing the break-even analysis on an ongoing basis is necessary for successful financial management. Profit is calculated as income less direct costs less indirect costs. Unless all three of these critical elements are continually measured, calculated and managed, the achievement of the business's objectives will be endangered. The aim of any business is to make profit, and the business manager/entrepreneur needs to make sure this is achieved.

6.7 Changes to the three critical factors

Any change to one of the three critical factors in the break-even analysis will have a significant impact on the profitability of the business. Price changes (in selling prices and/or direct cost prices and/or indirect costs) are common in business, and the manager/entrepreneur must have a sound understanding of the impact of these changes at all times. Only then will they be in a position to take corrective action. In Mary's case, the following three scenarios illustrate the impact of such changes.

6.7.1 If the selling price per unit changes

As an example, if the selling price is raised to R60 per unit, what will the new break-even point be (ie the number of units needed to break even)?

$$\text{Break-even point} = \frac{\text{Total indirect costs}}{\text{Selling price per unit} - \text{Direct cost per unit}}$$

$$= \frac{\text{R3 300}}{\text{R60} - \text{R20}}$$

$$= 82.5 \text{ hamburgers}$$

So Mary now needs to sell only 82.5 hamburgers in order to break even (instead of 110 when the selling price was R50 each). The 82.5 figure should of course be rounded off to 83.

6.7.2 If indirect costs change

If one or more of the indirect costs increase, for example if the landlord raises the site rental to R1 800 (previously R1 600) and the trailer company raises the trailer rental to R600 a day (previously R400), the break-even point will be:

$$\frac{R3\ 800}{R50 - R20} = \frac{R3\ 800}{R30} = 126.7, \text{rounded up to 127 hamburgers}$$

So Mary will now have to sell 127 hamburgers (previously 110) in order to break even after these increases in operational costs/overheads.

6.7.3 If the direct cost per unit changes

Say, for instance, that the cost price of the ingredients for the hamburger increases from R20 to R25 per unit. The new break-even point will then be:

$$\frac{R3\ 300}{R50 - R20} = \frac{R3\ 300}{R25} = 132 \text{ hamburgers}$$

So Mary now has to sell 132 hamburgers (previously 110) for her hamburger stall to break even.

> **NB!** You can see that a change in any one of the three factors influencing the break-even point has a direct impact on the profit, loss and break-even results of the business initiative. Each of these factors must be monitored continually.

6.8 Summary

In this chapter, we looked at the importance and the critical elements of break-even analysis. You learned that management has to identify three critical elements in order to do such an analysis: the selling price per unit, the direct costs to acquire or manufacture a unit (this can also be expressed as a gross profit percentage) and the total cost of indirect but necessary operational activities (overheads). Many of these are the result of the enterprise's pricing policies and practices.

By using the example of Mary's hamburger stall, we identified many issues that all kinds of management in all kinds of enterprises must continuously consider. You learned the important difference between direct and indirect costs, eg as applied to Mary's business. By using these data, two different formulas were used to calculate Mary's break-even point, expressed in terms of number of units required to be sold as well as in terms of the monetary sales income Mary requires. We stressed that you should always verify the calculation of the break-even point.

Lastly, we looked at how the break-even point changes when one (or more) of the three critical elements changes. The important thing to remember is the need to recalculate the break-even point continually and then to take the needed corrective action in time.

SELF-EVALUATION QUESTIONS

1. Name and explain at least six different factors to consider before starting up your own hamburger stall or any other kind of undertaking *(see sections 6.1.1 to 6.1.2)*.

2. Explain the following concepts in your own words and give an everyday example for each one:
   a) Fixed costs *(see Section 6.3.1)*.
   b) Variable costs *(see Section 6.3.2)*.
   c) Marginal income *(see Section 6.3.3)*.
   d) Gross profit percentage as opposed to mark-up percentage *(see Section 6.3.3 and calculations)*.
   e) Break-even point *(see Section 6.2)*.

3. Give the formula for each of the following:
   a) break-even point (number of units) *(see Section 6.4)*
   b) break-even point (monetary volume of sales) *(see Section 6.5)*
   c) marginal income percentage *(see Section 6.3.3)*.

4. Lucky Ali is considering starting his own business manufacturing and selling fishing rods. The cost of the components needed to manufacture one rod amounts to R160 and direct labour costs for one rod are R140. The rental of premises amounts to R500 per month (his father's garage at home) and other indirect costs will be R11 500 per month (including his own part-time salary). Lucky is confident that he will be able to manufacture and sell 100 fishing rods per month. His budgeted selling price is R600 per rod.
   a) How many fishing rods should Lucky manufacture and sell per month to break even?
   b) Verify whether your answer in (a) is correct.
   c) How many rods must Lucky manufacture and sell to make a net profit of R6 000 each month?
   d) Verify the correctness of your answer.
   e) If the price of rod components changes to R180, what happens to the break-even point in (a)?
   f) Draw a graph to illustrate the break-even point in (c).

ANSWERS

4. a) Fixed/indirect costs are R12 000 (R500 rent + R11 500). Variable costs are R160 + R140.

$$\text{Break-even point in units} = \frac{\text{Total indirect costs}}{\text{Selling price per unit} - \text{Direct cost per unit}}$$

$$= \frac{\text{R12 000}}{\text{R600} - \text{R300}}$$

$$= 40 \text{ unit sales (rods sold) needed to break even}$$

   b) Verification:

Sales/Gross income (40 rods @ R600 each)	=	R24 000
Less: Direct costs (40 rods @ R300 each)	=	R12 000
Gross profit	=	R12 000
Less: Overheads/fixed costs	=	R12 000
Net profit/loss	=	NIL

(The answer is correct.)

   c) Calculation to gain R6 000 monthly:

$$\frac{\text{Total indirect costs} + \text{Required profit}}{\text{Selling price per unit} - \text{Direct cost per unit}} = \frac{12\,000 + 6\,000}{600 - 300}$$

$$= \text{60 unit sales (rods sold) needed per month to achieve a R6 000 net profit}$$

   d) Verification:

Sales/Gross income (60 rods @ R600 each)	=	R36 000
Less: Direct costs (60 rods @ R300 each)	=	R18 000
Gross profit	=	R18 000
Less: Overheads/fixed costs	=	R12 000
Net profit/loss	=	R6 000

(The answer is correct.)

e) Calculation when costs/prices change:

Fixed/indirect costs are R12 000 (R500 rent + R11 500), and variable costs are R180 + R140.

$$\text{Break-even point in units} = \frac{\text{Total indirect costs}}{\text{Selling price per unit} - \text{Direct cost per unit}}$$

$$= \frac{\text{R12 000}}{\text{R600} - \text{R320}}$$

$$= \frac{42.857 \text{ (say 43) unit sales (rods sold)}}{\text{now needed to break even}}$$

Verification:

Sales/Gross income (42.857 rods @ R600 each)	=	R25 714
Less: Direct costs (42.857 rods @ R320 each)	=	R13 714
Gross profit	=	R12 000
Less: Overheads/fixed costs	=	R12 000
Net profit/loss	=	NIL

(The answer is correct.)

f) Graph to illustrate the break-even point in (c):

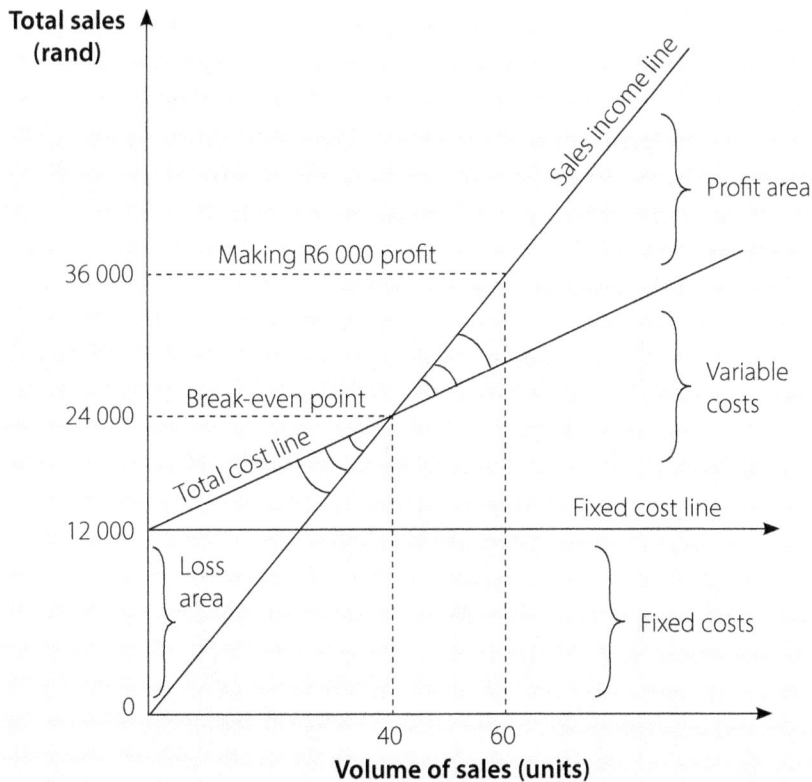

7

Budgets

WELMA FOURIE

Learning outcomes

After reading this chapter, you should be able to:

- give reasons for items included in your marketing budget
- distinguish between the various components (which include marketing) used to compile a master budget
- draw up the budgeted income statement and balance sheet
- draw up the cash flow budget
- draw conclusions and make decisions on the basis of the completed budgets
- compare actual costs with budgeted costs and draw conclusions.

7.1 Introduction

Whether you are budgeting your time or your available funds, everyone uses a budget in one way or another. Budget formats may vary from one organisation to the next, but the principles remain the same. For a business to be successful, strategic planning for the following year must be done and these plans (especially budgets) must be worked out on paper or electronically.

As strategic objectives need to be planned, the budgeting process is a tool to achieve those objectives. A business needs to identify what marketing campaigns will be necessary to achieve the budgeted sales, and to budget for any product launches (eg a new car model will require a big launch) and all related operating expenses.

DEFINITION

A **budget** is a written financial plan showing management's financial goals and forecasts for a specific future period.

7.2   Why do we draw up budgets?

A budget is merely a set of goals that are converted into figures. In this chapter we will look at the process involved in translating goals into figures. The budgeting cycle at Figure 7.1 shows how budgeting works.

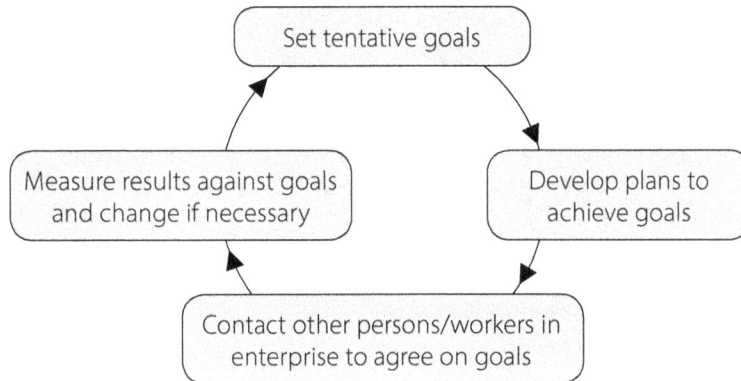

Figure 7.1: A budgeting cycle

Some of the advantages of budgets are that they:

- provide a formal framework for the marketing department to put campaigns into action to be able to achieve goals for the next period
- allow marketing management and staff to evaluate whether goals have been achieved
- allow comparisons between actual and budgeted results, thus aiding financial planning
- require people in charge of the different departments to be accountable for their actions and decisions
- create cost awareness among staff
- show where problems could arise in future
- coordinate the goals of the business and contribute to the effective use of resources
- give the business the opportunity to take external factors into account during financial planning – for example competition and economic cycles.

QUESTION

When and for what period is a budget drawn up?

ANSWER

Budgets are drawn up a reasonable time before the end of the financial year so that they are ready for the following year, when they will come into effect. The marketing budgeting process involves collecting the necessary information from the various components of the marketing expenses in the budget. A medium to large enterprise will have its budget ready in September for the following 12-month period from January to December.

7.3 Master budget

A master budget is compiled from a number of different budgets, each drawing on different components of the business. This is illustrated in Figure 7.2, which shows the sources of a master budget.

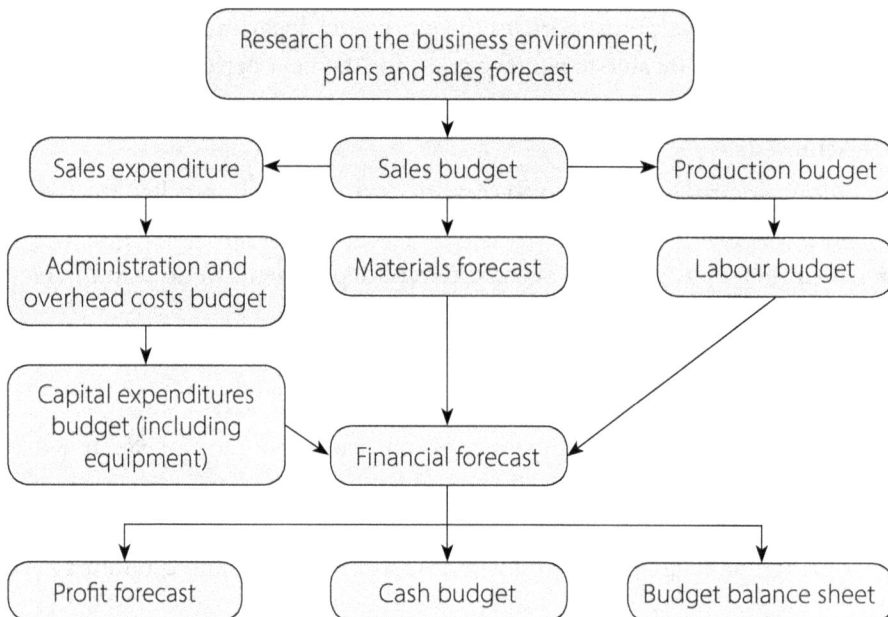

Figure 7.2: Sources of a master budget

All information contained in the budgets must be based on challenging but realistic goals. Thorough research must be done on existing circumstances – for example current sales and growth in the market – before a budget can be drawn up.

A budget will only work and be applied effectively if all interested parties in the business, such as salespeople and the marketing department, are consulted in the process. It is important that the budget includes their inputs. In a small business, the owner usually has knowledge of all levels of activity in the business.

When a budget is reasonable and realistic, it motivates staff to attempt to reach the goals set. Conversely, an unreasonable and unrealistic budget will have a negative influence on the staff. The first budget that must be completed is the sales budget.

7.4   Sales budget

The starting point of the budgeting process is the sales budget. It is important to remember that you can only draw up the sales budget if you have already determined your sales forecast. The sales forecast is an estimate or prediction of the sales of the enterprise for a future period.

First do some research to confirm your instinct on sales or add to your current knowledge of expected sales. The basis of a sales budget is to break the expected sales down into manageable parts, for example by:

- individual project/product or item
- month for a period of one year.

Add up the relevant sales records to get total sales per product or project for the year. You can add months together to get the total sales for a specific period/year. When you are doing a sales forecast in components, it becomes easier to establish later which sales were not achieved, the number of units sold or the price difference per unit sold against the budget. You can also draw up a sales budget for shorter periods – especially in cases where sales can fluctuate dramatically from month to month. The small business enterprise should review the sales forecast on a monthly basis so that it is in a position to make swift adjustments if necessary. The sales forecast is the point of departure for the sales and other budgets.

> **NB!** The sales budget is regarded as one of the most important budgets because it has an influence on so many other budgets. This is why it is drawn up first.

Table 7.1 shows an example of a sales budget for one year.

Table 7.1: An example of a sales budget

Sales estimates for product A	Jan	Feb	Mar	Apr	May	Jun
No. of units in Area 1	1 700	2 040	1 100	440	105	64
No. of units in Area 2	1 200	1 350	950	1 400	360	100
Total no. of units	2 900	3 390	2 050	1 840	465	164
Est. price per unit (R)	315	315	315	280	280	280
Total value of units (R)	913 500	1 067 850	645 750	515 200	130 200	45 920

Sales estimates for product A	Jul	Aug	Sep	Oct	Nov	Dec	Total
No. of units in Area 1	900	120	190	270	220	400	7 549
No. of units in Area 2	1 200	450	250	350	120	500	8 230
Total no. of units	2 100	570	440	620	340	900	15 779
Est. price per unit (R)	295	295	295	295	295	295	303.22
Total value of units (R)	619 500	168 150	129 800	182 900	100 300	265 500	4 784 570

EXAMPLE

The basic calculations of a sales budget are as follows:

Step 1: Determine the expected sales

Expected sales = Expected number of units sold × Unit price

If you have determined that you are going to sell 20 000 units with a value of R40 per unit the following month, your sales will be 20 000 × R40 = R800 000. This amount will be used for the profit and loss budget.

Step 2: Determine the expected cash collection

For the cash flow forecast, we need to determine the cash collection during the period. If the company sells on credit, cash is received over a specific period usually established by past trends and the effectiveness of the debt collection process. These amounts can be determined as shown by the following example:

For sales of R800 000, 20% were for cash and 80% were on credit. The credit sales will be collected as follows: 60% in the month following the purchase (30 days later) and 40% in the next month (60 days later).

⫸

	Month		
	1	**2**	**3**
Cash sales: R800 000 × 20%	R160 000		
Credit sales:			
R800 000 × 80% × 60%		R384 000	
R800 000 × 80% × 40%			R256 000

Check your answer: R160 000 + R384 000 + R256 000 = R800 000

We are going to draw up the annual budget for Timber to Table, a company selling chairs. The following information was collected:

- After thorough research, the owners determined that expected sales would be 3000 units for the first quarter, increasing by 500 units per quarter.
- The selling price remained constant for the year at R60.
- 60% of sales were for cash and 40% were on credit.
- Debtors paid 30 days after purchase.
- The outstanding debts of R65000 at the beginning of the year should all be collected in the first period.

The sales budget for Timber to Table is as follows:

Sales budget per quarter

	1	**2**	**3**	**4**	**Year**
Expected sales	3 000	3 500	4 000	4 500	15 000
Unit price	× R60	× R60	× R60	× R60	× R60
	R180 000	R210 000	R240 000	R270 000	R900 000
Cash collections	R	R	R	R	R
Balance b/f	65 000				
Cash sales	108 000	126 000	144 000	162 000	540 000
Credit sales		72 000	84 000	96 000	252 000
Total cash	173 000	198 000	228 000	258 000	
Debtors (R900 000 − R540 000 − R252 000) = R108 000					

The sales budget can be divided up by shop or region or salesperson.

EXERCISE 7.1

You are asked to draw up the sales budget of Manuella (Pty) Ltd. The company sells umbrellas that are in reasonable demand. The following information must be taken into account:

- Sales for the next year will increase from the second quarter by 10% every quarter. The sales for the current year is 3 200 units per quarter. Selling price per unit is R45, and this will increase by 10% in the third quarter.
- Cash sales amount to 50%.
- Manuella's outstanding debtors amount to R85 000, of which 50% is collected in period 1 and 50% in period 2.
- Debtors usually pay 60% in the first period after sales and 40% in the second period after sales.

Draw up the sales budget of Manuella (Pty) Ltd by filling in the missing fields in the following table:

Sales budget per quarter

	1	2	3	4	Year
Expected sales	3 200	3 250	_____	_____	_____
Unit price	× R45	× _____	× _____	× _____	× _____
	R_____	R_____	R_____	R_____	R_____
Cash collections	R	R	R	R	R
Balance b/f	45 000				
Cash sales	72 000				
Credit collection 60%		43 200	_____	_____	
Credit collection 40%			28 800	_____	
Total cash	**117 000**	_____	_____	_____	

7.5 Production budget

Now that you know how much you can sell, you must calculate how many units you need to manufacture. Here you must take into account the stock you already possess as well as what you want to retain. The calculation will be as follows:

Expected number of sales – Opening stock + Final stock = Expected number of units to manufacture

If the expected sales are 200 000, opening stock is 50 000 and final stock is estimated at 70 000 (to have enough stock on the shelves to sell), what is the expected number of units that you must manufacture?

200 000 – 50 000 + 70 000 = 220 000 units

It is important that the business carries the right amount of stock. Too much could lead to liquidity problems and the dismissal of staff, and too little could lead to loss of sales. This is why the production budget is so important.

EXAMPLE

Suppose the owners of Timber to Table have decided that they want to manufacture 15% of a future quarter's stock in the preceding quarter and have it on the shelves in advance. (This is their stock of finished products.)

1. We can now calculate what the opening and final stock must be for each quarter:

   Opening stock (15% × 3 000) = 450 units

   Closing stock (15% × 3 500) = 525 units

2. Timber to Table wants to create a production budget per quarter.

   - Direct material costs are R4.90 per unit.

   - Direct material purchases are paid 50% in cash in the quarter of purchase and 50% in the following quarter (30 days later). Accounts payable of R11 500 at the beginning of the year will be paid in full in the first quarter.

Timber to Table production budget

	1	2	3	4	Year
Expected sales (in units)	3 000	3 500	4 000	4 500	15 000
Less: opening stock	(450)	(525)	(600)	(675)	(450)
Plus: closing stock	525	600	675	750	750
Number of units to produce	**R3 075**	**R3 575**	**R4 075**	**R4 575**	**R15 300**
Material purchases:	R15 068	R17 518	R19 968	R22 418	R74 970
Units × R4.90	R11 500	R8 758	R9 984	R11 209	R11 500
Materials payment:	R7 534	R7 533	R8 759	R9 984	R37 485
Balance b/f cash credit					R26 276
Total payments	**R19 034**	**R16 291**	**R18 743**	**R21 193**	**R75 261**
Creditors	(R74 970 – R37 485 – R26 276) = R11 209				

The production budget is closely related to the sales budget since enough stock must be produced to meet the demand for goods.

EXERCISE 7.2

Complete the production budget for Manuella. Opening stock amounts to 25% of expected sales. Closing stock must be 25% of the following period's sales.

- Manuella pays cash for 50% of its materials in the quarter of sales, then pays 60% of the creditors in the following quarter and the outstanding 40% in the second quarter following the sales.
- Manuella's outstanding accounts at the beginning of the period were R42 000 and this will be paid in equal instalments over the following two periods.
- Material costs are R5 per unit.

Manuella (Pty) Ltd production budget per quarter

	1	2	3	4	Year
Expected sales (in units)	3 200	3 520	_____	_____	_____
Less: opening stock	−800	(_____)	(_____)	(_____)	(_____)
Plus: closing stock	880	_____	_____	_____	_____
Number of units to produce	3280	_____	_____	_____	_____
Material purchases: units × R materials payment:	_____	_____	_____	_____	_____
Balance b/f	**R21 000**	_____			
Cash (50%)	_____	_____	_____	_____	
Credit (60%)		_____	_____	_____	
Credit (40%)			_____	_____	_____
Total payments	_____	_____	_____	_____	_____

If a small business does not produce goods but buys and sells, it must draw up a purchases budget. The number of products that must be purchased is determined in the same way as the number of products that need to be manufactured. You must therefore determine the quantity that must be purchased for each quarter. After completing the purchases budget, you should immediately complete your cash flow budget (see Section 7.9).

7.6 Labour budget

It is necessary to draw up a labour budget to determine the need for, and cost of, human resources. Without a labour budget, you might find that you do not have enough staff to complete the required production within the given time.

EXAMPLE

It takes two hours of labour per unit at an average wage of R10 an hour to make Timber to Table's product – a tea tray. Draw up Timber to Table's labour budget.

Labour budget per quarter

	1	2	3	4	Year
	3 075	3 575	4 075	4 575	15 300
	× 2	× 2	× 2	× 2	× 2
Expected production (units) × Hours of labour per unit = Total × Cost per hour	6 150	7 150	8 150	9 150	30 600
	× R10	× R10	× R10	× R10	× R10
Total labour cost	**R61 500**	**R71 500**	**R81 500**	**R91 500**	**R306 000**

EXERCISE 7.3

Manumeter takes three hours to manufacture one digital thermometer, and the average labour cost is R15 an hour. Complete the labour budget for Manumeter.

Manumeter (Pty) Ltd labour budget per quarter

	1	2	3	4	Year
Expected production	3 280	_____	_____	_____	_____
× Hours of labour per unit	×_____	×_____	×_____	×_____	×_____
= Total labour (hours)	9 840	_____	_____	_____	_____
× Cost per hour	×_____	×_____	×_____	×_____	×_____
Total labour costs	**R147 600**	R_____	R_____	R_____	R_____

7.7 Budgeted income statement

Expense budgets for larger entities can be drawn up for every department. Such an expense budget is then assigned to the person responsible for that department or corresponding expense line and who must control and authorise all expenses in that department. The budgeted income statement is an important summary of all the previous budgets. It allows all income and expenses to be evaluated as a whole. Large marketing drives and other expenses such as marketing research need to be within a certain limit. The company might have guidelines, such as '5% of profit may be spent on marketing'. It therefore also indicates the expected profit for the following period. Since the income statement is a summary of all the previous budgets, it also serves as an excellent way to evaluate actual results against budgeted results.

EXAMPLE

Timber to Table had the following expenses in the preceding year and wants to make provision for an adjustment for inflation of 12% for the coming year:

Rent paid	R50 000
Telephone	R5 000
Salaries (administration)	R40 000
Repairs and maintenance	R4 000
Travel expenses	R1 000
Additional expenses:	
Interest obligation (a year)	R35 000
Taxation	R5 000
Operating expenses	R306 000

Here is the budgeted income statement of Timber to Table:

		R
Sales		900 000
Less: cost of sales		373 500
Opening inventory	(450 × R24.90)	11 205
Materials		74 970
Labour		306 000
Less: closing inventory	(750 × R24.90)	18 675
Gross profit		526 500
Current expenses		508 880
Rent paid	(R50 000 × 112%)	(56 000)
Telephone		(5 600)
Salaries (administration)		(44 800)
Repairs and maintenance		(4 480)
Marketing		(56 000)
Interest paid		(35 000)
Travel expenses		(1 000)
Operating expenses		(306 000)
Net income before tax		17 620
Tax		5 000
Net income		**12 620**

EXERCISE 7.4

Using the budgets that you have already completed, draw up a budgeted income statement for Manuella, the company that makes umbrellas. The company has already incurred the expenses listed. You should allow for inflation of 10% in your calculations.

Marketing   R2 000

Rent paid   R10 000

Stationery   R1 500

Telephone   R3 000

Travel costs   R18 000

Interest paid is R6 000 for the year and taxation will be 25% of the net income before taxation.

Budgeted income statement of Manuella (Pty) Ltd:

R

Sales
Less: cost of sales
Opening inventory
Materials
Labour
Less: closing inventory
Gross profit
Current expenses
Marketing   (_____)
Rent paid   (_____)
Stationery   (_____)
Telephone   (_____)
Travel costs   (_____)
Interest paid   (_____)
Net income before tax   _____
Tax   _____
Net income   _____

7.8 Budgeted balance sheet

Timber to Table had the following balance sheet at the end of the year:

Balance sheet of Timber to Table at 31 December

Fixed assets	133 000	
Current assets	141 829	
Inventory (750 × R24.90)		18 675
Debtors		108 000
Cash		15 154
	274 829	
Share capital	100 000	
Accumulated profits	13 620	
Loan (R150 000 – R5 000)	145 000	
Current liabilities	16 209	
SARS (tax)		5 000
Creditors		11 209
	274 829	

7.9 Cash flow budget

Let us say you have forecast the profit and loss. The difference between the forecast profit and loss and the cash flow budget is that you concentrate on when you will receive cash and when cash payments are made. The cash flow budget is the main lifeline of the business and is the most important result of drawing up the other budgets. The cash flow budget indicates the expected flow of cash and can help management make early provision for cash shortages and to consider the necessary financing possibilities. This allows cash planning to take place, and any excess cash can be invested.

NB! You have bought a vehicle for R100 000. This amount will appear in the cash flow budget as an outflow (expense), but in the balance sheet it will be capitalised and the depreciation will be written off in the income statement.

The cash flow statement does not take into account non-cash items, such as depreciation and bad debts.

EXAMPLE

Timber to Table has collected the following information to do their cash flow budget:

- The enterprise's bank account should show a positive balance of R40 000 at the beginning of the year.
- An investment of R4 000 will be sold for cash in the second period.
- Purchases of all current costs are spread evenly over the quarters.
- Direct labour costs are settled in the period in which they are incurred.
- Management wants to purchase a new truck for R133 000 in the second quarter.
- The enterprise pays its tax monthly in equal instalments.
- Loans are paid in the third quarter when there is sufficient cash (rounded off to the nearest R5 000).
- A loan of R150 000 will be granted in the second quarter.

Timber to Table cash flow budget

Cash flow budget per quarter (all figures are in rand)

	1	2	3	4
Receipts:				
Debtors and cash	173 000	198 000	228 000	258 000
Sale of investment		4 000		
Total receipts	**173 000**	**202 000**	**228 000**	**258 000**
Less: payments				
Direct material	19 034	16 291	18 743	21 192
Direct labour	61 500	71 500	81 500	91 500
Rent paid	14 000	14 000	14 000	14 000
Telephone	1 400	1 400	1 400	1 400
Salaries	11 200	11 200	11 200	11 200
Repairs and maintenance	1 120	1 120	1 120	1 120
Marketing	14 000	14 000	14 000	14 000
Purchase of vehicle		133 000		
Interest paid	8 750	8 750	8 750	8 750
Current costs	76 500	76 500	76 500	76 500
Tax	1 250	1 250	1 250	1 250
Total payments	**208 754**	**349 011**	**228 463**	**240 912**
Surplus/deficit	(35 754)	(147 011)	(463)	17 088
Cash balance	**40 000**	**4 246**	**7 235**	**1 772**
Financing				
Loans		150 000		
Repayments			(5 000)	
Closing cash balance	**4 246**	**7 235**	**1 772**	**18 860**

EXERCISE 7.5

Builder (Pty) Ltd's cash balance is R25 000 at the beginning of the year. A vehicle is bought for R20 000 in the second quarter, and in the third quarter, an investment of R20 000 is paid back. Tax is divided throughout the period and paid in equal instalments. Complete the cash flow budget in the suggested format for Builder.

Builder (Pty) Ltd cash flow budget

Quarter	1	2	3	4
Receipts:				
Debtors				
Sale of investment				
Total receipts				
Less: payments				
Direct material				
Direct labour				
Manufacturing				
Overheads				
Sales and administration				
Purchase of vehicle				
Tax				
Total payments				
Surplus/deficit				
Cash balance	25 000			
Financing				
Loans				
Repayments				
Closing cash balance				

7.10 Financial forecast

Budgets can also be drawn up on the basis of financial forecasts. This method relies on relationships and forecasts that are based on past data and trends.

EXAMPLE

Advertising costs have increased by 9% per year in the last five years, and amounted to R15 000 last year. What will next year's advertising expenditure be if you do a financial forecast?

R15 000 × 109% = R16 350

EXERCISE 7.6

The following is an income statement of Textile (Pty) Ltd for the past two years. Sales for the coming year are estimated to be 20% more than the current year. Current operating expenses are expected to follow the latest trend. Other income will remain constant. Interest paid will increase to R20 000 because of a new long-term loan that has been negotiated. All the other costs will remain in the same proportion (or ratio) to sales as they are currently. Tax for the coming year will amount to 30%. Now complete the budgeted income statement.

Textile (Pty) Ltd	Last year (R)	This year (R)	Next year (R)
Sales	700 000	750 000	_____
Cost of sales	(373 000)	(400 000)	(_____)
Gross profit	327 000	350 000	_____
Operating expenses	(112 500)	(125 000)	(_____)
Operating profits	214 500	225 000	_____
Interest paid	(9 500)	(12 500)	(_____)
Other income	5 000	5 000	_____
Income before tax	210 000	217 500	_____
Tax	(80 000)	(87 000)	(_____)
Net income	130 000	130 500	_____

ANSWER

	Next year (R)	Explanation
Sales	900 000	20% increase
Cost of sales	(480 000)	53.33% of sales
Gross profit	420 000	
Operating expenses	(138 750)	11.1% trend
Operating profit	281 250	
Interest paid	(20 000)	Given
Other income	5 000	Constant
Income before tax	266 250	
Tax	(79 875)	30%
Net income	186 375	

7.11 Compiling your marketing budget

When compiling your marketing budget, always try to include as much detail as possible and state the purpose of the expenses. This will make the budget easier to understand, especially by employees who are not financially oriented.

EXAMPLE

Objective for 2020: Increase inbound qualified opportunities through marketing efforts. Inbound opportunities include phone calls, emails website registrations and referrals.

Strategies	Goals	Tactics	Budget (R)
Internet marketing	Drive more activity to website	Advertising payment to www.xyz.com to appear higher in search engine results Google – R10 000 Yahoo – R10 000 Google AdWords budget – R20 000 Website hosting – R40 000	80 000
Direct marketing	Build awareness in target market	Water bottles, pens and T-shirts with company name for events	600 000
Brand development	Networking and building relationships	Organise events	180 000
Total expense			**860 000**

The following example shows a detailed marketing budget with monthly expenses broken down into the different types of marketing expenses.

Note that the budget is for R13.5 million (numbers rounded to R'000) for the whole department.

Marketing budget

	Jan R'000	Feb R'000	Mar R'000	Apr R'000	May R'000	Jun R'000	Jul R'000	Aug R'000	Sep R'000	Oct R'000	Nov R'000	Dec R'000	Total R'000
Personnel													
Salaries, wages	150	150	150	150	150	150	170	170	170	170	170	170	1 920
Benefits	5	5	5	5	5	5	7	7	7	7	7	7	72
Commissions and bonuses						60						70	130
Personnel total	R155	R155	R155	R155	R155	R215	R177	R177	R177	R177	R177	R247	R2 122
Market research													
Primary research	5	5	5	5	5	5	5	5	5	5	5	5	60
Secondary research		3				5			8			4	20
Library management						6							6
Market research total	R5	R8	R5	R5	R5	R16	R5	R5	R13	R5	R5	R9	R86
Marketing communications													
Branding		14			20				15			3	52
Advertising	5	12		10		5		40	20	32			124
Websites	5	5	5	15	5	5	5	5	5	25	5	5	90
Direct marketing	3	20	5	40	5	20	8	4	12	30	16	1	164
Internet marketing			16					24					40
Press relations	7	7	7	7	7	7	7	7	7	7	7	7	84
Public relations	10	35	10	10	10	10	10	10	15	5	5 000	5 000	10 125
Events			120							150			270
Marketing communications total	R30	R93	R163	R82	R47	R47	R30	R90	R74	R249	R5 028	R5 016	R10 949

	Jan R'000	Feb R'000	Mar R'000	Apr R'000	May R'000	Jun R'000	Jul R'000	Aug R'000	Sep R'000	Oct R'000	Nov R'000	Dec R'000	Total R'000
Customer acquisition and retention (CAR)													
Lead generation													70
Customer loyalty	10	10	10	10	10	10	10	10	10	10	10	10	50
CAR total	10	10	10	10	10	10	10	10	10	10	10	10	120
Other postage					4						2		52
Telephone travel	3	4	6	3	3	6	10	3	4	6	3	1	36
Computers and office	3	3	3	3	5	3	3	3	3	3	2	3	66
equipment	2	5	10	2	10	10	12	4	2	10	20	2	30
Other total	R8	R12	R19	R8	R22	R19	R25	R10	R9	R19	R27	R6	R184
Total marketing budget	R218	R288	R362	R270	R249	R317	R257	R302	R293	R470	R5 257	R5 298	R13 581

7.12 Actual against budget

An important control measure when budgeting is to measure the actual costs against the budgeted costs. This allows you to exercise control over the budget and cash flow.

When actual costs are compared with budgeted costs, reasons must be given for any deviation from budget. This allows the business to establish where problems lie.

EXAMPLE

If you have the actual money spent on the previous marketing budget, the results can be interpreted and explained.

Strategies	Tactics	Budget	Actual	Reason
Internet marketing	Search engine payments to www. xyz.com	80 000	85 000	Expense is based on people visiting the website. In April more people visited the website resulting in higher expense.
	Directory A	10 000	10 000	
	Directory B	10 000		Expense for Directory B replaced with additional AdWords
	Google AdWords	20 000	30 000	
	Website hosting	40 000	45 000	The website had to be updated with new product information
Direct marketing	Water bottles, pens and T-shirts with company name	600 000	620 000	Increase in water bottle prices created the overspend
Brand development	Organise events	180 000	170 000	Secured a cheaper location for event
Totals		860 000	875 000	

EXAMPLE

Cycle Supplies specialises in the sale of bicycles. The owner, Mr Wise, has drawn up a monthly sales budget. The business has cash flow problems and he suspects that the sales do not agree with the budget. The budgeted and actual sales figures for the bicycles are as follows (actual figures are only available up to June):

	Budgeted sales	Actual sales	Difference
	(R)	(R)	(R)
January	20 000	10 000	(10 000)
February	20 000	15 000	(5 000)
March	20 000	20 000	NIL
April	30 000	25 000	(5 000)
May	40 000	30 000	(10 000)
June	45 000	40 000	(5 000)
July	40 000		
August	30 000		
September	30 000		
October	20 000		
November	20 000		
December	30 000		

Mr Wise's conclusions:

- When he drew up the budget, he thought he would sell more bicycles because of a big race that was due to take place locally in June/July.
- January's sales are lower than budgeted (due to over-expectation), but still show a 2% growth over the previous year's figures.
- February's budgeted figures were still based on over-expectation and also show a 2% growth over last year's figures.
- March showed no deviation, as Mr Wise had a major advertising campaign.
- April's sales still show 2% growth over last year's sales, but did not meet expectations.
- Sales for May are weaker, as all race participants had already bought their bicycles from a competitor, Wheely Warehouse, located two kilometres down the road from Cycle Supplies.
- Sales for June are not as budgeted, but it was a good month, as the shop was crowded with visitors who arrived for the Freedom Challenge Race across South Africa. June showed a 20% growth over the previous year's figures.
- Mr Wise concludes that he should examine not only the sales budget but also his expenses to determine where he overspent.

7.13 Using a computer to draw up budgets

There are a number of computer programs available to help businesses draw up budgets. The advantage of using one of these programs is that you can change a single figure and the program will automatically revise your budget. If you do not have a purpose-built computer package, you can also draw up your budgets using Microsoft Excel or any other spreadsheet program. If you are working in Excel, remember to apply your formulas to the tables as well, since the program does not automatically recalculate budgets when individual figures are amended.

When using a computer program, it allows you to create sales charts to forecast future sales and can be used retrospectively to review actual sales achieved. Sales charts are also useful for understanding sales forecasts. The chart in Figure 7.3 is an example of how budgeted sales, as well as previous and current year sales are reflected in rands. This presents a visual interpretation of the growth of sales and whether budgets have been met.

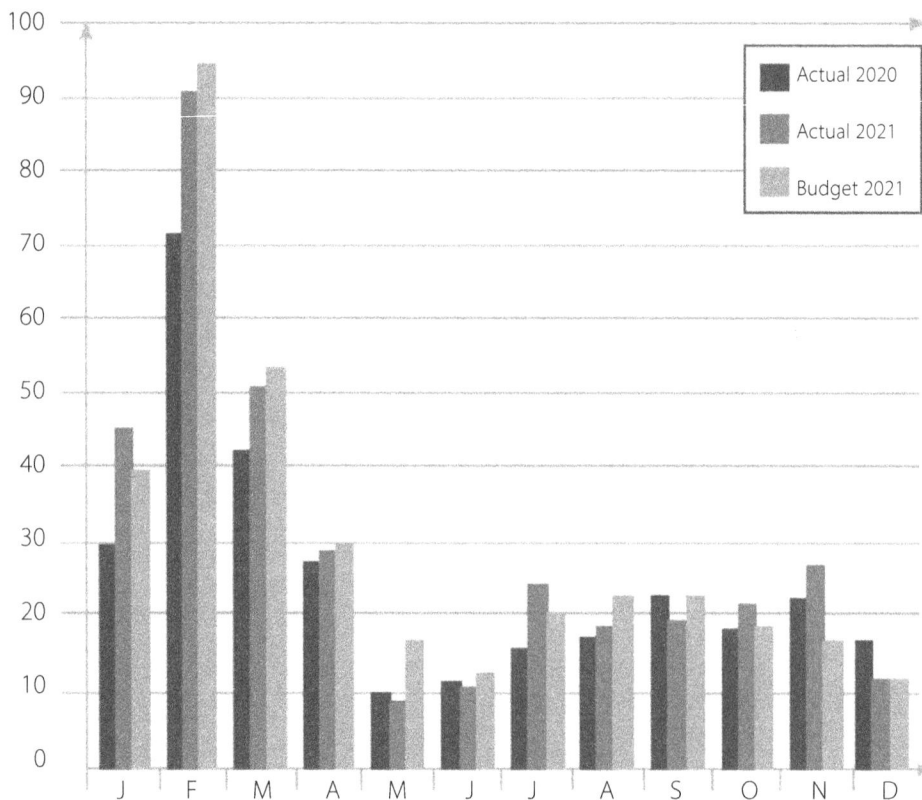

Figure 7.3: Actual sales against budget (2020 and 2021)

7.14 Summary

In this chapter we looked at how to draw up budgets. A business uses many budgets, and together these make up the master budget. The sales budget is the first budget drawn up, and it depends on the sales forecasts. We discussed the production budget, labour budget and cash flow budget, and how these affect the income statement and the balance sheet. Finally we learned about assessing the difference between actual and budgeted figures, and the advantages of using computer programs for budgeting.

SELF-EVALUATION QUESTIONS

1. What is the definition of a budget?
2. List the reasons why it is necessary to draw up a budget.
3. Which factors must you take into account when drawing up a sales budget?
4. What is the formula that you use to determine expected sales?
5. List the steps you would follow when drawing up a cash flow budget.
6. Current expenses have risen by 8% a year for the last four years. Last year the current expenses amounted to R150 000. What will next year's current expenses be if you do a trend sales forecast?
7. The cost of sales was 70% of total sales last year. Next year's sales are budgeted at R1 050 000. What will the cost of sales be?
8. Over the past few years the sales of the business were as follows:

	2018	2019	2020	2021	2022
Sales (rand)	100 000	110 000	121 000	133 000	147 000

   Calculate the sales for 2023 using a trend analysis.

9. Mike intends to start trading on 1 January 2022. He intends to market and distribute a travel mouse with a pointing laser packaged in a zip-up presentation folder as marketing merchandise in KwaZulu-Natal. The merchandise will be manufactured in South Korea. He is confident that he can sell an average of 5 000 presentation folders per month, but he recognises that there will be a start-up phase – it will take time to become known and established in the marketplace. He would like to formulate a profit and loss projection and cash flow forecast before starting the business.

   These are some details pertinent to the proposed business:

   - The Korean manufacturer wants a committed monthly order, confirmed for a six- month period at a time.

- The cost price per presentation folder is R80 and the payment method is cash on delivery. Orders for the six-month period must be placed two months prior to the first delivery. Mike has decided that his first order will be 2 000 units per month for the first three-month period. The order for the next three months will be 2 200 units per month. The first shipment will arrive in South Africa on 5 January 2022.
- Mike's sales projections, expressed as a percentage of the monthly purchases, are as follows:

Jan 2022	Feb 2022	Mar 2022	April 2022	May 2022	June 2022
80%	80%	90%	100%	110%	120%

- The selling price of presentation folders in KwaZulu-Natal will be R120 per unit. The majority of customers are likely to be businesses. Mike believes that while his customers will be given 15 days' credit after invoice, in reality an average of 30 days is taken for payment, even after implementing strict credit control procedures.
- Mike intends to employ a sales representative and pay them a fixed salary of R5 000 per month, as well as a sales commission of 2% on sales achieved. The sales commission is paid in the month following sales achieved. Mike believes that the sales representative will make 30% of the sales, and that he will make 70%.
- Rental expense would be R2 000 per month, payable at the end of each month. A refundable deposit, equivalent to one month's rent, is to be paid when Mike takes occupancy of his premises on 1 January 2022.
- Mike needs to acquire the following for his business:

Item	Cost	From date	Depreciate over
Computer equipment	R14 400	1 January 2022 Cash	3 years (straight line)
Motor vehicle	R96 000	1 January 2022 Credit agreement with a monthly repayment of R3 200pm	5 years (straight line)

- Other monthly overheads are expected to be:

	R	
Accounting fees	3 000	(one month's credit)
Electricity and water	1 200	(paid in the following month)
Petrol	2 000	(paid in the month incurred)
Mike's salary	30 000	
Telephone	1 500	(paid in the following month)
Advertising	10 000	

- Mike has R160 000 of his own money to invest in the venture. He calculates that he might qualify for a R170 000 overdraft and he has the option to offer his house as security to the bank.

a) Calculate the closing stock (in units) per month for the period 1 January to 30 June 2022. Use the following layout:

	Jan 2022	Feb 2022	Mar 2022	April 2022	May 2022	June 2022
Opening stock						
Add: purchases						
Less: sales						
Closing stock						

b) Prepare a monthly profit and loss budget for the period 1 January to 30 June 2022.

c) Prepare a monthly cash flow forecast for the period 1 January to 30 June 2022.

10. Prepare a marketing budget for quarter 2 for the car dealership LC Retailer, with a service centre, selling both new and used cars. In this environment, the initial budget allocation is based on the sales target for the next quarter. There is a marketing allocation of R12 000 for each new car sold.

The following are the total targets supplied by the sales team:

New cars – 10 units

Used cars – 17 units

For the marketing expenses, the budget is divided into four sections, which must total the marketing allocation as indicated in the marketing planner. This amount must be divided among the following activities as follows:

- national and retailer activities
- media activities
- local activities
- service-related activities.

The following information was used in the previous quarter 1 and should be used to compile the marketing budget:

LC Retailer Marketing Planner 2022 Q1

Customer experience		
National and retailer activity	**Budget in Q1**	
Email marketing	10 000	This amount will increase by 10%.
SMS communications	500	Fixed per quarter
Family day sponsorship	?	The dealership agrees to sponsor a family day of R6 000.
POS nameplates	?	It is necessary to replace the marketing nameplates on the cars for R2 000.
Road race sponsorship	?	A road race requires a sponsorship of R10 000.
Ladies' spa day	?	The budget in this section of R45 500 can be spent on a ladies' spa day to increase awareness of the product in the female market.
Media activities		
Cost of display in shopping centre	17 000	This will increase by 15% from the previous quarter amount.
Advertising of vehicles on various websites	?	The remainder of the budget for this section (30% of total) can be spent on web-related advertising.
Local activities		
Live broadcast Saturday	20 000	Fixed quarter amount
Wash and evaluate day	?	Remainder of budget spent allocated to this section (20% of total) to be spent here.

Customer experience		
National and retailer activity	Budget in Q1	
Service-related activities		
SMS service reminders	750	A quarterly cost of SMS reminders for clients to bring their cars in for service will remain the same.
After-sales brochures	?	New after-sales brochures need to be printed at a cost of R5 500.
Email communications	1 800	This amount will increase by 10% in the next quarter.
Accessories voucher campaign	?	A total of R14 500 is allocated to the after-sales customer experience, with the remainder to be spent on the accessories voucher campaign.

ANSWERS

1. A budget is a written financial plan showing management's financial goals and forecasts for a specific future period.

2. Reasons to draw up a budget:
   - provides a formal framework for the business to put strategic objectives into action to be able to achieve those goals in the next period
   - allows management and staff to evaluate whether goals have been achieved
   - allows comparisons between actual and budgeted results, thus aiding financial control
   - requires people in charge of the different departments to be accountable for their actions and decisions
   - creates cost awareness among staff
   - shows where problems could arise in future
   - coordinates the goals of the business and contribute to the effective use of resources at the business's disposal.

3. Factors to consider:
   - give the business the opportunity to take external factors into account during financial planning, eg Covid19
   - competition
   - economic cycles
   - weather conditions (if applicable, eg drought)
   - political calendars, eg elections.

4. Expected sales = Expected number of units sold × Unit price

5. Steps for a cash flow budget:
   - Calculate actual cash received.
   - Calculate the actual cash payments to be made.
   - Calculate the net cash movement per month and add/deduct to/from previous month cash balance.

6. Next year's expenses: R150 000 x 1.08 = R162 000

7. The cost of sales is: R1 050 000 x 70% = R735 000

   Sales for 2023: increase 10% pa over the last 5 years, therefore R147 000 x 10% = R161 700

8. 147 000 x 1.10 = R161 000

9. a) Calculation of closing stock per month per unit

	Jan 22	Feb 22	Mar 22	Apr 22	May 22	Jun 22
Opening stock	–	400	800	1 000	1 000	780
Add: purchases	2 000	2 000	2 000	2 200	2 200	2 200
Less: sales	1 600	1 600	1 800	2 200	2 420	2 640
Closing stock	400	800	1 000	1 000	780	340

b) Profit and loss for budget for period 1 Jan 2022 to 30 June 2022

Profit and loss for 6 months	Jan R	Feb R	Mar R	April R	May R	June R
Sales	192 000	192 000	216 000	264 000	290 400	316 800
Less: cost of sales	128 000	128 000	144 000	176 000	193 600	211 200
Opening inventory	–	32 000	64 000	80 000	80 000	62 400
Purchases	160 000	160 000	160 000	176 000	176 000	176 000
Less: closing inventory	–32 000	–64 000	–80 000	–80 000	–62 400	–27 200
Gross profit (loss)	64 000	64 000	72 000	88 000	96 800	105 600
Current expenses	57 852	57 852	57 996	58 284	58 442	58 600
Rent paid	2 000	2 000	2 000	2 000	2 000	2 000
Depreciation (400 + 1 600)	2 000	2 000	2 000	2 000	2 000	2 000
Accounting fees	3 000	3 000	3 000	3 000	3 000	3 000
Electricity and water	1 200	1 200	1 200	1 200	1 200	1 200
Petrol	2 000	2 000	2 000	2 000	2 000	2 000
Mike's salary	30 000	30 000	30 000	30 000	30 000	30 000
Salesperson's salary	5 000	5 000	5 000	5 000	5 000	5 000
Commission	1 152	1 152	1 296	1 584	1 742	1 900
Telephone	1 500	1 500	1 500	1 500	1 500	1 500
Advertising	10 000	10 000	10 000	10 000	10 000	10 000
Net income before tax	6 148	6 148	14 004	29 716	38 358	47 000
Tax	–1 721	–1 721	–3 921	–8 320	–10 740	–13 160
Net income	4 427	4 427	10 083	21 396	27 618	33 840

c) Monthly cash flow forecast for the period 1 January to 30 June 2022.

	Jan	Feb	Mar	April	May	June
	R	R	R	R	R	R
Opening bank balance	0	–68 600	–95 652	–122 704	–141 900	–113 384
Receipts	160 000	192 000	192 000	216 000	264 000	290 400
Sales		192 000	192 000	216 000	264 000	290 400
Other: capital contribution	160 000					
Less payments:	–228 600	–219 052	–219 052	–235 196	–235 484	–235 642
Purchases	–160 000	–160 000	–160 000	–176 000	–176 000	–176 000
Motor vehicle payment	–3 200	–3 200	–3 200	–3 200	–3 200	–3 200
Rent paid	–4 000	–2 000	–2 000	–2 000	–2 000	–2 000
Computer equipment	–14 400	–	–	–	–	–
Accounting fees	–	–3 000	–3 000	–3 000	–3 000	–3 000
Electricity and water	–	–1 200	–1 200	–1 200	–1 200	–1 200
Petrol	–2 000	–2 000	–2 000	–2 000	–2 000	–2 000
Mike's salary	–30 000	–30 000	–30 000	–30 000	–30 000	–30 000
Salesperson's salary	–5 000	–5 000	–5 000	–5 000	–5 000	–5 000
Commission	–	–1 152	–1 152	–1 296	–1 584	–1 742
Telephone	–	–1 500	–1 500	–1 500	–1 500	–1 500
Advertising	–10 000	–10 000	–10 000	–10 000	–10 000	–10 000
Net cash flow for the month	–68 600	–27 052	–27 052	–19 196	28 516	54 758
Closing bank balance	–68 600	–95 652	–122 704	–141 900	–113 384	–58 626

10. Total marketing spend to be calculated on new car sales:

    Target marketing spend based on sales in Q2 = 10 cars × R12 000 = R120 000

    Based on the costs from the previous quarter, complete the budget as follows:

LC Retailer Marketing Planner 2022 Q2

National activity	Budget
Email marketing	11 000
Retailer activity	**Budget**
SMS communications	500
Family day sponsorship	6 000
POS nameplates	2 000
Road race sponsorship	10 000
Ladies' spa day	16 000
	45 500

Retailer activity	Budget
Cost of display in shopping centre	19 550
Advertising of vehicles on various websites	16 450
	36 000
Retailer activity	**Budget**
Live broadcast Saturday	20 000
Wash & evaluate day	4 000
	24 000
Retailer activity	**Budget**
SMS service reminders	750
After-sales brochures	5 500
Email communications	1 980
Accessories voucher campaign	6 270
	14 500
Total marketing budget for Q2	**120 000**

Managing credit

WILLIE CONRADIE

Learning outcomes

After reading this chapter, you should be able to:

- define debt and credit, as well as debtors and creditors, and demonstrate how these concepts are related
- explain what is meant by the term 'credit transaction'
- describe at least four different forms of credit
- explain at least eight possible advantages (including marketing advantages) to the enterprise or organisation of granting credit purchasing facilities to its customers
- explain at least five possible disadvantages to the enterprise or organisation of granting credit purchasing facilities to its customers
- identify at least eight issues that must be addressed in a credit policy document
- explain and give examples of the seven major elements indicating a customer's creditworthiness
- demonstrate the contents, importance and advantages of using a formal credit application form
- give at least three important factors relating to the effective implementation of credit decisions
- explain the importance of effective control of debtors' accounts.

> **NB!** There are many excellent videos available on credit management, from the most basic to the very sophisticated. One is *Introduction To Credit Management* (https://www.youtube.com/watch?v=5Fz5od7XKx0).

8.1 Introduction

You have probably heard the old saying: 'Neither a borrower nor a lender be.' Many people, including many managers and entrepreneurs, believe this to be excellent advice. Almost 50% of all businesses that use banking facilities do not borrow anything from the bank. However, extending credit to customers and making use of credit facilities is a valid practice, especially when the economy is not doing very well and consumers cannot presently afford all the things they need or want. Lending facilities are widely offered by both private and public enterprises. Because of its importance, this aspect of financial management deserves special attention.

In this chapter, we will explore some of the major issues concerning the management of credit in a business enterprise (even in a governmental or a not-for-profit institution). These issues include:

- the meaning of the terms 'credit' and 'debt'
- the various forms of credit
- the advantages and disadvantages of granting credit
- the most important elements to manage when extending credit to customers so as to ensure credit-granting success and avoid bad debts.

> **NB!** It is important to note that this chapter deals mainly with how an enterprise extends credit to its clients, but in general does not cover the ways in which an enterprise uses the credit facilities available in the marketplace to purchase goods/services (eg suppliers' credit, bank overdraft facilities or long-term loans). However, remember that granting credit to a customer also involves the other party taking up the credit you have extended.

8.2   Defining credit and debt (creditors and debtors)

The word 'credit' is derived from the Latin word *credo* ('I believe'), and in essence this is what credit is all about. Whenever an entrepreneur/manager supplies goods and/or services to a customer or a client without receiving full payment immediately, the business says to the customer/client: 'I believe that you will pay me in future as agreed.'

The word 'debt' is derived from the Latin word *debeo* ('I owe' or 'I am supposed to'). Whenever a client or customer takes products or uses the services of an organisation without paying in full at the same time, we say that the customer/client is in debt and becomes a debtor ('I owe you') to that business.

DEFINITIONS

The accounting term **outstanding debtors** refers to the sum total of all the monies owed to an enterprise by customers/clients at any given time. The enterprise has granted credit to these customers/clients, and the outstanding monies still owed to it on a certain date will represent the value of the business's **debtors' book**.

We can define the concept of **creditors (or trade creditors and other creditors)** as the sum total of all the monies owed by the enterprise to suppliers of the business or organisation. These suppliers are usually the suppliers of goods/services to the enterprise – for example, manufacturers and wholesalers from whom the business has purchased goods/services on credit (buying now, paying later).

NB! All suppliers of finance, goods or services to the enterprise who do not immediately receive full compensation for what they have supplied can be regarded as the creditors of that enterprise. For example, when a bank/financial institution lends money to an enterprise (say in the form of a mortgage loan or a bank overdraft), the financial institution becomes a creditor to that enterprise. However, in financial management terms, such loans are considered long-term loans and bank overdrafts in the financial statements (the balance sheet) and not as creditors.

The term 'trade creditors' is used to indicate monies owed to the suppliers of goods and services intended for resale purposes, while the term 'other creditors' refers to money owed to the suppliers of goods and services meant for supportive, operational purposes. An example of the latter is stationery (eg letterheads and invoice books) needed for administrative purposes or money owed to a company for fitting new display cabinets in a retail shop.

DEFINITION

Credit is the debt that results whenever goods or services are rendered without full payment at the same time, ie at the time of the transaction.

The concepts of debt and credit are therefore linked, and you cannot have one without the other. The moment an enterprise supplies goods/services to a client without receiving full payment at the same time, both a credit and a debt are created: the enterprise (the creditor to the customer/client) extends credit to the customer/client (the debtor to the enterprise) and the customer/client is in debt to the enterprise.

Similarly, the moment a business receives goods/services from a supplier without paying in full, both credit and debt are created: the business receives credit from the supplier (creditor) and is therefore in debt to this supplier (it is obliged to pay in future, because it owes a debt to the creditor).

8.3   The credit transaction

The most important identifying characteristic of a credit transaction is that goods/services are supplied without receiving full payment at the same time from the receiver.

DEFINITION

A **credit transaction** is any business activity where goods and/or services are supplied but where the receiver does not immediately pay for them in full.

The credit transaction can be more fully explained by means of a table (see Table 8.1).

Table 8.1: The credit transaction

Supplier (creditor)	Receiver (debtor)
Supplies goods/services	Receives goods/services
Has the right to be paid	Has an obligation to pay the supplier
Believes that payment will be made in the future	Does not pay the supplier in full immediately Indicates that full payment will be made at a later stage

8.4   Forms of credit

There are many ways in which an entrepreneur/manager can choose to extend credit to customers, and a combination of these forms may often be applicable. These are discussed below.

8.4.1   Open account

An open account is a form of credit in which credit is extended regularly to a customer/client, but the customer/client has to pay the full amount of each of the specific purchases within the subsequent agreed-upon period. A variation is where an agreed-upon minimum amount of debt is payable at regular intervals (eg when it is agreed that the debtor will pay a minimum of, say, 25% of their debt at the end of each month).

EXAMPLE

XYZ Business regularly needs and receives goods supplied by ABC Manufacturer. Their mutual understanding is that XYZ Business will pay ABC Manufacturer all purchases during a certain month to the full before the seventh day of the following month.

8.4.2 Revolving credit

Revolving credit is a form of credit where the client (debtor) is restricted to a maximum limit (or ceiling) of the accumulated debt owed. As long as this limit is not reached, the difference between the limit allowed and the actual amount owed is available as credit. The client is allowed to purchase goods/services on credit until the limit is reached.

8.4.3 Instalment credit

Instalment credit is a form of credit that applies mainly where high-priced goods/services are supplied on credit and the client is obliged to make regular instalment payments until the full debt is paid to the supplier. There are many forms of instalment credit, but the best known is hire purchase (which also has many forms). Normally, this is when a physical item (such as a commercial vehicle) is supplied to a client for use, but the legal ownership remains with the supplier/financier until the item is paid for in full. Usually the client pays an initial deposit, with monthly interest and other financial costs forming part of the agreement. Leasing and rental agreements are also forms of instalment credit.

EXERCISE 8.1

Do some research. For example, visit a local SMME retailer and ask the manager/entrepreneur to explain these two concepts to you, and list the major characteristics of leasing and lay-by (two forms of credit).

8.4.4 Other forms of credit

Previously, post-dated cheques (where the cheque is a type of promissory note) were used as another form of credit. But from 2021 banks no longer accept cheque payments or physical cheques. Other forms of credit are secured loans (against collateral assets that can be seized) and lay-bys (where the seller keeps an item until the client pays off the full amount in instalments). We will now look at some typical business transactions.

EXERCISE 8.2

Test your understanding of credit management by indicating whether or not the examples given are credit transactions.

1. The client receives goods from XYZ Marketing Services on 1 June and promises to pay the full amount at the end of the same month.
2. The client wants a particular unique piece of equipment. The seller promises not to sell it to anybody else and to keep it until the client has saved up and paid the full purchase price of R30 000. The client has already paid the seller R3 000.
3. The client buys marketing equipment for a total price of R100 000 and offers a valid and legal credit card as full payment. The transaction is concluded automatically by means of the normal electronic procedures; the client then signs the slip and leaves with the equipment.
4. The client buys the goods in example 3 and pays hard cash for the full amount.
5. The client buys the goods in example 3 and pays by cheque for the full amount.
6. The client pays for the equipment in example 3 by means of four cheques: one dated for today and the other three dated for the end of each of the following three months.
7. Reasons for granting (or not granting) credit.

8.5   Advantages and disadvantages of granting credit

Whenever an entrepreneur/manager considers the possibility of extending credit facilities to existing and new customers or clients, they should carefully consider the advantages and disadvantages of doing so.

8.5.1   Advantages of granting credit

One of the primary aims of a private enterprise is to ensure the best possible return on its investment over the longer term. For a not-for-profit enterprise the aim is to render products/services in the most effective and efficient ways possible. The advantages identifiable in extending credit to clients should contribute to reaching these objectives.

Increasing sales

Many clients/customers prefer not to buy services/products on a cash basis, and therefore make most (or all) of their purchases on credit. There are a variety of reasons for this: they need the goods/services immediately, but do not have the cash resources to pay for them right away; they feel it is risky or inconvenient to carry cash with them; or their purchases are paid for by other people (eg a student who buys textbooks on account, and the debt is later paid by their parents).

Thus clients who prefer, or are forced by circumstances, to buy/acquire services/ products on credit will not support a business without credit facilities.

Increasing market share

A continuous growth in sales leads to an increase in market share. Extending credit may increase sales.

Facing competition

If your competitors offer credit purchasing facilities to customers/clients, one way of competing would be to match the competitors' credit facilities. In a highly competitive market, an entrepreneur/manager who decides not to give credit will need to offer unique and more attractive products/services to the target market in order to remain competitive.

Selling more expensive products/services

Some products/services are too expensive for many individuals if they are available on a full cash basis only. The more luxurious and expensive products and services (eg equipment, specialised furniture and vehicles and homes/property) are especially open to credit facilities. Businesses that wish to sell more expensive and/or luxury items and services would be advised to consider extending credit to customers and the marketplace.

Cross-selling to existing customers

Sending out account statements and receiving regular payments from customers opens up many opportunities to ensure ongoing business transactions with them. Such customers can be made to feel that they enjoy special treatment (eg by informing them that an upcoming special offer is only open to account holders during the first two days or months of the promotion).

Retention of customer base

It is very important to ensure that as many trustworthy customers as possible return to the business for follow-up transactions. It costs a business seven to 10 times as much to recruit a new client than it does to retain an existing one. Using credit as an instrument to build up a long-term relationship with a client is a strong advantage linked to credit extension.

Easier to exchange and adjust returned goods

Because credit transactions involve more extensive and detailed administrative records, it puts the business in a good position to assess the legitimacy of requests to return and/or to exchange and/or alter purchased goods/services.

Aiding advertisements and communications

Although price, place, and the range and quality of products are all important parts of successfully doing business and attracting customer support, offering easy, trouble-free and extended credit facilities also helps to get the advertising message into the marketplace. This applies to all advertising media (social media, TV, radio, newspapers and even direct emailing lists). An existing list of customers further enhances the advertising message because the messages can be personalised (eg 'Dear Lindiwe' or 'Hi John'). This might always be meaningful to a targeted (potential) customer.

Increasing profit

The business entrepreneur/manager may argue that clients who buy on credit are not as price conscious as those who pay cash. This gives the business the opportunity to achieve bigger profit margins. In fact, all the advantages mentioned should help to increase net profits to the enterprise and its owner(s).

EXERCISE 8.3

What do you think are the practical reasons that make each of the possible scenarios mentioned above advantageous for businesses?

8.5.2 Disadvantages of granting credit

While there are many advantages to granting credit, there are also a number of real and potential disadvantages.

Higher administrative and operational costs

Formulating a credit policy; getting customers to complete application forms; assessing and verifying the information supplied by the customer; keeping records of clients' personal information; and setting and monitoring credit limits, credit purchases and payments all result in increased operational and administrative costs. The extra costs (along with opportunities for errors and mistakes) can be substantial. Businesses that sell only for cash do not have to carry this additional burden.

Possibility of late payment by debtors

It is realistic to expect that not all clients/customers owing monies to the enterprise will honour their obligations to the business at all times. Payments expected but not received can place huge (and sometimes unbearable) burdens on the enterprise's finances and future existence.

Likelihood of bad debts

It is realistic to expect that there will be some clients/customers who, either intentionally or unintentionally, will not pay their debts at all, even over the long term. From time to time businesses that sell on credit have to write off monies owed to them as irretrievable bad debt. Debt not paid has a direct detrimental impact on cash flow and net profit as well.

Increased need for capital

The moment a business does not receive full payment for products/services supplied, this creates an increased need for capital (the enterprise must find capital to replace the sold goods and services – this is to finance the debtors' book). The increased administrative and operational costs (eg management's time and attention) in extending credit also contribute to this increased need for capital.

Slowdown in cash inflow

Because the business now has to wait longer before it receives full compensation for goods/services already supplied, this places greater stress on the business to find additional sources of capital. The business still needs to pay for its own purchases and overheads (rent, wages and transport), but now has to contend with a shortage of income needed to do so, and must find other and additional sources of capital to fill the gap caused by extending credit to customers. The importance of a positive cash flow for any enterprise is explained elsewhere in this book, and its utter importance must never be ignored by management.

EXERCISE 8.4

Give five reasons applicable to the management environment for why you agree or disagree with any one of the possible disadvantages of extending credit.

EXERCISE 8.5

The decision to grant credit (or not to do so) requires a solid knowledge of the variety of options, as well as the advantages and disadvantages involved. In considering these factors, the entrepreneur/manager must keep the bottom line in mind – will granting credit enhance the enterprise's major objectives?

8.6 The importance of a realistic and sound credit policy

Once the decision has been made to extend credit, an enterprise needs to develop a credit policy, preferably in the form of a written policy document. A policy document is compiled after careful analysis and planning, and lays out management's decisions regarding the what, where, why, when, who and how of desired credit practices. Typical issues addressed in such policy documents are as follows:

- Will we sell on credit? What percentage of total sales should be credit sales?
- What kinds of goods/services will qualify for credit sales? Will all our goods/services be offered on credit?
- Will there be a selling price differentiation between credit and cash sales?
- What criteria and procedures will the business use for assessing clients' applications for credit?
- Who will be authorised to assess and decide how to extend credit to a customer?
- What will the terms and conditions be? Examples of conditions that need to be decided upon are demanding a deposit, adding monthly interest to outstanding debt, and requiring a specified minimum of the outstanding balance to be paid at the end of each month.
- How will we manage accounts in arrears?
- Who is responsible and accountable for each part of our credit practices? For example, can any staff member agree to a client's request to buy on credit? Who must take what steps and how soon when a client is in arrears making an agreed payment?
- A sound and realistic credit policy, set down in written form, gives guidance and information to the owner/manager and employees as well as to the customers of a business. It tells all stakeholders: 'This is the way we extend credit to customers in our business.'

The most basic factors ('The ABC of a credit policy') must therefore be taken into consideration when formulating a sound credit policy.

The credit policy should be drawn up in a written document, which should be periodically updated and implemented.

8.7 Assessing the creditworthiness of customers

It does not help an enterprise very much if few customers make use of its credit facilities. In order to maximise the advantages of extending credit to customers (see Section 8.5), the entrepreneur/manager must ensure that their decision to sell on credit is promoted as effectively and efficiently as possible – and on a continual basis.

Existing clients as well as potential customers should therefore be informed of this facility and persuaded to take up the offers of credit being made. One of the most common and popular ways to start this process is to convince existing and potential customers to complete an application form requesting that they be permitted to buy on credit from the business.

8.7.1 Indications of creditworthiness

The primary objective of extending credit to customers is to increase the profits of the enterprise over the longer term, but all the advantages of credit sales will be cancelled out and even turned into a net disadvantage to the business if credit customers do not fulfil their obligations to the business. It is therefore important that the business successfully assesses whether a particular client is worthy of receiving credit facilities.

> **NB!** South African law stipulates that it is the responsibility of credit suppliers to ensure that their potential debtors have the ability to repay their debt.

The business will suffer severe losses if a large percentage of customers (debtors) do not pay on time (or do not pay the agreed amount at all). If a large number of debtors become aggressive and hostile about their obligations to the business, and refuse or are unable ultimately to pay their debts, the future of the business will be jeopardised.

It is therefore important that the entrepreneur/manager takes precautions to minimise (and preferably eliminate) the potential disadvantages of selling on credit. The 'seven Cs' of assessing a potential client's creditworthiness are excellent guidelines that should be followed at all times. These are as follows:

1. credit history
2. capital
3. conditions
4. capacity
5. character
6. collateral
7. common sense.

Credit history

A common way of assessing an applicant's creditworthiness is to obtain full particulars of their credit history, as well as detailed credit references.

Another important and effective way of assessing an applicant's credit history is to consult a credit bureau. These agencies specialise in collecting important information about the past and present credit behaviour of individuals, businesses and organisations. Credit bureaus sell their information, and any credit manager is advised to make use of these services. Individuals, businesses and organisations that have been blacklisted (eg for having court judgments against them for not paying their debts) can be declined very early in the assessment process.

Capital

Capital refers to the monetary value of credit purchases in question. How much value does the customer wish to buy? Will this be a single once-off transaction or will the customer regularly buy on credit?

This aspect of credit assessment involves setting a credit limit (or ceiling). For example, a client might apply to be allowed to make credit purchases regularly during a particular month, indicating that the total amount of purchases will not exceed, say, R10 000 per month. Another example could be a customer who wishes to buy marketing services to the value of R50 000 and can only pay a R10 000 deposit. The capital amount of this request would be the outstanding R40 000 plus possible interest and other potential service charges.

Conditions

The agreement between client and business involves many conditions that need to be negotiated and agreed upon. Examples of such conditions are the following:
- the agreed interest rate (if applicable)
- the agreed starting date and amount of the first instalment
- the agreed other dates and amounts of regular instalments
- the agreed methods of payments (cash, cheque, debit order)
- the agreed credit limits
- the agreed methods of communication (eg for account statements, dealing with queries, acknowledging payments, etc)
- the agreed reassessment of the credit agreement
- the agreed steps to be taken when an account is in arrears.

Capacity

The entrepreneur/manager must also assess the applicant's means and ability to honour the regular payment of due monies as stipulated under the conditions of the credit agreement.

The important question to ask is whether the client can afford to make the required payments. To answer this question, the business needs to look at things like proof of regular income (having a full-time job, and proof of monthly salary and deductions) and recent bank statements.

When the applicant is another business, assessing the applicant's audited annual financial statements may provide valuable information.

Most banks and other financial institutions will not grant a home loan to a person if the required monthly instalment will exceed 30% of the client's regular monthly income. They believe (and have evidence to back this up) that when this limit is exceeded, the ability of the client to honour their obligations is placed under severe pressure, which will very likely lead to default. The supplier of trade credit does not need to be so meticulous, but should always carefully consider the customer's ability to repay debt.

Character

Assessing the character of an applicant is never easy. In trying to assess character, the entrepreneur/manager tries to determine what kind of person the applicant is.

- Is the client trustworthy, or will they look for excuses for not meeting the agreed conditions of payment?
- Will the client give priority to their own interests when things get tough, or will the client do everything possible to meet their obligations to other parties?
- How punctual is the applicant and how important is a 'good name' to the applicant? Ethics and integrity are important issues in assessing the character of an applicant.

Collateral

Collateral is what an applicant offers as a guarantee in order to convince the giver of credit that the applicant will meet all the obligations of the credit agreement. Examples of collateral are as follows:

- The parents of a student sign a document guaranteeing that they will pay the student's debts.
- The owners/shareholders of a business sign in their personal and individual capacities to guarantee payment to the giver of credit (another business or the bank).
- The credit applicant makes share certificates and paid-up insurance policies available to the creditor with a signed letter of authority to liquidate these assets under certain conditions and circumstances.

- The applicant allows the creditor to register a first, second or even third mortgage bond over fixed property (land and buildings). In the case of default, the land and buildings may be sold by the creditor to cover the debt.

Entrepreneurs/managers often accuse bank managers of being willing to authorise a loan only if more than enough collateral for the loan is available. However, remember that every business – including banks – tries to add value and realise a satisfactory profit. Businesses do not prefer to use collateral offered by customers, but would rather have customers fulfil their obligations so that they avoid bad debts as far as possible.

Common sense

Once the information about an applicant has been collected, and the seven Cs of credit analysed, the entrepreneur/manager must exercise sound judgment. A well-assessed and well-motivated decision needs to be taken. Research shows that the more knowledgeable and experienced the person assessing the application, the better the final decision and its outcomes. But remember the saying: 'Common sense is very important, but not very common!'

EXERCISE 8.6

Try to remember the core concept of each C to be assessed. Give a short description and everyday example of each core concept

8.7.2 The credit application form

To assess the creditworthiness of a customer or potential customer, the business entrepreneur/manager needs reliable and valid information from a range of sources. One way of collecting part of this information is to ask the customer to complete (and sign) a credit application form. Standard forms are available from local stationery suppliers, but some entrepreneurs may wish to draw up their own.

Figure 8.1 is an example of a typical thorough credit application form.

Credit application form
I . . . .(full names) hereby apply to be granted credit purchasing facilities by . . . . (name of business). I certify that all the information supplied herewith by me is 100% correct, valid and reliable.

. . . . SIGNATURE OF APPLICANT	. . . . DATE

1. Surname:		
2. First names:		
3. Title:	4. Marital status:	
5. ID no.:		
6. Tel no. (h):	(w):	(cell):

7. Residential address:

code:

8. Postal address:

code:

9. Name and address of employer:

Period employed:

10. Number of years staying at present residential address:

11. Number of years staying at previous residential addresses (give details):

12. Name and address of previous employer:

13. Period employed there:

14. Present gross salary per month:

(proof of present salary to be supplied)

15. Name and address of bank:	
16. Bank account number:	
17. List and values of present assets:	
18. List of present debts and amounts owed:	
19. Credit references (past three years only):	
1. Name: Address: Tel no.: Account no.:	2. Name: Address: Tel no.: Account no.:

Figure 8.1: Example of a credit application form

NB! An important part of credit management is to verify the correctness of the information supplied on the application form. Insufficient and/or incorrect information will immediately alert the entrepreneur/manager to the potential of dishonesty and/or carelessness. It is essential to check in time and follow up on the information supplied on the application form.

8.8   Implementing credit decisions

8.8.1   Confirming the outcome of an application

It is good manners to let a customer know as soon as possible about the outcome of their application for credit. This is also an excellent opportunity to foster a good relationship with the customer (especially when the outcome of the credit assessment is positive).

It is important to send the applicant a formal but friendly letter informing the customer of the outcome of their application.

8.8.2   Signing a formal agreement with the customer

Sound business management requires good communication practices, especially with your customers. All aspects of any credit agreement must be fully explained, discussed and understood by the client before the first credit transaction takes place. To formalise the credit agreement, both parties must sign a contract. This will ensure that there is less chance of misunderstanding and dispute later on.

8.8.3   Ensuring efficient and effective administration

A business cannot be successful in the long term if it is not supported by a sound, effective and efficient administrative support system. Remember the wise saying: 'If you do not measure something, you cannot manage it.' Sound business decisions are always influenced and guided by sound administrative recording and reporting systems.

The effective recording of every credit agreement, credit sales transaction and payment (or lack thereof) is essential for successful credit management. Accurate accounts must be sent out to debtors timeously and regularly and any deviation from the agreement must be brought to the attention of management for them to take the appropriate corrective action.

8.9   Controlling debtors' accounts

One of the advantages of extending credit to customers is that the enterprise can use debtors' records for marketing its products/services. However, diligence is required to ensure that all debtors fulfil their obligations as initially agreed upon.

To control debtors' accounts – as with all aspects of business management – the entrepreneur/manager must exercise the FAD (fanatical attention to detail) principle.

8.9.1   Sound administration

We have already emphasised the importance of a sound administrative system (see Section 8.8.3). Account statements and requests for payment must never be sent out late. These must be precise, valid and correct in every detail. For example, the title of the client, the spelling of names, and the up-to-date postal address should not contain a single error. No opportunity should be given to the client to delay or dispute payment.

8.9.2   Follow-up

The dedicated and disciplined follow-up of accounts in arrears, as well as debt collection procedures, is important to ensure effective and efficient credit extension practices. If an account is in arrears, do not neglect or ignore it for even a single day. Businesses around the world know that the longer an account is in arrears, and is allowed to remain that way, the more likely it is that such debts will never be paid. You do not want to have to write these monies off as bad debts.

A business can avoid a substantial number of bad debts by taking steps to follow up on accounts in arrears and recover monies at the first sign of delayed payment.

The ability to collect instalments when due, and particularly the ability to follow up effectively on accounts in arrears, can mean the difference between success and failure for an enterprise. No enterprise can afford slow payments, and no entrepreneur/manager should allow debts to be written off because of negligent debtors' control.

EXERCISE 8.7

Give at least five good reasons why an effective and efficient administration is so important in credit management (think about all aspects of credit management).

8.10 Things to remember

Each industry has particular characteristics that have a direct impact on sound credit management practices in that industry.

For example, the credit policies and practices of a business buying and selling new and custom-made vehicles (such as off-road filming vehicles) will be quite different from those of a marketing retailer selling billboards.

The following are useful and practical hints that apply to most industries:

- Never underestimate the importance of having a formal credit policy, a sound administrative system, and a dedicated and disciplined follow-up system for accounts in arrears.

- The business must achieve all the possible advantages of credit sales – not only higher turnover figures, but also higher profit margins, increased profits, the retention of clients and the building of long-term relationships with customers.

- The business must maintain effective and efficient communication with customers. 'Out of sight, out of mind' is vital to remember for effective credit management. Communication is vital at all times – not just when accounts are in arrears – as it affects the business's relationship with all of its customers.

- Always be friendly and professional when you deal with customers in arrears. You do not want to lose them, but only want them to honour their obligations. Even when you reach a point where you do not want such a customer any more, you should still behave in a disciplined and professional way.

8.11 Summary

In this chapter we explained the concepts of debt and credit, as well as debtors and creditors. The nature of the credit transaction and a variety of forms of credit were discussed and illustrated. We discussed the rationale for granting credit purchasing facilities to customers, as well as the possible negative results of such business practices. When the entrepreneur/manager does decide to grant credit to customers, it is essential to draw up a well-planned credit policy document. Part of this document should indicate the major elements to be assessed in determining the creditworthiness of a potential debtor. Policies and plans are not enough, however. Professional implementation and control systems are required to ensure the maximum advantages and the minimum disadvantages to the enterprise.

SELF-EVALUATION QUESTIONS

1. Explain the meaning of the concepts 'credit', 'debt', 'creditors' and 'debtors' *(see Section 8.2)*.

2. Illustrate the relationship between credit and debt by explaining the credit transaction *(see Section 8.3)*.

3. Explain in your own words, and give examples of the following forms of credit:
   a) an open account *(see Section 8.4.1)*
   b) instalment credit *(see Section 8.4.3)*
   c) revolving credit *(see Section 8.4.2)*
   d) hire purchase *(see Section 8.4.3)*.

4. Peter Nkosi, the owner of a retail business, is considering offering credit purchase facilities to his present and potential customers. Indicate at least eight possible advantages as well as five possible disadvantages such a step may mean to his business *(see sections 8.5.1 and 8.5.2)*.

5. After careful consideration, Peter has decided to offer credit to his target market. Can you advise him by explaining and illustrating the following concepts?
   a) assessing a client's creditworthiness *(see the seven Cs in Section 8.7)*
   b) the importance of a credit policy document *(see Section 8.6)*
   c) the major issues to be dealt with in the credit policy *(see Section 8.6)*
   d) the importance of having and using a formal credit application *(see Section 8.7.2)*
   e) the importance of implementing credit decisions in a professional manner *(see Section 8.8)*
   f) the major elements involved in effective and efficient control of debtors' accounts *(see Section 8.9)*.

9 Managing stock/inventory

WILLIE CONRADIE

9.1   Introduction

Business is only possible when products and/or services are effectively and efficiently offered for sale and are bought by many customers. However, it is a waste of money and effort for a business entrepreneur/manager to keep a huge variety and range of goods and services available on display shelves, with more stock in warehouses, unless these goods and services pass through the cash registers and credit sales invoices of the enterprise promptly.

The aim of business is to make profit, which can be achieved only if enough income is generated by transforming ample available goods and services into paid for sales. The same principle applies to any not-for-profit enterprise: the services and products must be made available in the most effective and efficient ways possible to the potential target markets.

> **DEFINITION**
>
> The basic aim of **stock/inventory management** is to ensure that the appropriate and optimum level of goods and services are available at the right time, at the right place and at the right price so as to achieve the most profitable sales.

NB! **Stock (inventory)** refers to those goods that will be acquired by the business for sale/distribution to the marketplace. Goods and services that are needed in a business's operations, but that are not normally for sale (eg own office stationery and furniture) are not regarded as stock (inventory). However, they must also be managed effectively.

In this chapter we will look at the most important elements of stock management, as well as a number of closely related matters.

9.2   Classifications of stock (inventory)

The economy of a country has a wide variety of industries (sectors), for example mining, manufacturing, transport, accommodation, services, telecommunications and retail, to name a few. Each industry or sector has a range of types of business. If we take manufacturing as an example, there are manufacturers of photographic equipment, specialised vehicles, paint products and all kinds of furniture, among others. You can see therefore that there is a wide variety of stock classifications. In this chapter, we will use three major categories to classify stock, namely:

1. manufacturing (and related industries)
2. the retail industry
3. the services industry.

Each industry has its own methods of stock classification.

9.2.1   Manufacturing (and related) industries

Raw and supplementary materials, semi-finished goods and finished goods are classifications of stock used in the manufacturing (and related) industries.

Raw and supplementary materials

Raw and supplementary materials are those goods needed to manufacture the finished products that will ultimately be sold directly and/or indirectly to the target market. For example, the raw and supplementary materials for a manufacturer of office furniture could be:

- aluminium
- varieties of wood, steel, plastic, etc
- wheels and all their accessories
- rubber/plastic hand grips and footrests
- upholstery material.

Semi-finished goods

Semi-finished goods are those goods in which an investment of raw and supplementary materials (as well as labour and other costs and resources) has been made, but which are not yet finished and not ready yet for selling. The term 'finished' can have a variety of meanings.

Finished goods

Finished goods are those goods that have been through the full manufacturing and production cycle and are ready to be sold to the ultimate user. In our example of the manufacturer of office furniture, the manufacturer's finished stock will consist of completed desks, chairs and other items, ready to be supplied to a customer.

9.2.2   The retail industry

Businesses such as furniture stores normally deal only with finished goods, which they buy from manufacturers and other suppliers to sell to their customers.

> **NB!** Sometimes retailers will also add value to the goods they have bought for resale purposes – for example a pharmacist who buys pills in bulk and then repacks them into smaller bags as the final finished stock offered for sale.

9.2.3   The services industry

Stock management in the services industry is just as important as in any other industry, but is quite different to that of the manufacturing and retailing industries. You should be able to explain how stock management in manufacturing and/or retailing also relates to the services industry.

EXAMPLE

Let us consider a guesthouse (the accommodation industry) as well as a mechanical workshop, where office furniture is repaired, restored and serviced (the mechanical services industry). The guesthouse sells 'sleeping nights' and breakfasts to tourists and tourist agencies. The workshop sells an artisan's labour hours and various parts, such as new drawers, to its potential customers.

For any specific day, the guesthouse has five double rooms available as 'stock' to sell to prospective customers. In the same way, the workshop's 'stock' is 21 labour hours per day (seven hours each for the three artisans employed).

Services are another type of stock (inventory), but are not acquired, stored and/ or sold in the same way as physical, tangible stock. In the services industry, stock/ inventory mainly consists of labour hours of different levels of skill – for example the labour services made available by the above-mentioned mechanical workshop.

EXERCISE 9.1

For each of the following two types of business, indicate which goods you would regard as stock (inventory). Give reasons for your decision. (You may wish to refer to Chapter 4, Section 4.3 and Exercise 4.1, in which the nature of assets of a business enterprise is discussed).

Business A

Business A makes and sells hotel and restaurant kitchen units. The business has machinery and equipment to the value of R6 million, raw materials (mainly stainless steel and supplementary materials) to the cost price value of R8 million, semi-finished kitchen units to the cost price value of R9 million, office furniture to the value of R15 000, and R1.5 million (cost price) in finished kitchen units available for sale.

Business B

Business B is a retail business buying and selling large appliances (washing machines and refrigerators) mainly to the hospitality industry (hotels and lodges). The business owns a showroom building valued at R8 million, appliance stock with a cost price of R2 million, and broken and malfunctioning washing machines (to be repaired by the business's repair shop) to the value of R600 000 (at cost price). Apart from these, the business uses shelving/display equipment to the value of R250 000 and transport vehicles to the value of R1.3 million.

9.3   Why stock management is important

There are many reasons why stock management is important to management and eventually to business and enterprise success. Some of the most important of these are explained.

9.3.1 Stock is a huge investment

To many enterprises, the investment in stock could represent between 30% and 80% of the enterprise's total investment. For manufacturing industries, the percentage of stock compared to total assets is lower (25% to 50%), because manufacturing requires bigger investments in machinery and equipment. For retailers and enterprises in the services industry, this figure could be as high as 95% of the total investment.

9.3.2 Stock-keeping costs

Apart from the huge investment in stock, an enterprise incurs significant costs to hold stock. These costs relate to storage, security, financing and stock losses.

Storage

The space taken up by stock is very seldom (or never) available at no cost. Normally, rent must be paid to a landlord, and the rental of storage facilities (including that of the display and selling areas) may be quite substantial. Even when the business owns the storage space, there are other storage costs to be paid as well as opportunity cost (what else the storage space could have been used for).

Security

Security costs are the costs required to ensure that stock is safeguarded against damage, theft, fire and pilferage, for example insurance and the cost of security systems.

Financing

Every investment in stock has a financing or opportunity cost. A financing cost could be the interest charged by a bank for the loan used to buy and store the stock. An opportunity cost could be the difference between the lower cash price you could have paid if you had cash available, and the higher price you paid because you purchased the goods on credit.

Stock losses

Apart from costs incurred to ensure that all stock is safeguarded against damage, theft and pilferage (insurance and security costs), substantial costs are incurred when stock is actually damaged and/or stolen. Linked to this is the problem of stock being sold at a discount because of obsolescence (going out of fashion and/or being superseded by newer, better goods entering the market).

9.3.3   Enhancing purchases management

NB!   Stock management is also important because it enhances effective and efficient stock purchases (buying or acquiring only enough of those items/services that are required by the applicable target markets).

Stock management and purchases management (also linked directly to production and marketing management) are closely related and integrated business functions, although each has its own speciality areas. For example, purchasing is concerned with selecting appropriate suppliers, ensuring the best products and services are available to the enterprise at the best terms, and enhancing relationships with existing and potential suppliers.

The more effective and efficient the stock management practices in an organisation or enterprise, the more effective and efficient the purchases management, and vice versa. An example of this is the ability of stock management to identify fast- or slow-selling stock. When this information is known, the business can concentrate on purchasing only goods that are popular and selling fast at acceptable cost and profit margins.

9.3.4   Calculating profits

Profit is the positive difference between the income and operating expenses of doing business. If the cost of sales (or cost of manufacturing) is not precisely known and accurately verified, any calculation of profit will be mere guesswork and unreliable.

NB!   Calculating profit (or loss) is impossible without appropriate stock management practices.

If the entrepreneur/manager does not know the specific value of opening stock, the value of all purchases of stock during that period of time, and the end value of stock, then cost of sales/manufacturing cannot be accurately calculated. It would then be impossible to reliably calculate and to determine profit or loss.

9.3.5   To ensure minimum over- or under-stocking

NB!   Stock management should aim to ensure that stock levels are not too low or too high at any time.

Ideally, a business should never hold more or less than a certain minimum amount of stock. Over-stocking occurs when a business carries more than the absolute minimum of stock. Under-stocking occurs when a business experiences stock-outs. This could occur when a sale is lost because the stock item is not available when a customer wants it, or it could be when the production process breaks down because of the unavailability of raw or supplementary materials. Such stock-outs always negatively affect the way customers and potential customers perceive the business.

EXERCISE 9.2

Yerefan Davids hopes to open the doors of his newly established marketing supplies business in two months' time. In your own words explain why an effective and efficient stock management system is very important to Yerefan's business's chances of success. Mention at least five major reasons, and relate each one to his specific business.

9.4 Over-stocking and under-stocking

Both over-stocking and under-stocking have negative effects on a business.

9.4.1 Too much stock

These are the disadvantages of carrying too much stock:

- **Higher-than-required investment in stock**: Often enterprises and organisations may experience a shortage of cash or may need additional capital because they have invested too much in stock. In such cases it is wise to bring stock levels down to the minimum required. This turns the over-investment in stock into available cash that can be used for other more profitable applications, for example to reduce a bank overdraft.

- **Higher-than-required levels of stock-keeping costs**: The minimum stock-keeping levels can be ensured by renting or financing the minimum physical space and facilities to carry stock (in storage, in the manufacturing process and in display areas). This keeps storage costs down, as carrying too much stock leads to unnecessary storage costs. The same applies to the other stock-keeping costs, such as insurance, security, financing costs and actual stock losses.

9.4.2 Too little stock

These are the adverse effects of carrying too little stock:

- **Loss of potential sales and real customers:** When an existing or potential customer wants a product that is unavailable or out of stock, or a service that cannot be provided because of a staff shortage, the business loses income. Even more damaging is the negative perception created in the minds of customers and potential customers that it may be better to switch to another supplier.

- **Loss of production (time and capacity):** Whenever the production process is stopped because a required raw or supplementary material is unavailable, this triggers a series of related consequences such as unnecessary labour costs of idle employees, expensive machinery and equipment standing idle, and the delay in manufacturing processes (causing bottlenecks). The customer may receive the product late or not at all.

- **Fighting fires instead of doing business:** Insufficient stock adds to the demands on successful business management. Remember that stock-outs represent crises: the missing raw materials have to be supplied as soon as possible in order to ensure that production can continue. Generally, dealing with this kind of crisis, which is called fire-fighting, requires additional attention from management, which also carries a high cost. Management could have instead used its valuable time on important strategic issues, such as working out a marketing initiative to increase sales.

9.5　The economic order quantity

Keeping stock is an essential part of any business. Without stock in one form or another, it is virtually impossible to do business. The costs involved in the acquiring, changing, storing, marketing and selling of stock are therefore unavoidable in any business.

To understand this, we use the concept of the economic order quantity (the quantity of a business's regular stock order that minimises the total cost of acquiring and keeping stock). Essentially, this refers to holding the correct amount of applicable stock at the right price and the lowest possible stock-keeping costs. The business must find a balance between the cost of acquiring stock and the cost of keeping stock.

One element of the challenge of stock management is to weigh the costs of keeping stock against the costs of ordering and acquiring it. If you need to, refer to Section 9.3.2, where we looked at stock-keeping costs (storage, insurance, security, financing costs and stock losses).

The entrepreneur/manager must also consider the cost of ordering and acquiring stock. There is always a cost for stock purchases: the time and direct costs involved in placing orders, following them up, transportation, receiving and checking deliveries, and administration all have a cost implication.

The more stock carried by a business, the lower the cost of acquiring stock, mainly because the frequency of ordering stock will be lower. The less stock carried, the higher the required frequency of ordering and receiving, and therefore the higher the ordering costs, eg phoning each day to order stock, or phoning only once every month to order stock.

Management must therefore try to achieve an optimum balance between these two costs. Figure 9.1 illustrates such an optimum level.

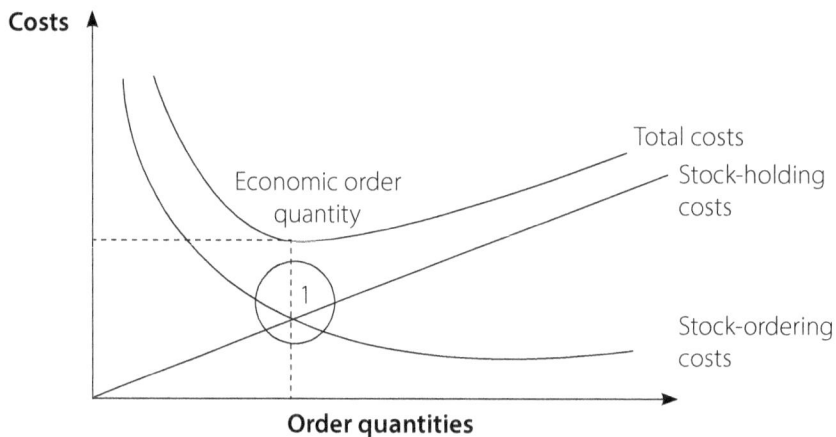

Figure 9:1: The economic order quantity

9.5.1   Stock-keeping costs

Figure 9.1 shows that the costs of keeping stock show a direct correlation with the increase in the number (and value) of stock units on the business's premises. The higher the number of units per order and delivery, the higher the stock-keeping costs.

9.5.2   Stock-acquiring costs

The higher the frequency of ordering and receiving single stock items, the higher the acquiring costs (more telephone calls, more paperwork, relatively high transportation costs per product unit and more time and effort spent checking and receiving ordered stock). Ordering costs should decrease when more units are ordered per single order.

9.5.3 Total costs

Total costs indicate the balance or trade-off between the advantages and disadvantages of having too much stock and having too little and the balance between the advantages and disadvantages of a high or low frequency of ordering and receiving stock.

The point where the two cost lines (stock-acquiring or ordering costs, and stock-keeping costs) intersect, given the minimum total costs, is where the economic order quantity is located (point 1 on the graph in Figure 9.1).

9.6 Ordering, receiving, storing and selling stock – the just-in-time (JIT) principle

The basic aim of stock management is to ensure the applicable product/service at the right price at the right place and at the right time (see Section 9.1). Timing is therefore a very important aspect of effective stock management.

> **EXAMPLE**
>
> Thomas Rodolo is the owner of a retail enterprise (selling a variety of hardware equipment). Thomas prides himself on his professional approach to management practices (including effective stock management practices).
>
> His goal is to have a fully stocked display area, with no large empty spaces between the items on display. This is because he knows that potential customers view empty shelves in a negative way and he also does not have additional storage facilities (too costly), and therefore has to use all the space available in his retail venue for display purposes.

What should Thomas take into consideration regarding the timing of stock management activities?

Thomas should consider:

- the order date
- the receiving date
- the lapse of time between the ordering and receiving dates
- the lapse of time between the receiving and selling dates
- the just-in-time (JIT) principle (see Figure 9.2).

All of these factors have implications for:

- the costs of acquiring stock
- the costs of keeping stock
- the negative consequences of stock-outs or over-stocking.

In order to avoid stock-outs or over-stocking, the enterprise must synchronise the times between ordering, receiving, storing and selling stock.

The ideal is for stock to arrive just in time in order to be consumed (manufactured) or sold. In business, this ideal is known as the just-in-time (JIT) principle, which is illustrated in Figure 9.2.

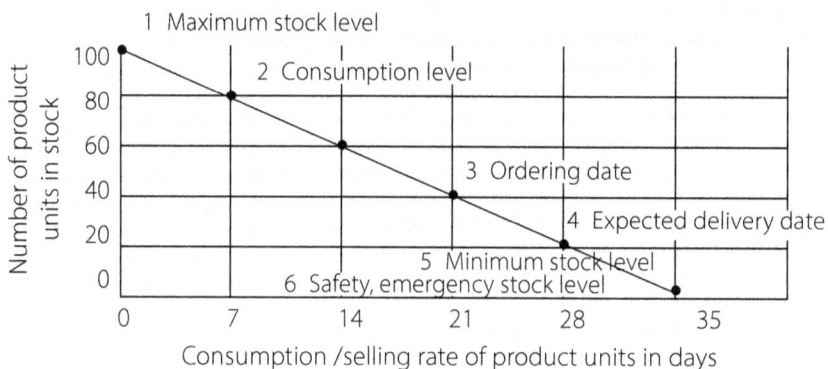

Figure 9.2: The JIT principle

Point 1 indicates the predetermined maximum level of stock. If more stock is kept, it is costing the business too much.

Point 2 is the consumption level. From past experience, a consumption (or selling) level is calculated, and this number of products will be consumed or sold on an average day. At any point in time, a fairly accurate forecast can be made of how long the existing stock will last.

Point 3 is the ordering point/date. Because the relevant supplier needs seven days between receiving the order and making the delivery, the order should be placed seven days before the minimum stock level is reached.

> Point 4 is the delivery date. The expected delivery date of products is arranged to synchronise with the date the minimum stock level will be reached so that the ordered goods will arrive just in time (JIT).
>
> Point 5 indicates the minimum stock level, which is determined as a safety precaution.
>
> Point 6 represents the safety/emergency stock level. If something happens and delivery of ordered goods is delayed, an emergency stock level (say to last another three days of demand) is kept.

9.7 Valuing stock

Raw and supplementary materials, and semi-finished and finished goods are purchased, acquired and stored on a continual basis. In order to know and calculate all the costs involved in doing business, the manager/entrepreneur needs to know the value of these different types of goods.

> **NB!** The assessment of the value of stock carried by the business at any given time is therefore a very important issue as profit cannot be measured and/or managed unless the correct value of every kind of stock is known at different intervals.

> **NB!** For sound bookkeeping and accounting reasons, stock needs to be valued at least at its cost price to the business (marking the value at selling price is an additional option, but not a prerequisite like cost price is).

There are various methods of arriving at the cost price of stock at hand, including the following:

- actual purchasing costs
- the first-in-first-out (FIFO) method
- the last-in-first-out (LIFO) method.

(FIFO and LIFO will be discussed in sections 9.7.2 and 9.7.3.)

Factors to bear in mind are:

- inflation and its effect
- the necessity of prudent administration.

9.7.1 Actual purchasing costs

All products (or groups of products) should be marked with the actual price paid to the supplier. This price is then regarded as the value (at cost) of the product, regardless of any other consideration (eg that the product was bought six months ago and that a similar product's price today may be 50% higher).

This method may result in a weighted average cost price of similar products, where the cost prices of older products (normally lower prices) and those of new arrivals (normally higher prices) are aggregated.

9.7.2   First-in-first-out (FIFO)

According to the first-in-first-out (FIFO) method, older products are sold (or used for production) first. These goods are therefore sold (used) in the same sequence as they were acquired. Remaining stock is valued at the cost price of later (more recent) consignments of that stock (because the previous stock has been sold).

9.7.3   Last-in-first-out (LIFO)

The last-in-first-out (LIFO) method is the inverse of the FIFO method. The most recently acquired stock is sold first, so the value of the remaining stock will depend on the previously paid (earlier) cost prices for that stock.

9.7.4   Inflation and its effect

The inflation rate is defined as the percentage change in the prices of similar goods and services during a certain period. If the cost price of a product increases from R100 to R110 in 12 months' time, the applicable inflation rate will be 10%.

This means that the valuation of a business's newly acquired stock may be 10% higher than last year, even though the number of stock units remained exactly the same. An entrepreneur/manager should always bear this in mind.

9.7.5   Prudent administration

Many entrepreneurs/managers are unaware of the threat of huge losses caused by poor administration. Owners and managers must always make sure that only ordered goods are delivered by suppliers, and also that the delivered goods are 100% correct and fully correspond with the actual order, the delivery notice and the invoice *before* paying for those goods and services.

Huge amounts of money can be lost when a business pays blindly for purchases (without carefully checking every order, delivery, delivery note, credit or debit note, invoice and account statement).

> **NB!** Consider that the total annual purchases of raw materials of any manufacturer, or that all the goods purchased for resale purposes by any retailer, usually amount to one of the biggest expense items of that business. This is an indication that prudent administration should never be neglected.

9.8   The importance of physical stocktaking

A wide variety of stock management systems are available today. The information age has led to holistic management systems that integrate information on all business activities (purchases, sales, cash, credit, debt, gross profit and stock analysis).

EXAMPLE

Macy's of New York (the largest department store in the world and with more than 850 stores) monitors the movement of approximately 800 000 different types of products on an hourly basis using data from its cash registers. Store managers not only know exactly how much shelf space a certain item is taking up at the start of each business day, but they also know exactly what the stock-keeping costs of that item are for that day. As the sales of the items are recorded, an hourly analysis indicates whether an item is 'earning its living'. The managers decide this according to a predetermined minimum number of sales per hour to make the item profitable. If not enough items are being sold, they are replaced by others that should have a better chance of adding profit to Macy's bottom line.

Entrepreneurs/managers should not rely blindly on the sophisticated computer systems that are available today. Even the most powerful computer system requires correct inputs – as the saying goes, 'rubbish in, rubbish out'. The faster and more powerful the computer, the worse are the potential consequences when the input is wrong.

No amount spent on sophisticated record-keeping systems can replace an effective and efficient physical stocktaking programme to keep track of stock purchases and sales and ensure the validity and correctness of the numbers, and the value of stock at hand.

The more often physical stocktaking is done, the more often stock management will be able to assess its efficiency and effectiveness.

Managers should not regard physical stocktaking as too physically demanding or as a waste of time and energy. They cannot depend solely on administrative (ie not actual/real) information to value stock and to make usage and profit calculations. When a business is liquidated or declared bankrupt, entrepreneurs and managers can't afford to be dumbstruck or unable to see where things went wrong.

> **NB!** You cannot avoid the need for physical stocktaking in business. The entrepreneur/manager who ignores this principle is simply inviting serious problems in the future.

There are a number of ways to approach the necessity of physical stocktaking, but no matter which option (or combination of options) is chosen, the end result must always be the physical validation of the quantity and value of all stock on hand in a business – at least once a year.

9.8.1   Focusing on critical stock items

Stock can be categorised by their unit costs and/or whether items are top, average or poor sellers. As far as cost price per unit is concerned, it is logical to focus more effort on items with a high unit cost (eg stinkwood furniture is much more valuable than pine furniture).

Here the Pareto principle (also known as the 80/20 principle) provides a useful guideline. In general, 20% of the stock in a business will contribute to 80% of sales, and/or 20% of the stock will contribute to 80% of the profit (not necessarily the same items in each case). Do not, however, ignore the other stock, which is also important and needs to be managed.

9.8.2   Doing interim spot checks

As an ongoing business practice, it is advisable to do regular spot checks, comparing the 'administrative' stock figure – derived from the internal administrative and bookkeeping and computer systems – of the number and value of stock at that point in time with the actual amount. Rotating this practice at intervals and among a variety of ranges of products will reveal any serious irregularities and errors in the administrative or security systems.

9.8.3   Choosing between chaos and order

Stock management also depends on neatness, order and systems. Untidy stock areas cause a lot of confusion and irritation, and make effective and efficient stocktaking very difficult and sometimes even impossible. Problems include lack of coding (indicating the cost price of any stock item), lack of product identification (is this a 300 g or a 320 g jar of petroleum jelly?) and untidy shelves or store rooms.

If products are neat and orderly, and correctly marked – type by type, size by size, age by age, supplier by supplier, etc, physical counting and valuating will be so much easier.

EXAMPLE

A large retailer of academic and other books and stationery takes fewer than six hours (on a Saturday evening) each year to physically count all its stock on hand, which is worth more than R40 million. Management attributes this achievement to their meticulous stock management approach and preparations made on a continuous basis.

9.8.4 Sound administrative and effective cost accounting practices

The backbone of sound decision making in business management is the quantity, quality, timeliness and relevance of accurate and valid management information. The same applies to stock management. If you do not know the purchase price of an item on the shelves of your business or enterprise, you will find it very difficult and troublesome to trace the appropriate value accurately. The more items of unmarked stock you have, the more difficult (and even impossible) it will be to arrive at a correct valuation of stock on hand.

NB! There are many excellent videos available on stock/inventory management, from the most basic to the very sophisticated. One is *What Is Inventory Management? – Whiteboard Wednesday* (https://www.youtube.com/watch?v= sl5zEPRkp0U).

9.9   Summary

In this chapter, we discussed effective and efficient stock management practices and why they are important. We outlined the basic aim of stock management and looked at the different ways to classify stock in different enterprises. Disadvantages of stock-outs and over-stock situations were given, as well as the costs of acquiring and keeping stock. Finally, we suggested methods for valuing stock, as well as prerequisites for physical stocktaking practices.

SELF-EVALUATION QUESTIONS

1. Define the basic aim of stock management *(see Section 9.1)*.

2. Explain and illustrate the different forms of stock in the manufacturing, retailing and services industries *(see sections 9.2.1–9.2.3)*.

3. Name and explain five major reasons why stock management is important *(see sections 9.3.1–9.3.5)*.

4. What are the differences between the four different cost items making up stock-keeping costs? *(see Section 9.3.2)*.

5. Give five practical examples of what happens when an enterprise carries too little and/or too much stock *(see sections 9.4.1 and 9.4.2)*.

6. Explain why the entrepreneur/manager should also consider the costs involved in acquiring stock. List three kinds of such costs *(see sections 9.5.1–9.5.3)*.

7. Use a graph to indicate the relationship between the timing of ordering, receiving, storing and selling stock and the required minimum stock levels *(see Figure 9.2)*.

8. Discuss the different ways of valuing stock *(see sections 9.7.1–9.7.4)*.

9. Explain the importance of physical stocktaking practices and discuss four important aspects of stocktaking *(see Section 9.8)*.

10

Making sense of data

RENÉ PELLISSIER

It is easy to lie with statistics, but easier to lie without them.
(Mosteller, F, cited in *Time*, August 2006, p10)

Learning outcomes

After reading this chapter, you should be able to:

- distinguish between numerical and non-numerical data
- differentiate between levels of data measurement
- collect relevant data
- summarise and interpret data using descriptive statistics
- summarise and interpret data using graphical displays.

10.1 Making sense of data matters

What is data? Data comes in various guises – all valid but not equally useful. Data is the name given to basic facts and entities, like names and numbers, prices, costs, numbers of items sold, employee names, product names, addresses, tax information, stock prices, etc. It can even be text, images, sounds or multimedia.

Edward Deming asserted years ago that 'without data you are just another person with an opinion'. To add to that, *Forbes* magazine declared that 'without an opinion, you are just another person with data'. But how useful is data? Data in itself is 'raw' and fairly useless unless we give meaning to it. Rarely, at any previous point in the history of humankind, have the requirements of useful, validated information been stronger. Modern society, be it in business, social, political or research spheres, all require data and information to make informed, substantiated decisions. Without it, we are lost in a sea of data without meaning, living in a society of subjective information. With the advent of the internet and the huge proliferation of social media ventures, there is an abundance of information available. Whereas before there was a need for *information*, the shift is towards the need for *reliable* information.

With the advent of big data, the value of data lies not in having it but in using it, and ensuring that data and its sources can be trusted so that the information and knowledge derived from it can be used to the benefit of society. The value is in our ability to derive meaning from data using some of the statistical techniques discussed in this chapter.

There is another problem. We are all exposed to data and information. Much of what we receive are inferences based on a certain sector of the population. Some such inferences are valid; others are not. Some are based on adequate sample sizes; others not. Some are based on appropriate samples; others not. Yet, all bear at least some truth and semblance of reality.

There exists the contention that data and statistics can be used to support almost anything. Some even believe that it is easy to lie with statistics. So how do we know the truth? The techniques we discuss here are the ways in which we can be sure that the information we provide, especially in a financial setting, is truthful and objective.

EXERCISE 10.1

Study the following statements:
1. I think Gauteng is the best province in which to live.
2. Chocolate cake is the most delicious kind of dessert.
3. Nearly 65% of teenagers are overweight.
4. Taylor Swift is the greatest singer ever!
5. We live in the best neighbourhood in the city.
6. I believe that summer is the best season.
7. Spring is the best season.
8. I think that spaghetti is a delicious meal.
9. The *Sunday Times* is a newspaper.

You may agree or disagree with these statements. That is your subjective view. In statistics, we try to make sense of the data by providing information and knowledge that represents the entire environment or population. For each of these statements, give your subjective opinion, whether you agree or not. Now, try to write a plan on how you will 'check' these statements (see Table 10.1).

Table 10.1: Checking the validity of statements

	My first reaction Yes, no or maybe …	I suggest the following plan to 'test' this statement
I think Gauteng is the best province in which to live.		
Chocolate cake is the most delicious kind of dessert.		
Nearly 65% of teenagers are overweight.		
Taylor Swift is the greatest singer ever!		
We live in the best neigh-bourhood in the city.		
I believe that summer is the best season.		
Spring is the best season.		
I think that spaghetti is a delicious meal.		
The *Sunday Times* is a newspaper.		

10.2   Statistics as the science of sensemaking of data

We have a responsibility to make sense of data using statistical thinking and analytical tools that can be relied upon and remove doubt in decision making. From a business perspective, anyone involved in the world of work needs to deal with this sensemaking process – the chief executive officer, the manager, the customer, the negotiator, the entrepreneur, the shop steward or the financial manager. This sensemaking process used in statistics follows a four-step approach (see Figure 10.1).

Step 1: Collecting data

Step 2: Organising and summarising the data

Step 3: Analysing and describing the data and obtaining information

Step 4: Presenting the outcomes using the relevant technique

Figure 10.1: The four-step process in making sense of data

This chapter will discuss these steps: collecting the data, then organising and summarising it, analysing the data to reach a decision and, finally, presenting it using relevant techniques. We will start by defining statistics.

DEFINITION

We say that **statistics** is the science and practice of making sense of empirical data by expressing it in a (mostly) quantitative form.

Statistics is based on statistical theory, which is a branch of applied mathematics. Within statistical theory, randomness and uncertainty are modelled (ie viewed) by probability theory. Because one aim of statistics is to produce the 'best' information from available data, some authors consider statistics a branch of decision theory. Thus, the objective of statistics is to draw conclusions about a population of interest based on data obtained from a sample of measurements from that population. We will therefore spend a considerable amount of time understanding data, measuring data and collecting data before we transform the data into information.

EXAMPLE

Consider the use of polls to determine the public opinion concerning a specific political candidate. The question arises whether these pollsters can really claim to capture the opinion of the total population. Certainly, they will have a hard time to contact every voter. What they therefore do is to sample the opinion of a smaller number of voters – thus estimating the consensus based on the findings from the smaller group. Consequently, they believe that the opinion of the smaller number matches (or estimates) that of the total population at that point in time. From your perspective, do you think that all pollsters will necessarily select the same sample group, and can you guarantee that all sample groups will necessarily agree to the same outcome?

Consider another example where an auditor samples 1 000 financial accounts from a set of more than 20 000 and finds that 94 are incorrect (that is, 9%). What does this imply about the full set of 20 000 accounts? In other words, what inference can be made about the percentage of incorrect accounts in the total population based on the information obtained from the sample of 1 000 accounts?

Data only has value in terms of *how* we collected it and for what purpose we want to use it to make decisions.

10.2.1   From statisticians to data scientists

What do statisticians do? The immediate response might be, they sit in a dark office and make the data confess to anything! The reality is that, in the context of making sense of data, statisticians are involved in all aspects of gathering, summarising, analysing and reporting results. As mentioned before, there are correct and incorrect ways of collecting and interpreting data and it is quite easy to use the wrong methodology and come up with results that are untruthful. Living in the Fourth Industrial Revolution means that we are all confronted with data and information because there is such an abundance of it. We do not need to be statisticians, but we do need to be data scientists and ensure that we treat data with respect and make sense of data using the correct principles. As data scientists, we share the responsibility to ensure that the information we share is truthful and reliable. For that, we need to examine the course of the data carefully, the data collection practices and the relevant techniques to make sense of the data.

10.2.2   What do we do with statistics?

If statistics makes sense of data, it follows that we need to consider carefully how the data was obtained and whether it was indeed for the specific use we have in mind. Thereafter we must select the relevant and appropriate statistical measure and subsequently make a decision based on that result. If there is no output or decision to follow, there was no need for the experiment in the first place.

10.3   Data and information

It is easy to distort the truth for the uninformed. In Mark Twain's words: 'Get the facts first and then you can distort them as much as you please.' However, reality and the focus on meaningful information and knowledge will not allow for this. Everything in statistics has to do with making sense of data. Its value lies in the meaning it gives data by transforming it into information, even to knowledge. Just as data is different from information, knowledge is different from information or data. To clarify these key terms, let us look at the following definitions:

DEFINITIONS

Data is an element of analysis, a collection of raw facts in isolation. It conveys meaning but is not useful by itself.

Information is data with meaning or context.

Knowledge refers to information with meaning; concepts, experience, insight that provide a framework for creating, evaluating and using information.

Wisdom refers to knowledge plus insight.

One can view these terms in a value chain (or transformation process), moving from operational functionality (starting with data as relatively meaningless) to strategic value (where the data is of huge long-term benefit) as value is created from the data. The first transformation (from data to information) is merely a matter of trying to understand relationships between entities, while the second transformation (from information to knowledge) is about patterns and trends. See Figure 10.2.

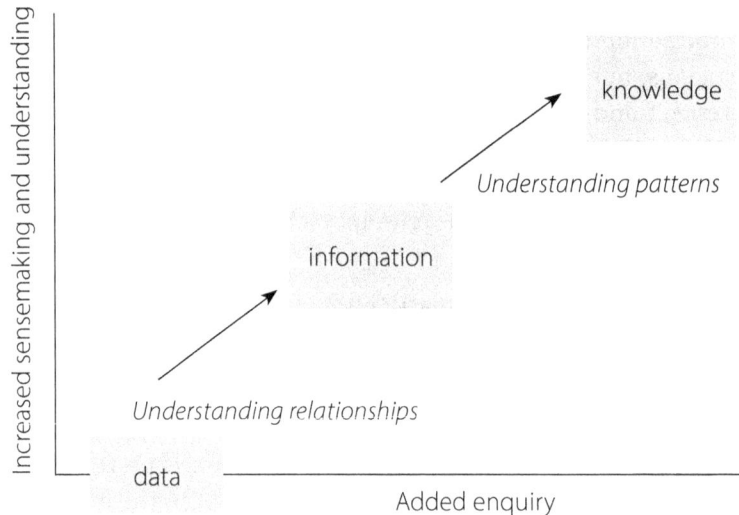

Figure 10.2: Making sense of data following a value creation process

Data is used in a variety of fields such as marketing, sociology, business, public health, and so on. Data can be used to describe a situation in words, pictures or even feelings, or it can be used to describe opinions and activities using numbers. Different types of data thus exist, depending on different situations and needs. The subject of statistics requires data to be in number format so that we can conduct mathematical calculations with it using statistical techniques. Other forms of data require other ways of summarising them. Indeed, in cases where the data is large, it is beneficial to describe such data using summary statistics, which we call descriptive statistics. This summarises numerical data sets in terms of specific measures, which cannot be undertaken with non-numerical data. We therefore distinguish between (at least) two forms of data: numerical (also known as quantitative) data and non-numerical (also known as qualitative or categorical) data.

10.4 Variables and data

10.4.1 Variables

To discuss data, we need to discuss the concept of a variable first. To perform a statistical analysis of data, it is important to get to grips with the concept of a variable and how variables are measured. Any quantity whose value can change every time it gets measured is called a variable. For instance, consider a sample of employees. The variables for this population can be industry, location, gender, age, skills, job-type, etc. For each employee, there are different values or outcomes. The value of the variables will differ for each employee. These values (or numbers) are then used to do statistical calculations, as we will discuss in Section 10.6.

10.4.2 Data types

Certainly, numerical data (we call this quantitative data) is preferred, since this enables the decision maker to perform calculations and thus summarise the data into more usable outcomes. There are different ways in which we can categorise data.

Numerical and categorical data

Data can be broadly classified into numerical (quantitative) data and categorical (qualitative) data.

1. **Numerical data:** Numerical data is measurable; it has numerical values and can be used for calculations. Examples are salaries, ages, hours of work, etc. Numerical data refers to data about quantities (ie data about 'how many'). This type of data is used when we measure and count, for example how many tickets were bought for a soccer match or how many trees there are in a street. Numerical data can further be subdivided into two main groups depending on whether the observations can only assume fixed values (we call this *discrete data*) or whether the observations can assume all possible values within a specified interval (we call this *continuous data*).

2. **Categorical data:** There are many variables that cannot be numbered or measured. Categorical data refers to data that is not in numerical format, for example discussions, open-ended questionnaire responses, unstructured interviews and unstructured observations. Take, for example, data that relies on your senses or feelings such as a person's attitude to his employer or the colour of their eyes. This type of data is known as categorical (also known as qualitative) data. Although we distinguish between numerical and categorical data based on the fact that the first can take on numerical values, it is possible to turn categorical data into a form of numerical data using coding, ie attaching a numerical number to

217

a non-numerical concept. It is possible to present such data in a quantitative (numerical) manner. For example, if attitude towards employer is represented according to 'poor', 'fair' or 'excellent', these attitudes can be assigned ratings 0, 1 or 2. This is known as ordinal qualitative data, since there is mention of some sort of order. On the other hand, if the data is of a qualitative nature, but there is no concern about order, the information is deemed nominal and has little value.

Figure 10.3 gives a useful representation of these different types of data.

Making sense of the data types

The primary difference between numerical and categorical data lies in the purpose of the data (ie what the data is collected for and what needs to be achieved using the data). Both numerical and categorical data are valuable and have their uses. In general, we say the following:

- The data type that classifies based on some characteristic (quality) is called categorical data. On the other hand, data that can be counted and expressed in numbers and values is called numerical data.

- Qualitative data normally *explores*, to provide insights and understanding. On the other hand, numerical data normally concludes and focuses on examining relationships between entities.

- The approach to enquiry in the case of categorical data is *subjective* and holistic, whereas numerical data has an *objective* and focused approach.

- When the data type is categorical, the analysis is non-statistical, whereas numerical data can be statistically summarised and analysed as in sections 10.5 and 10.6.

- In categorical data, there is an unstructured collecting of data, while data collection in numerical data is structured and methodical.

- While categorical data can determine a lot of depth of information and understanding, numerical data is very wide and lacks that depth of understanding of a specific topic.

- Numerical data is all about '*How much or how many?*'. On the contrary, categorical data asks '*Why?*'.

- In categorical data, the sample size is small and likely drawn from non-representative samples. Conversely, the sample size is large in numerical data that is drawn from representative samples.

- Categorical data develops initial understanding (ie it defines the problem), whereas numerical data can recommend a final course of action.

Therefore, Table 10.2 illustrates the two forms of data (numerical and categorical). From an enquiry and decision-making point of view, categorical and numerical data allow for different outcomes and present different viewpoints of which both are reasonable but achieve different outcomes.

Table 10.2: Comparison between numerical and categorical data

Characteristic	Numerical data	Categorical data
Definition	Deals with quantities, values or numbers	Deals with quality
Measurability	Measurable	Generally not measurable
Nature of data	Expressed in numerical form	Descriptive rather than numerical
Decision-making outcome	Conclusive	Exploratory
Quantities measured	Measures quantities such as length, size, amount, price, duration	Narratives often make use of adjectives and other descriptive words to refer to data on appearance, colour, texture, and other qualities
Method of collection	Statistics is used to generate and subsequently analyse this type of data	Mostly through observation
Approach	More objective	More subjective
Data structure	Structured	Unstructured
Determines	Level of occurrence	Depth of understanding
Reliability	More reliable and objective	Less reliable and objective
Data-collection techniques	Numerical surveys, interviews, experiments	Categorical surveys, focus group methods, documental revision, etc
Sample	A large and representative sample	A small and non-representative sample
Possible outcomes in sensemaking	Provides specific outcomes with justification	Provides broad themes

Continuous and discrete data

Not all data can be deemed as similar. Statisticians distinguish between data that can take on discrete values and data that can take on continuous values. This is important because statistical techniques depend on the nature of the data available. Numerical data can take on discrete values (ie, only loose, isolated integer values are allowed) or numerical data can be continuous (ie, all real numbers are possible). Examples are age (as a continuous data) and number of children per household (as discrete data). Continuous data can be grouped into histograms and frequency distributions that represent bundles of data, while discrete data can be presented as bar charts, pie diagrams and scatter plots. We will examine this more in Section 10.5.

EXAMPLE

An example of numerical, discrete data is the number of individuals in Sun Tzu's army (only discrete integers are possible because people are counted as integer numbers). On the other hand, the time spent to conduct his war will constitute a quantitative continuous data set since time can be measured on a continuous line (all time values, not only integer ones are possible).

10.4.3 Levels of measurement of data

Now that you are aware of the difference between numerical and qualitative data, we can go one step further. When we measure the variables, discussed in Section 10.3.1, there are four data measurement scales with varying degrees of uses. Look at Figure 10.3.

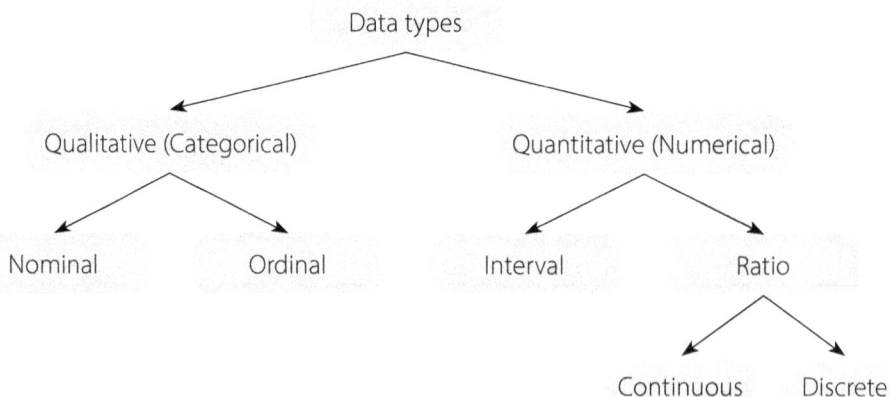

Figure 10.3: Schematic representation of the different data types

Figure 10.3 represents the order of preference of the kinds of data we can collect based on the possible value we can get from the data (with preference increasing from left to right). That is, we can derive far more value from ratio scale data (numerical) on the right than we can from nominal scale data at the other end of the sensemaking spectrum on the left. Put differently, ratio data is the highest level of measurement and nominal scale data the lowest level of measurement in terms of the value we can get from that information. Let us look at the four data measurement scales in more detail. These numerical data measurements scales are depicted in Figure 10.4.

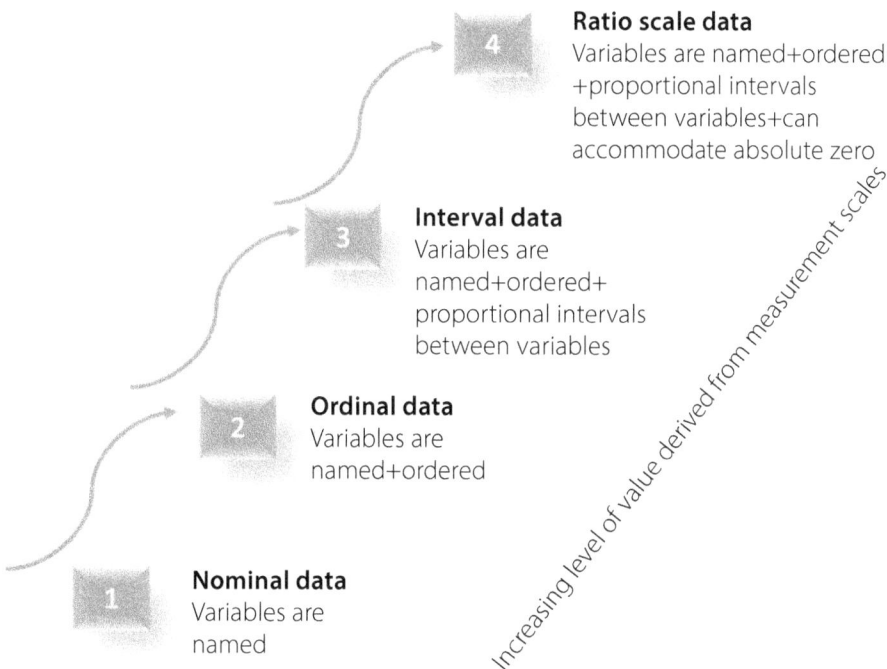

Figure 10.4: The increasing levels of use of data measurement scales

Level 1 data measurement scale: nominal scale data

This is the simplest of the four variable measurement scales. Nominal scale data (also known as categorical data) is used to categorise variables into distinct classifications where the order of the classification does not matter. There are not many calculations that can be done due to the nature of the data and lack of numerical values. Nominal scale data is often used in research surveys and questionnaires where only variable labels hold significance.

> ### EXAMPLE
>
> Where do you live? (1 – Suburbs, 2 – City, 3 – Town)
>
> Which brand of smartphones do you prefer? (1 – iPhone, 2 – Samsung, 3 – Huawei)
>
> In both examples, the data is merely classified and all we can do is count the number in each category. From a statistical analysis point of view, that means that one can only count *how many* of each category was found and report on that.

Level 2 data measurement scale: ordinal scale data

Ordinal scale data is a measurement scale used to depict the order of variables and not the difference between each of the variables. Hence, it is also a form of categorisation, but it ranks the variables in terms of their level of importance. It measures ideas such as satisfaction, happiness, a degree of pain, etc. It is easy to remember this scale because 'ordinal' refers to the 'order' of something, which is exactly the purpose of this scale.

> ### EXAMPLE
>
> Status at workplace, tournament team rankings, order of product quality, and order of agreement or satisfaction are some common examples of the ordinal scale. For instance: How satisfied are you with our services? (Very unsatisfied – 1, Unsatisfied – 2, Neutral – 3, Satisfied – 4, Very satisfied – 5). Here, the order of variables is of prime importance and so is the labelling. Very unsatisfied will always be worse than unsatisfied and satisfied will be worse than very satisfied. And this is where ordinal scale differs from nominal scale – the order is relevant to the value of the outcomes.

Level 3 data measurement scale: interval scale data

Interval scale data is a numerical scale where the order of the variables is known as well as the difference between these variables. Variables that have familiar, constant, calculable differences are classified using the Interval scale. It is easy to remember the primary role of this scale too, 'interval' indicates 'distance between two entities', which is what an interval scale helps to achieve. Interval scale data contains all the characteristics of the ordinal scale data, but, in addition, one can do calculations on the differences between the variables. The main characteristic of this scale is the equidistant difference between objects.

> **EXAMPLE**
>
> Consider a Celsius/Fahrenheit temperature scale. 80 degrees is always higher than 50 degrees and the difference between these two temperatures is the same as the difference between 70 degrees and 40 degrees. Furthermore, the value of 0 is arbitrary because negative values of temperature do exist – which makes the Celsius/Fahrenheit temperature scale a classic example of an interval scale.
>
> Another application is where people's opinions and attitudes are measured using the interval data scale. For example, work performance (as excellent, average, poor) can be assigned numerical 'rankings' (for instance, 1, 2, 3, respectively). We often see this in questionnaires where such values (we refer to them as Likert scale values) are replacement integer values which can then be used in calculations. For instance, we can use a Likert scale to determine perfections on a range of topics, where 1 equates to 'absolutely disagree' and 5 is 'absolutely agree'. Doing this, we are forcing numbers on people's opinions and that allows us to do statistical calculations to make the decisions.

Level 4 data measurement scale: ratio scale data

Ratio scale data is numerical, meaning it uses everyday numbers. It is defined as a variable measurement scale that not only indicates the order of the variables but also distinguishes between variables as well as information about the value of true zero.

It is calculated by assuming that the variables have an option for zero, the differences between the variables are the same and there is a specific order between the options. Hence, a ratio scale does everything that a nominal, ordinal and interval scale can do, but in addition, the true zero is included.

> **NB!** The best examples of ratio scales are weight and height. Why? Because weight and height both adhere to the principles as above: (1) the number zero can exist (0 kg), (2) the differences between numbers are equal (2 kg, 3 kg) and (3) there is a sense of increasing order (2 kg is one less than 3 kg, etc). In financial management, a ratio scale is used to calculate market share, annual sales, the price of an upcoming product, the number of consumers, etc.

Ratio scale data provides the most detailed information that the financial manager can use to perform statistical manipulations. It is superior to all three other forms of data measurement scales because the distances between numbers are equal and because there is a true zero.

Making sense of the data scale measurements

Table 10.3 provides a summary of the four data measurement scales we discussed.

Table 10.3: The data measurement scales

Categorical data		Numerical data	
Nominal data	**Ordinal data**	**Interval data**	**Ratio data**
The variables are named but there is no particular order or ranking indicating levels of importance, eg yes/no responses to questions	The variables are named *and* there is a sense of ranking or level of importance, eg level of skin burns (first-, second- or third-degree burns) indicate seriousness	The variables are named, are ordered and there is a relative order to the distance between them, eg an increase of temperature in a centigrade scale: 40 °C is not twice as hot as 20 °C, but both have value relative to 0°	The variables are named, ordered and the relative distance between them is the same, eg regular numbers in our numbering system.
Hair colour (brown, black, blonde, red, etc)	Likert scale responses		

Study Table 10.4 and decide on the data measurement scale.

Table 10.4: Data scale measurement examples

Example	Measurement scale	Justification
A fund manager decides to assign the number 1 to small-cap stocks, the number 2 to corporate bonds, the number 3 to derivatives		
A list of 500 managers of mutual funds is ranked by assigning the number 1 to the best-performing manager, the number 2 to the second best-performing manager		
A fund manager that is ranked 1 probably did not outperform the fund manager ranked 2 by the exact same amount that a fund manager ranked 6 outperformed a fund manager ranked 7		
Monthly salaries, monthly expenditures, number of employees		

We now turn to the four steps of the sensemaking process.

Step 1: Collecting data

Step 2: Organising and summarising the data

Step 3: Analysing and describing the data and obtaining information

Step 4: Presenting the outcomes using the relevant technique

10.5   Collecting data

10.5.1   Where do I look for data?

We now know that not all data is alike, or even equal. But where do we look for data? Although data and information are all around us, we need to plan carefully where we look for data and where the data source is. There are two types of data sources available: primary and secondary data sources.

DEFINITIONS

Primary data denotes data collected from scratch for a specific purpose.

Secondary data is data that is already available and that has not necessarily been collected for the specific purpose.

Secondary data saves time and money because it has already been collected, although care should be taken that the data matches the requirements and has not been collected for an opposing purpose. Well-known secondary data sources include StatsSA, the World Health Organisation, publications from the World Bank and the World Economic Forum.

10.5.2   A sample and a population

Fundamental concepts in understanding the dynamics of statistics are the introduction of a population and a sample.

DEFINITION

The **population** can be defined as the set of measurements, existing or conceptual, that is of interest to the person involved in the research. It is also called the universum. It denotes a comprehensive list of all people, markets or whatever is of interest to the researcher. Examples are: the complete list of employees in an organisation, times to complete tasks, etc.

Samples are subsequently selected from the population.

DEFINITION

A **sample** is defined as any subset taken from the population, like a group of employees selected for a task. A sample is simply a subset of the population, so the sample size is always less than the population size.

Moreover, sampling literally means obtaining relevant data to reach a decision. Sampling involves two issues: first, representing the population and, second, estimating the characteristic of interest as best as possible. In a census, the data is obtained from every member of the population.

10.5.3 The need for sampling

It is not always feasible or possible to study the entire population, with the result that a sample taken from the total set is selected and, using statistical techniques, a decision is made based on the sample information. Reasons for drawing a sample include:

1. Necessity: It is not always possible to study the entire population due to its size or inaccessibility.

2. Practicality: It is easier and more efficient to collect data from a sample due to financial or time constraints.

3. Cost-effectiveness: There are fewer laboratory, equipment or resource costs involved as well as fewer participants.

4. Manageability: Storing and conducting analyses on smaller data sets is faster and simpler.

If the sample is designed scientifically, this decision will then hold for the population as well. By 'scientifically', we mean that the elements in the sample should show the same characteristics as that of the population as a whole, otherwise the final conclusion could be incorrect. In other words, the sample should be representative of the population. For instance, a random sample would constitute a representative sample. This notion will be discussed in more depth in the following section.

The main concern with sampling lies in the fact that the conclusions drawn using the sample information are not 100% foolproof. They remain uncertain, meaning that we can attribute the probability of their outcomes being completely true for the population itself. In statistics, this is the degree of confidence we attach to the conclusions enabling the decision-maker to determine the accuracy of their decisions. For example, if the probability that a statement is true, is .95 (or 95%), then we say that that statement is true 95% of the time the statement is made – and it is false 5% of the time. (All probabilities around a certain event or outcome have to add up to 1.)

Population

Sample 1 = a subset
of population

Sample 3
= a subset
of population

Sample 2
= a subset
of population

**Population =
total set of all
elements under
investigation**

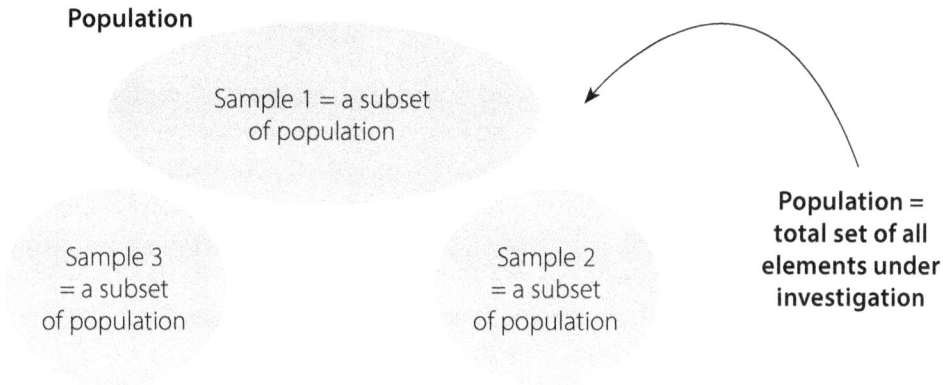

Figure 10.5: The population with several samples of different sizes drawn from it

It is important to note that it is possible to draw several, different, samples from the same population. All of these samples may be representative. The largest sample, however, may be the most accurate as it contains the most information from the population (not all of it). However, it is also possible to draw a sample that most accurately represents the entire population but that is not the largest. Here it gets tricky.

> **NB!** The golden rule here is: the more data (ie the larger the sample size), the better, provided that all characteristics of the population are incorporated in the selection.

EXAMPLE

Consider the case of a retail business trying to determine the weekly wages of all its employees. If time is the issue, it will prove easier to draw a representative sample including all units within the business, then determine the weekly wages in the sample and use this as an estimate for the whole company. However, if two people were asked to conduct this research, it is quite possible for them to come up with different samples, even consisting of different sizes. However, if they are both sure that their samples are representative of the total set, generally, their conclusions should be the same.

The first step in making sense of data is to gather data on the issue at hand. However, scientific data collection does not just happen. It needs a conscious and concerted effort focusing on:

- the specific objective of the data-gathering exercise
- the variable(s) of interest (eg weekly wages)
- the choice of design for the survey or study
- the collection of the data.

In statistics, data can be gathered by means of a survey or a scientific study – or a combination of both. Surveys are passive; they aim to collect data on existing opinions, conditions, attitudes or behaviours. For example, the management of a manufacturing company would use a survey to sample the opinions of the operations managers on the merits of a new incentive plan. Scientific studies, on the other hand, tend to be more active in that the person conducting the interview would tend to deliberately vary certain conditions to reach a conclusion. For example, if a plant manager is interested in the effect of noise level in his manufacturing plant, he could vary the noise levels and certain controlled conditions to determine the gain or loss in productivity.

10.5.4 Collecting data using a sample

Collecting data means that we either need to access the entire population or that we need to gather data for a subset of that population. Gathering data from such a subset is called sampling.

The steps in collecting data

Collecting data is a simple step-wise process.

Step 1: Identify the sample frame, which is the complete list of all cases representing the entire population.

Step 2: Decide on a suitable sample size.

Step 3: Select the most appropriate sampling technique.

Step 4: Check that the sample is representative of the population.

We can divide sampling methods into two large groups, namely probability and non-probability procedures.

Probability sampling techniques

In probability sampling all elements in the population are equally likely to be selected. The population characteristics are known. The size of the population is known (ie how many units there are), and the units can be listed or accessed. Therefore, every element in the population has a known probability of being included. There are four possible probability sampling techniques, depending on the specific situation. It is up to you to decide which one is preferable to ensure the data are valid and representative of the greater population.

Table 10.5 summarises the advantages and disadvantages of probability sampling techniques.

Table 10.5: Advantages and disadvantages of probability sampling techniques

Advantages	Disadvantages
Can generalise to the population	More expansive than non-probability samples
Less prone to bias	Take more time to design and execute
Allows estimation of magnitude of sampling error, from which one can determine the statistical significance	Requires that you have a list of all sample elements
Information from a representative cross-section	No advantages when small numbers of elements are to be chosen
Sampling error can be computed	
Results are projectable to the total population	

Figure 10.6 shows the most important probability sampling methods. These methods are:

- random sampling
- stratified sampling
- cluster sampling
- systematic sampling.

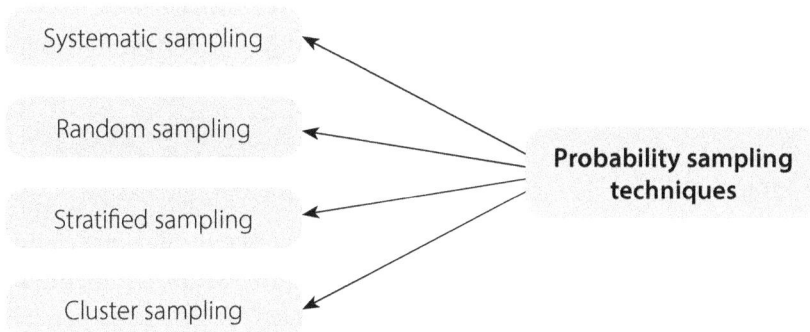

Figure 10.6: Probability sampling techniques

Random sampling

A random sample is one completely determined by chance. That means that every element in the population not already included has the same probability of being selected. In other words, it makes the sampling 'fair' and the selection of the elements is unbiased. Thus, a random sample will contain as much information on the population as the population itself. For example, assume that it is necessary to test the opinions of the production managers on the merits of the incentive plan. Every manager should have the same probability of being included for the sample to be considered a random sample.

Stratification

If there is reason to believe that there are specific groupings within the organisation that have differing points of view, the total population should first be subdivided into these natural groupings before the sampling is executed. These subdivisions are called strata or groups. We say that if the total population is heterogeneous with respect to the issue being tested, stratification should be used, whereby the population is divided according to natural groups before the sampling is conducted. This random sampling method is known as stratified sampling. The schematic representation in Figure 10.7 should make this clearer.

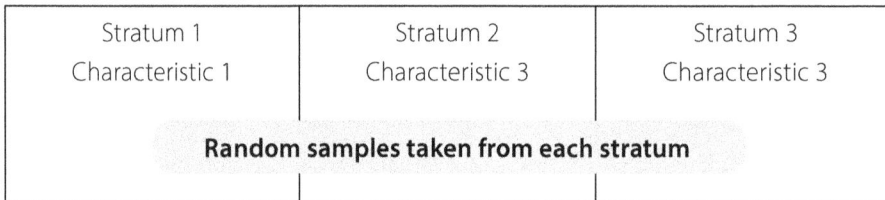

Stratum 1	Stratum 2	Stratum 3
Characteristic 1	Characteristic 3	Characteristic 3
Random samples taken from each stratum		

Figure 10.7: Schematic representation of stratified sampling

Hence, stratification can only be accomplished if there is sufficient knowledge about the population indicating that there are inherent differences in the population. This method increases the level of accuracy in the sample. If the sampling is done proportional to the size of the stratum, the accuracy is further enhanced. This is called proportional allocation in stratified sampling. Of course, one could also select equally from the different strata, but this is unreasonable if one stratum is much larger in size than another.

Cluster sampling

Although individual preferences are desired, a more economical procedure is to sample entire office blocks or buildings rather than individuals. The method entails that the total population be subdivided into clusters, each cluster representing all characteristics of the population. Clusters are then randomly selected for inclusion, hence the name 'cluster sampling'.

Hence, the total population is subdivided into clusters where each cluster contains all the characteristics of the population (see Figure 10.8).

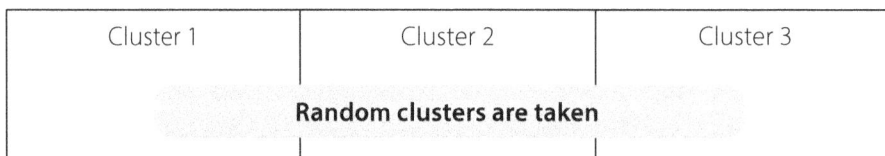

Cluster 1	Cluster 2	Cluster 3
Random clusters are taken		

Figure 10.8: Schematic representation of cluster sampling

Systematic sampling

The last probability sampling technique is often used when the names of people in the population are available in a list, such as a telephone directory or personnel files. For this situation, an economical technique is to draw the sample by selecting the first name near the start of the list and then to proceed from that point and select every tenth or fifteenth person thereafter. If sampling is conducted in this manner, we obtain a systematic sample. Some statisticians prefer to artificially form the list into a circle and then start anywhere within the circle and proceed as above.

Table 10.6 summarises the appropriate sampling scheme according to the specific population characteristic.

Table 10.6: Population characteristics lead to specific probability sampling schemes

Population characteristic	Example of population type	Appropriate sampling technique(s)
Population is generally a homogeneous group of individual units.	A particular variety of flower seeds, which a researcher wants to test for germination potential.	Simple random sampling
Population contains definite strata that are approximately equal in size.	A school with six grade levels: kindergarten, first, second, third, fourth and fifth.	Stratified random sampling
Population contains definite strata that appear in different proportions within the population.	A community in which residents are Catholic (25%), Protestant (45%), Jewish (15%), Muslim (5%), or non-affiliated (10%).	Proportional stratified sampling
Population consists of discrete clusters with similar characteristics. The units within each cluster are as heterogonous as units in the oveall population.	Travellers in the nation´s 20 leading air terminals (All air terminals are similar in atmosphere, purpose, design, etc. The passengers who use them differ widely in such characteristics as age, gender, national origin, socio-economic status, and belief system, with such variability being similar from one airport to the next.)	Cluster sampling

Non-probability sampling techniques

In non-probability sampling the elements are selected in a more personal way and thus may not represent the population as much because we may be biased towards some issue.

Non-probability sampling methods are far more subjective and could lead to bias in the final conclusions. The elements in the sample are selected based on convenience, rather than fairness and objectivity. Table 10.7 summarises the advantages and disadvantages of probability sampling techniques.

Table 10.7: Advantages and disadvantages of non-probability sampling techniques

Advantages	Disadvantages
Generally costs less than probability sampling techniques	Results cannot be projected to total population
Can be gathered more quickly	Sampling error cannot be computed
More flexible	Researcher does not know degree to which the data is representative
Less costly	
Produces samples that are reasonably representative	

Figure 10.9 shows some non-probability sampling techniques. These methods include:

- convenience sampling
- judgmental sampling
- purposive sampling
- quota sampling.

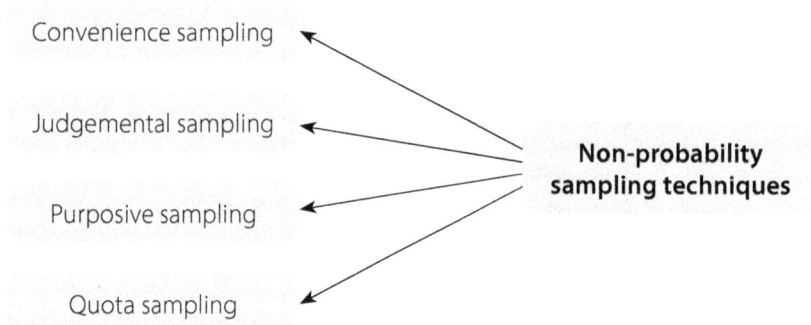

Convenience sampling

Judgemental sampling

Purposive sampling

Quota sampling

Non-probability sampling techniques

Figure 10.9: Some non-probability sampling schemes

Convenience sampling

The elements are drawn entirely at the convenience of the researcher and thus may not be representative of the population. The method is simple and not expensive, but results cannot be generalised to the population.

Judgemental sampling

The researcher judges which elements to include based on some criterium. The method is thus biased according to the researcher's preferences and cannot lead to generalisation.

Purposive sampling

The researcher selects the elements in the sample because of some previously agreed upon criterion. Although the results cannot be generalised to the extent that probability sample results can, the method has the advantage that elements are chosen specifically because of their fit for use. This method can provide a better solution than the probability sampling methods, but the results cannot be generalised.

Quota sampling

The researcher decides before the time to include a specific number of elements and terminates the selection when this number is reached. This may lead to bias of selection as, for instance, the first hundred respondents to a questionnaire/survey may have a specific strong opinion of the issue under investigation. The results cannot be generalised.

QUESTION

Which sampling technique best fits the situation?

Situation	Decide on the most appropriate sampling scheme
1. Travellers in the USA's 20 leading airport terminals. (All air terminals are similar in atmosphere, purpose, design, etc. The passengers who use them differ widely in such characteristics as age, gender, national origin, socioeconomic status, and belief system, with such variability being similar from one airport to the next.	
2. A community in which residents are Catholic (25%), Protestant (45%), Jewish (15%), Muslim (5%), or non-affiliated (10%)	
3. A school with six grade levels: kindergarten, first, second, third, fourth, and fifth.	
4. A particular variety of flower seeds, which a researcher wants to test for germination potential	

ANSWERS

1. Cluster sampling selecting one airport and then stratified random sampling according to the differences within that airport.
2. Stratified random sampling because of the differences in the population.
3. Stratified random sampling if the concept under investigation will produce different results for the different grades. If the concept under investigation will not be different for the different grades, a purposive sample according to the specific issue will work; for instance if they all needed to use a specific mode of transport to go to school.
4. Purposive sampling based on that specific variety of flower seed.

Note: There may be other solutions as well based on the specific issue to be investigated.

10.6 Organising and summarising the data

Now that we have collected data, we need to organise and summarise the data. With the first step in making sense of data being the gathering of the data in a useful format, we now come to the descriptive part. What trends do we see? Is there a recognisable pattern? Do most of the values fall near some central value? Does the data show substantial variability? The easiest way to summarise the data is to develop visual displays which you can do in Excel. There are three standard graphical displays, each based on the specific data measurement scale we discussed:

1. Histograms
2. Bar charts
3. Pie charts

10.6.1 Histograms

A histogram (see Figure 10.10) is the most commonly used graph to summarise data using a visual representation. A histogram can be used to summarise continuous data. Even if the data has already been summarised in a table, a histogram makes it easier to identify differences, trends and frequencies of occurrence.

It has two axes, one horizontal, one vertical. The data is transposed onto a graph with vertical blocks with the number of blocks depending on the categories of data. For example, if you are measuring the frequency of something that occurs in a week you would have seven sections along the horizontal line, one for each day of the week. The vertical line has numbers indicating how many times the event occurred. Here are some examples. Note that the bars are continuous and there are no gaps inbetween.

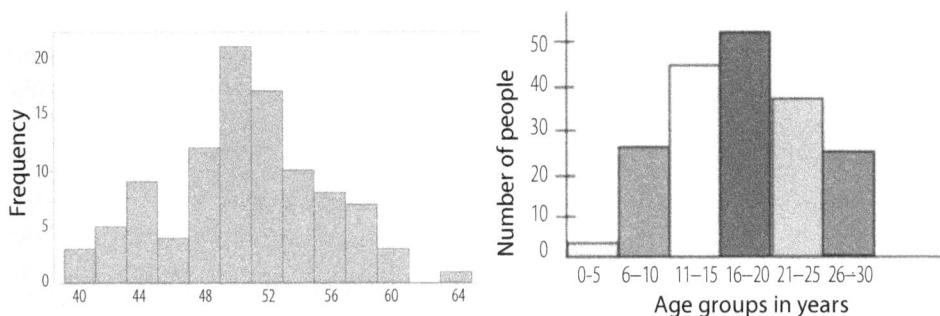

Figure 10.10: Histogram examples

The usefulness of histograms

The advantage of the histogram is that it provides a simple pictorial summary of the data. The following are some of the benefits:

■ **Statistical purposes:** Using data presented in the histogram, you can determine statistical information. This includes the mean value (the average across all the blocks); the maximum value (the highest block); and the minimum value (the lowest block). The number of blocks determines the number of items you are measuring, such as months in a year. The top of each block lines up to a number on the vertical line and may determine frequency.

- **Identifying trends:** Histograms track trends. For example, if you have split the horizontal line into 12 sections representing January through December and the vertical line is split into temperatures, you can see the trend of temperatures during the year. Another example is having sections on the horizontal line representing years and the vertical line representing household income. As the income data is put onto the histogram, you see a trend.

- **Checking out the distribution or shape of the data:** There are several common types of histograms, based on data distribution. The term 'normal' is applied when the shape of the histogram rises until it reaches the centre block and then falls again. 'Cliff-like' can be applied to a histogram when the first block is the highest and the height of each subsequent block is shorter than the preceding one. 'Skewed' applies when the blocks rise, but then fall, before reaching the centre of the blocks, while a 'plateau' is a histogram that has generally high blocks that are similar in height.

Weakness of histograms

Histograms have many benefits, but there are two weaknesses. A histogram can present data that is misleading. For example, using too many blocks can make analysis difficult, while too few can leave out important data. Histograms are based on two sets of data, but to analyse certain types of statistical data, more than two sets of data are necessary. For example, the blocks may denote the number of months in a year and the vertical line, the number of students attending college each month. However, it doesn't tell you the number of male and female students.

How to interpret a histogram

- The size of the class intervals and the number of classes are our choice. The number of classes depends mainly on the size and variability of the data set. Too many intervals or too few both detract from the value of the histogram as the first does not provide a summary and the latter does not serve as a simplification of the data at all. Usually, between five and 15 class intervals are preferred.

- It is preferable to use class intervals of equal length, since this makes comparison of the classes possible.

- There should not be any ambiguity as to which interval an observation belongs to, hence the class limits should not overlap. In this way, the intervals form a continuous line without overlapping.

- Open classes are sometimes used at the beginning or end of the data set. For instance, we could have used <20 for the first interval and >90 for the last one.

- The frequencies should add up to the sample size (ie the total number of observations) – this serves as a quick check that all observations are indeed included.

- In the process of summarising the data in a histogram, the actual data values are lost and replaced by intervals and frequencies per interval. Thus, we can identify which class interval comes up most, rather than the value.

The information could also be summarised using pie charts or any of the numerous pictorial techniques that make descriptive statistics so rich.

10.6.2 Bar charts

Bar charts do exactly what histograms do. The only difference is that they graphically summarise a discrete data set (that is when the elements of the data set are measured in integer values or natural numbers, and real values are not possible). They are easy to interpret, as the heights of the bars denote the relative importance of the differing categories. The frequency of each category is represented by a bar. The length of each bar is proportional to the frequency of each category. The length of the bars is important, not their widths (though their widths should be the same size, to avoid distorting a category's importance). Bar charts may be vertical or horizontal.

Figure 10.11 summarises a company report to its shareholders indicating the contributions to earnings from the various sources for 2020 and then a combined 2020/2021 bar chart.

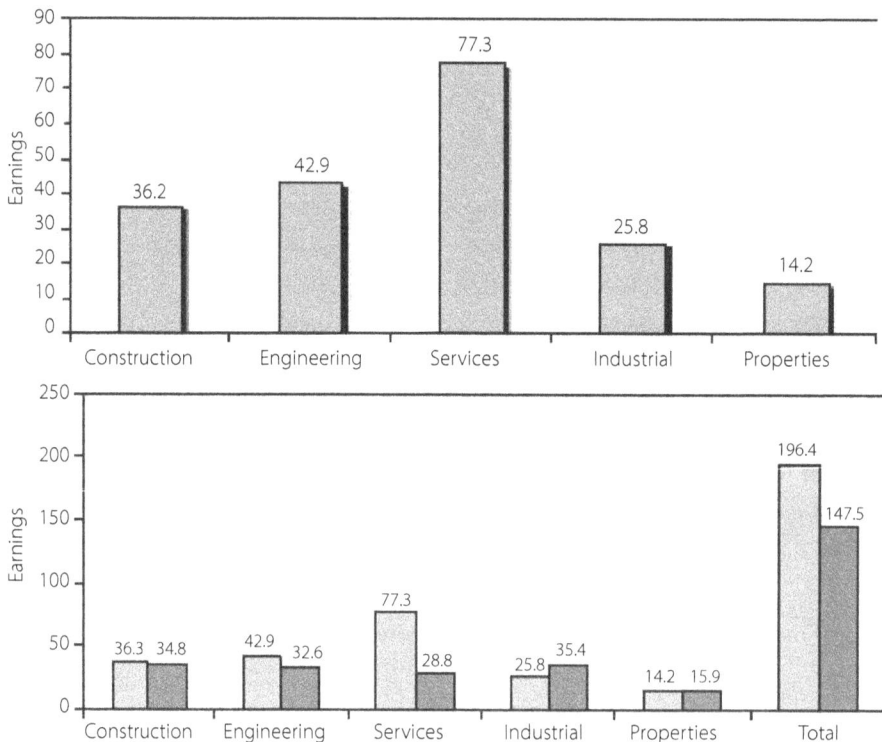

Figure 10.11: Combined bar chart of the contribution to earnings in 2020/2021

Figure 10.11 indicates that the contribution to earnings was generally higher in 2020 than in 2021 except in the industrial sector. The contributions were similar in the property area.

10.6.3 Pie charts

The pie chart (see Figure 10.12) is a very common tool for summarising *categorical* data. The pie chart is a circle, subdivided into a number of slices that represent the various categories. The size of each slice is *proportional* to the percentage corresponding to the category it represents. The concept of pie slices is used to show the percentage of particular data from the whole pie.

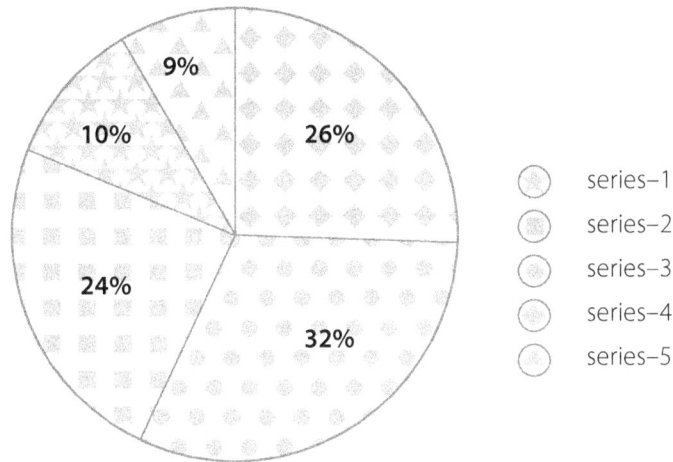

Figure 10.12: Example of a pie chart indicating the relative importance of each segment of the categorical data

10.6.4 Bar charts or pie charts?

The selection of a particular chart depends on your intention (see Figure 10.13). If comparison of categories is important, then use a bar chart. If observing the portion of the whole that is in a particular category is important, then use a pie chart. Pie charts are not useful if there are too many categories.

EXAMPLE

Here are the job grades of a sample of 40 employees.

B	A	A	D	B	A	C	C	D	A	B	C	D
D	D	D	B	C	B	A	D	B	D	D	D	
A	B	A	B	C	D	A	B	C	A	C	D	
D	D	A										

In this case, either a bar chart or a pie chart can work. If we see the job grades as categories, we can use a pie chart, remembering that the slices of the pie are percentages of each grade. If we see the grades as discrete data, we can represent the date as bar charts with each bar representing the number (or frequency) representing that grade.

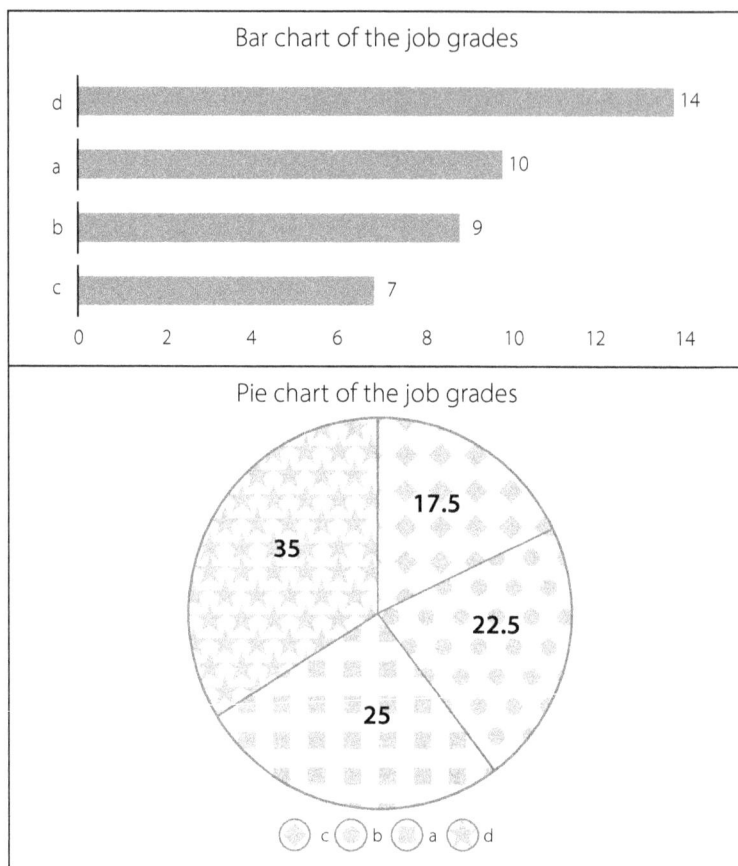

Figure 10.13: Data represented as a bar chart or as a pie chart

10.6.5 Histograms or bar charts?

Histograms are constructed by counting the number of observations that fall into a specified class interval. They are similar to a bar graph, except that the bars of histograms must be joined at the class limits, the class intervals cannot be displayed in any order as with the bar chart and the class width determines how wide the bars of the histograms will be. In a bar graph the width is arbitrarily set.

Table 10.8 offers a good summary.

Table 10.8: Summary of the three chart types

	Continuous data	Discrete data	Categorical data
Histograms	X		
Bar charts		X	
Pie charts			X

We have now discovered three distinct ways of graphically summarising tabulated data, namely histograms for continuous data, bar charts for discrete data sets and pie charts for categorical data. The histogram loses the actual information and we are left to the devices of so-called middle values for further calculations. In a bar chart the height of the bar denotes the relative importance of that category, while in the histogram it is not so much the height as the area of the bar that is indicative of the relative importance of that interval.

It is important to note, when creating graphical displays, that there is a tendency to start the axes at numbers significantly larger than 0. In other words, the lower part of the graph is cut off, thereby creating the wrong impression of the magnitude of the changes in the different categories or intervals. It is perfectly legitimate to do so, but care should be taken as it can influence what conclusions are drawn from the graph.

10.7 Analysing and describing the data to derive information

In our quest for the reduction of large volumes of data, we now come to issues pertaining to describing the data using statistical measures. These numerical measures can describe the centrality and shape of the data. These can be divided according to:

- measures indicating central tendency (or midpoint)
- measures indicating variability (or spread)
- measures indicating symmetry (or skewness).

We call these the descriptive measures, since they describe the shape of the data set according to the four notions above. Consider Figure 10.14 that we will refer to as we discuss the measures.

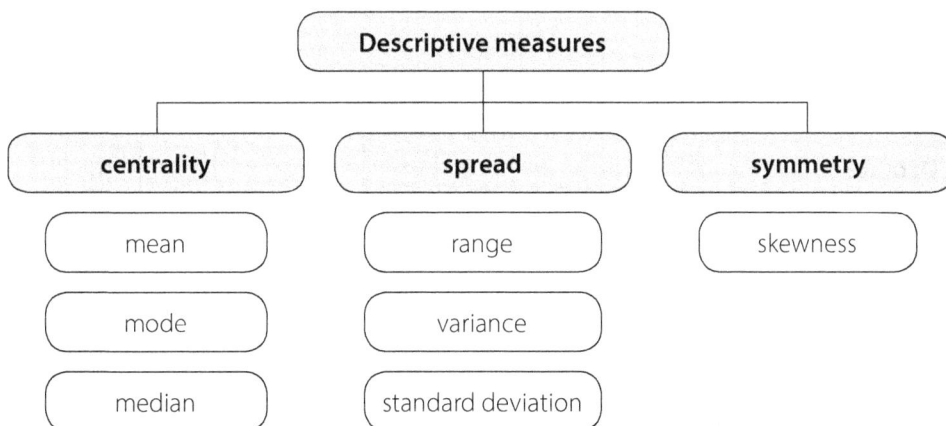

Figure 10.14: Summary of measures describing the data

10.7.1 Descriptive measures of central tendency

An average – also known as a mean – is a single value that is used to describe an entire population or data set. For example, gold trades at, on average, R26 101 an ounce; women wear, on average, a size 6 shoe; the average worker is paid R22 500 per month. This measure is used to describe a data set in terms of central tendency; that is, it summarises the data using a middle value. How good this single value is in describing the data is reflected by the other descriptive measures.

The mean

The mean is the average of a set of values. Let us say we have a huge data set of employee information of the time each person takes to complete a specific task. If you were asked to describe that data set using a single value, you could do so by calculating the arithmetic mean. This is done by adding up all the data values and then dividing them by the number of terms in the set.

The median

The median is simply the middle value. To find it you first arrange the data into a sequence in ascending order and then locate the middle position. This means that half of the values will be smaller than the median, and half of the values will be larger than the median.

The mode

The last measure of central tendency is also the easiest and most simplistic. The mode is defined as the observation that occurs most often.

To understand the mean, median and mode, let us consider the data series in Table 10.9.

Table 10.9: Middle values

Data set	9	6	8	5	12	11	8	8	5	10

See if you agree that the mean is 8.2, the mode is 8 and the median is 8. The mean and median both denote a midpoint in the data set while the mode indicates the value (of 8) that comes up the most often.

The fact that the median and the mean are not the same is because there is variation in the data, ie the values are not spread evenly around the middle point. We will discuss variation next.

10.7.2   Descriptive measures of spread or variability

The second descriptive measure actually describes the first because it tries to make sense of variation of the data around the middle value as we discussed. To follow this reasoning, consider the following.

The range

The range provides a basic form of measuring spread. It indicates the variability between the largest and the smallest values in the data set. It can be calculated using the following formula:

Range = Maximum value – Minimum value

Since it is based on only two of the data points, it has relatively limited use. Moreover, two data sets with the same maximum and minimum can have the same range regardless of the spread of the rest of the data points.

The variance and standard deviation

Although the mean is a great tool to summarise data, one needs to grasp the extent to which the data varies around that central value. This is the purpose of the variance and the standard deviation. The variance and standard deviation measure the same thing: The standard deviation takes the square root of the variance after the variance has been calculated. So, if the variance is 25, then the standard deviation is 5.

Consider the two data series in Table 10.10.

Table 10.10: Data sets differing in variability or spread

Data series 1:	9	6	8	5	12	11	8	8	5	10	Mean = 8.2
Data series 2:	10	5	9	4	12	14	10	9	3		Mean = 8.4

Here is a graphical display of the data sets. Clearly, they differ in terms of variation. We know this because the range of the two data series differ:

Data series 1: range = 7
Date series 2: range = 11

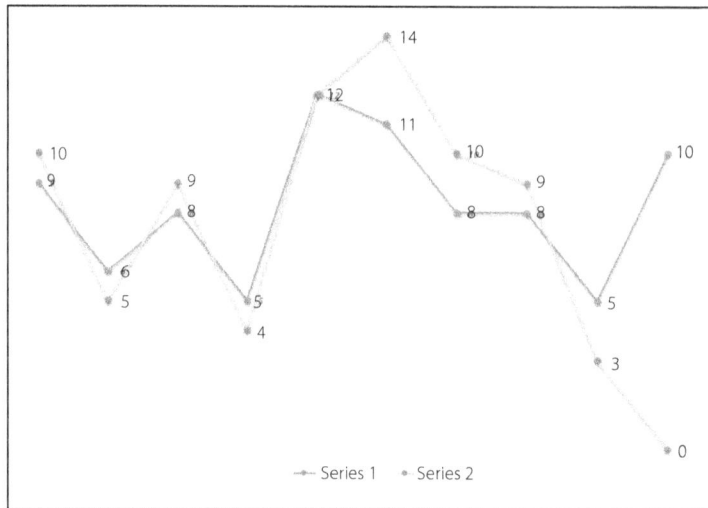

Figure 10.15: Graphical display of the data sets

Although the measures of centrality are close, the data sets differ in terms of spread. This can be accounted for by the variance (or the standard deviation). The larger the variance the larger the deviation of the data around the middle value.

Indeed, for data set 1 the variance is denoted by 5.2, while the variance for data set 2 is 12.2. Hence, the two data sets may have means that are close to each other, but the data sets differ greatly in terms of their spread around that middle point. (If you are worried about these calculations, remember that these are done using Microsoft Excel's data analysis functionality.)

We can now use Microsoft Excel to summarise the data series as follows. This allows us to compare the two data sets according to the midpoints and variability as we discussed.

Data series 1:		**Data series 2:**		
Mean	8.2	Mean	8.2	**Midpoints**: Means, medians and modes are slightly different.
Median	8.0	Median	9.0	
Mode	8.0	Mode	10.0	
Standard deviation	2.4	Standard deviation	3.7	**Variability**: Data series 1 shows less variability than data series 2 as indicated by the sample variances, standard deviations, range and minimum vales.
Sample variance	5.7	Sample variance	13.8	
Range	7.0	Range	11.0	
Minimum	5.0	Minimum	3.0	
Maximum	12.0	Maximum	14.0	
Count	10.0	Count	9.0	**Count**: The number of data in data series 1 is more than in data series 2.

10.7.3 Descriptive measures of symmetry

A symmetry measure indicates the degree of skewness of the data set. Symmetry or skewness is easily determined using measures of central tendency, namely the mean (the balancing point), the median (the halfway point) and the mode (the most frequent value). If we find that:

- mean ≈ median ≈ mode, then the distribution is more or less symmetric (Figure 10.16)
- mean < median < mode, then the distribution is more or less negatively skewed (Figure 10.17)
- mean > median > mode, then the distribution is more or less positively skewed (Figure 10.18).

Symmetry is important because it helps us identify the shape of the distribution.

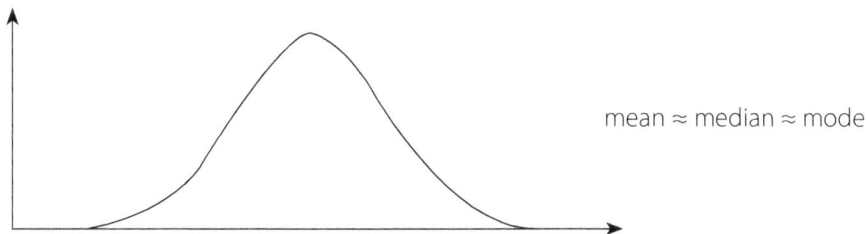

mean ≈ median ≈ mode

Figure 10.16: A symmetrical distribution

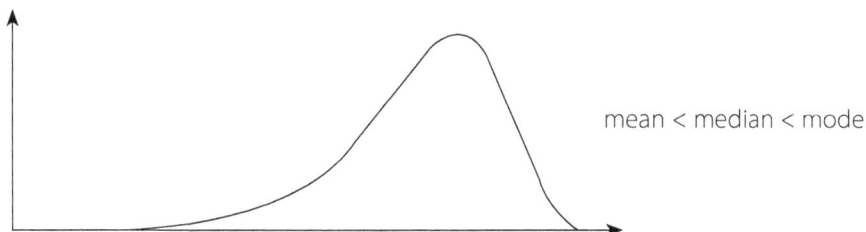

mean < median < mode

Figure 10.17: A negatively skewed distribution (ie, skewed to the left)

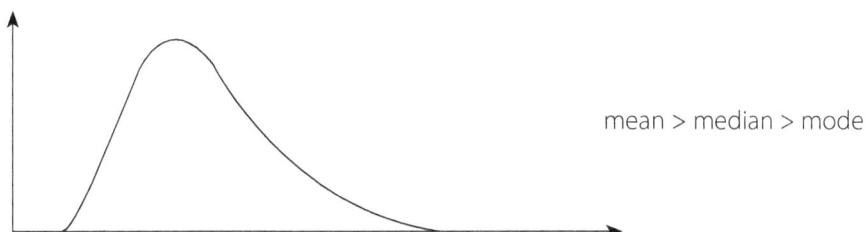

mean > median > mode

Figure 10.18: A positively skewed distribution (ie, skewed to the right)

EXERCISE 10.2

Consider the example of the two data sets.

Data set 1		Data set 2	
Mean	8.2	Mean	**8.4**
Standard error	0.7	Standard error	**1.1**
Median	8.0	Median	**9.0**
Mode	8.0	Mode	**10.0**
Standard deviation	2.3	Standard deviation	**3.5**
Sample variance	5.2	Sample variance	**12.2**
Skewness	0.1	Skewness	**−0.2**
Range	7.0	Range	**11.0**
Minimum	5.0	Minimum	**3.0**
Maximum	12.0	Maximum	**14.0**
Sum	90.2	Sum	**84.4**

Write a report about the differences and similarities of the two data sets based on this section. Hint: Follow the outline of Figure 10.16 and describe each group in terms of middle values, variability, count in order to compare the two groups based on these descriptors.

10.8   Presenting the data to make sense

Let's put all of this together. We have learnt how to collect data and we have learnt about data sources. We then discussed the different data scale measurements and the summarising techniques to describe the data. When we want to present our findings, we need to bring all of these together. Table 10.11 is a summary of which data type is applicable to which statistical technique.

Table 10.11: Linking descriptive measures to data measurement scales

	Data measurement scale available			
Descriptive measures available	**Nominal**	**Ordinal**	**Interval**	**Ratio**
The sequence of variables is established	–	Yes	Yes	Yes
Mode	Yes	Yes	Yes	Yes
Median	–	Yes	Yes	Yes
Mean	–	–	Yes	Yes
Difference between variables can be evaluated	–	–	Yes	Yes
Addition and subtraction of variables	–	–	Yes	Yes
Multiplication and division of variables	–	–	–	Yes
Absolute zero	–	–	–	Yes

We are now ready to present a report on the findings in terms of any project for which we gathered data. Mostly, the report or findings will describe the collected data using graphs or the calculated descriptive measures.

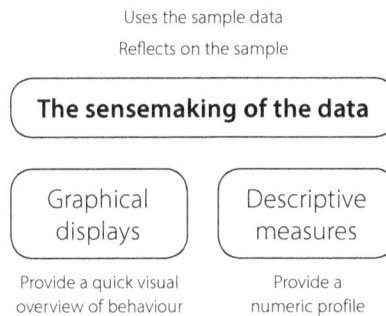

Uses the sample data
Reflects on the sample

The sensemaking of the data

Graphical displays

Descriptive measures

Provide a quick visual overview of behaviour

Provide a numeric profile

Figure 10.19: The statistical tools to make sense of the data

Your CEO intends to provide additional support to women in the organisation and tasks you to investigate the average length of time in a particular post level. You obtain the data in terms of duration of service in the position and find the following descriptive measures (see Table 10.12).

Table 10.12: Descriptive measures obtained at a specific position level in the organisation

Men (years' service)		Women (years' service)	
Mean	5.556209	Mean	5.491034
Median	3.65	Median	3.5
Mode	2.5	Mode	1.4
Standard deviation	5.362564	Standard deviation	5.576401
Sample variance	28.75709	Sample variance	31.09625
Skewness	1.463723	Skewness	2.046589
Range	29.2	Range	35.8
Minimum	0.1	Minimum	0.1
Maximum	29.3	Maximum	35.9
Count	306	Count	290

How do men and women differ according to the time in a specific post? What recommendations do you have? Use the above descriptive measures for the two data sets to draw conclusions and make recommendations.

10.9 Summary

This chapter introduced concepts of making sense of data. The sensemaking process took us from understanding the types and measurement scales of data, graphical displays and statistical measures to summarise and analyse the data. Before we can analyse data, we have to ensure that the data obtained is relevant and credible by understanding what data we require and finding the most reliable collection technique for the specific situation. To that end, we discussed the population and then various sampling techniques to select elements from the population. With so much data and information available, be sure that you remain scientific about the choices and treat the data and information with respect so that the decisions you make from these are reliable and truthful.

www.ingramcontent.com/pod-product-compliance
Lightning Source LLC
Chambersburg PA
CBHW051334200326
41519CB00026B/7421